# MATZO BALLS
# AND CORNBREAD

# MATZO BALLS
# AND CORNBREAD

## *A LOVE STORY*

*Tyree and Les Wieder*

LAZLO VIDOR PRESS
Chatsworth, CA
2017

LAZLO VIDOR PRESS
Chatsworth, CA
lazlovidorpress@gmail.com

ISBN: 978-0-692-84131-0
LIBRARY OF CONGRESS CONTROL NUMBER: 2017949752

Book design by Pablo Capra

# CONTENTS

# DEDICATED TO

*Our daughter*
*Shavonne Rebecca Wieder*

# PREFACE

## MATZO BALLS: LES

I'VE had a very interesting and exciting life; at least I think I have. I've met famous and some infamous people; had the chance to travel the world, had a wonderful career, fell in love with a beautiful African American woman, married her and fathered a lovely daughter.

Don't get me wrong, there were bumps along the way... a lot of bumps. But I learned to overcome them and found happiness and contentment.

It hasn't been boring, that's for sure. In fact, most of the time it's been pretty exciting: both the good and the not so good. Like I said, at least it's never been boring.

## *CORNBREAD: TYREE*

*BECAUSE of the dedication and love of Arthur Lorenzo Countee, my maternal grandfather, and my grandmother, Ethel, I grew up in a large extended, supportive family in South Central Los Angeles. My two brothers and I came to live with them shortly after the death of our mother and the departure of our father who had moved away. I was two years old at the time so Arthur became my "daddy" and Ethel became my "mama."*

*I always felt I wanted to live my life the way my grandparents would have expected, to work hard, do things for the right reasons and be an asset to my community. This was not a burden to me, but a road map to a life that gave me purpose. They had shown me that in spite of having come from hardship and humble means one could have a fulfilling life, and most importantly I could live my life the way it's "s'pposed to be."*

*My journey has included finding my soul mate, becoming a mother, recognizing the basic goodness in people and understanding there are those in the world whose actions I will never understand. My pathway has also taken me to places I would never have envisioned as a child, traveling the world, becoming a college president, serving as Chancellor of the largest community college district in the country, marrying someone who was not African American and, oh yes, converting to the Jewish faith.*

# INTRODUCTION

## *Spring 1978*

I'M sitting in the control room at Moorpark College directing another episode of the College's TV series, *On the Hot Seat*. The host is Tyree Allen. I look at a TV monitor and over my headset I tell the camera operator to zoom in for a tighter shot of Ms. Allen. Beside me Joyce, my assistant director, turns to me and says, "Les, why don't you just go up to her after the show and ask her out?"

"Is it that obvious?" I ask.

The entire control room, all 10 people, replied in unison, "YES!"

"Oh," I whisper and then look back to the wall of monitors facing me. "Wrap it up," I say and snap my fingers as the technical director taps the switcher and the credits begin to roll.

"Hurry up," Joyce yells at me, "before she leaves!"

"Okay," I reply and rip off my headset and make a dash for the control room door.

I'd had my eye on Tyree ever since I first saw her at orientation at the beginning of the semester. Now, it's been almost seven months and I still haven't asked her out. So now, suddenly, it's time.

I rush out of the control room, run down the hall and push open the door leading out of the studio. But I'm too late she's already out the door. I step outside and see her standing there reading a note.

Okay, I'm not too late, I think. So I walk up to her and say, "Hi." She turns to me and smiles and I stammer, "Ah, listen, Tyree... I wonder... Maybe some time we could go out... maybe have dinner or a drink?"

She looks at me for a moment not saying anything.

Now, Tyree knows who I am. She is the counselor for the theater department, we've been in meetings together and when I directed *The River Niger*, the first all-black play ever done at the college, she had been a guest at rehearsals and attended several performances.

So I'm standing there having just asked her for a date and she's looking at me and not saying a word. I'm thinking, "Oh shit... why isn't she saying anything?" Then she smiles and says, "I don't think so."

"Why?" I ask.

"Well, for one," she replies, "I'm married."

So I then say, "Well, then how about going for coffee?"

To which she replies after a short pause, "I don't go out with white guys."

"Wha... What," I stammer?

She says it again, "I don't go out with white guys." Then before I can say anything else she turns and walks away with just the hint of a smile on her face.

I stand there with my mouth open, shocked at: one, being turned down; and two, being turned down because I'm white. That's never happened before but there I am, watching this amazing woman walk away from me, and I'm thinking, "There's only two ways this can go: one, I walk away; or two, pursue her." It's a no-brainer... I pursued.

*I knew Les. He was the new Theater Arts instructor and my TV director for the past few months and we'd see each other around campus or in meetings. In the spring, he directed,* The River Niger, *the first all-black play at Moorpark College, and I came to appreciate his talents as a director. He was actually doing something to bring diversity onto our campus, and I was very impressed with the production.*

*So I knew Les but when he came up to me and asked me out for dinner I was actually surprised and flattered. But even though I might have wanted to have dinner with this man, I thought no... let's not tempt fate. And so I said, "I'm married."*

*That didn't stop him. Because he immediately came back with "How about coffee?" And right then I knew I wanted to say yes but instead I thought no... end it. So I said something to the effect of, "I don't go out with white guys."*

*I'll never forget the look on his face when I said that to him. He was really surprised and for a moment he looked stunned. Then before he could say anything else I walked away but felt flattered that he'd asked.*

For the next two months I pursued Tyree. I made a point to seek her out and sit with her whenever we were in the Campus Center. I regularly went to see her in her office to "talk about the theater program," but what I was really doing was getting to know her. What I found out was she was the real deal.

Then one day we were having lunch with a group of colleagues and the talk got around to stress. How stressed everyone was feeling and how he or she dealt with their stress. Tyree mentioned that she was a type A personality and it was hard for her to relax. That's when I said, "I live in Ojai and it's pretty stress-free up there. Come on up and I'll show you how to relax."

*During the semester Les seemed to find various reasons to stop by my office. Each time we met I learned a little more about him. The new theater professor was Jewish... and separated from his wife. He was cute, charming, smart, and he had a great smile. In addition I was still very impressed by his work on The River Niger. So one day at lunch when he offered to show me Ojai, I said, "OK", and mentioned it would be a good opportunity for us to discuss the theater program, at least that is what I told myself.*

We made a date for the first Friday in May... just a week away. I was excited. I mean... Tyree was beautiful, smart, funny, and had a great personality. I have to confess I was... smitten.

Friday arrives and we agree to meet in Ventura where Tyree can leave her car and I'll drive us to Ojai. I get there and see her walking towards me with a cup of coffee in hand. She has a funny look on her face but all I really see is this beautiful woman walking to me.

*I was nervous when I drove up to Ventura. I remember thinking, "What am I doing?" It was crazy... but I didn't care.*

She walked up to me and I leaned over and kissed her cheek. I took her hand and we walked over to my car. I helped her in and off we drove to Ojai.

# CHAPTER 1

## *Moorpark College*
## *1977–1980*

Since high school the theater has been an important part of my life. In fact, it has been the most important thing in my life ever since I performed in my first musical at North Hollywood High School. I respect the theater. For many years it was the only thing in my life that I truly loved. To me the Theater is sort of like my mistress. In truth I loved it more than my previous wives, harsh but true. It's what saved me until I met Tyree.

I have always felt the most important aspect of any successful theater arts program is its productions. If the productions are first rate then everyone can see what the product is you are teaching. High production values and achievement usually mean more students will be interested in enrolling in the program. It was just like sports. If you want to have a successful athletic program then you need to have winning teams. For a theater program that meant you needed winning shows. So my entire premise for building Moorpark College's theater department was to have great shows that I would direct. It was the cornerstone of what I did at the college.

Early in my first semester, there is a knock at my office door, and in walks a large black man maybe seven feet tall and weighing over 300 lbs. (At least he looked that big to me when he stepped into my office.)

"Hi, I'm Prince Hughes," he says. He tells me he's 28 years old, attending Moorpark on the GI Bill and is the President of the Black Student Union (BSU) at the college. And no he wasn't seven feet tall, just six feet four inches and 285 lbs.

"Tyree Allen," he says, "my counselor, told me you were the man to see regarding a theater project I have in mind."

"Okay," I say. "What's your idea?"

"I want to know how the Black Student Union can produce the play *The River Niger*, on campus, for Black History month this coming February."

I tell him I'd like to read the script first before deciding if it can be done by February, just five months away.

He hands me a copy of the script, gives me his phone number and leaves. That night I read the script. When I finish I realize two things: one, I love the script; and two, I want to direct it.

The next day I call Prince and tell him my feelings about the script and how I am interested in directing it myself. We meet and figure out the details.

It will be a co-production of the Theater Arts Department and the BSU. Prince agrees to act as co-producer and help recruit actors for the all-black cast needed for the production. (At the time there were just a few black students in the theater program.) Then he tells me he wants to play the lead role of the father. I ask him if he's ever acted before and he says yes he has. To make sure we read a scene from the play, and to my surprise I find he's very good. I cast him on the spot and quickly our production begins to take shape.

Prince is true to his word. He recruits actors for the play. Some are really bad while others are outrageously funny but can't act. A few have talent. In the end we get a cast. While half have acting experience, for the other half this will be their first time on stage. But I'm confident enough as the director that I can get a performance out of them.

There are 10 in the cast, seven men and three women. A couple of the actors are Army veterans like Prince. Three are former gang members who bring a definite verisimilitude, a real truthfulness to their roles. The women are energetic and talented. Everyone is very real. Oh, and one other thing, all the men are well over 6' tall. A couple guys are taller than Prince. One guy is 6'7", another is 6'5". During rehearsals I am the only white face in the room and the only person under 6' tall. Sometimes I have to stand on top of a table to get everyone's attention. Everyone thinks that's funny. (Anything to keep the troops happy.)

Not long after I start rehearsals, Tyree Allen, the theater department counselor, shows up to watch, saying she is curious to see how I am handling her students.

I'd first noticed Tyree when I met her during orientation. I mean, who wouldn't notice her? Everyone spoke glowingly of her and her work as a counselor at the college. Everyone said she was smart, attractive, personable and also married. Married or not, I must admit I was instantly attracted to this beautiful black woman.

Rehearsals begin. In the beginning, discipline is a big issue. That means you come early for rehearsals if you want to be on time. It means you know your lines as written and don't make them up as you go along. It means following directions. It means not socializing when rehearsing. And it also means not hitting on women in the cast during rehearsals.

Early on one of the male actors went to Tyree with some complaints. He told her I expected everyone to be on time to all the rehearsals and know their lines! She later told me when she heard that comment that she knew I was going to be all right. What can I say? I'm a disciplinarian when it comes to the theater.

*The complaints were actually that silly. I laughed and told the actors welcome to the theater, it's hard work. Well, they stuck it out, and the play opened in February to rave reviews. He actually pulled off an all-black play at a predominately white college. I invited a few friends and family to make the drive out to the college to see the finished product. The production was wonderful; I was truly impressed and after the show I told him so.*

To say I had a good time working on this production is an understatement. I had a great time. Once the cast got used to me telling them what to do and saw that I knew what I was doing, we got along famously.

The show opened and was an instant success, and for the first time there were lots of black people in attendance at a Moorpark College theater production. The local press gave it a lot of coverage and Prince Hughes was singled out as the driving force behind the production. I was very happy for him.

After the show closed Prince and I became good friends. He was only a few years younger than me, and when he and the woman who played his wife in the play told me they were getting married I was thrilled for them.

At the end of my first year I found I enjoyed teaching college students. I was putting my mark on the theater program and was satisfied with what I was doing. However, for me, the most satisfying thing that first year was meeting Tyree.

*When I went to work at Moorpark College I was assigned to be primary counselor for the Fine and Performing Arts Department working with art, music, dance and theater students. I also covered career and personal counseling in the Women's Reentry Center. In addition I hosted a weekly television show called,* On the Hot Seat.

*The half-hour program focused on a specific career field. I interviewed a faculty member, a professional in the field, and a student interested in the field. In the fall of 1977, the theater arts and television departments hired a new instructor, Les Wieder. One of his assignments was to direct the half-hour program. Unfortunately during the taping I actually did not see him. He was in the control room and I was in the studio during the shoot. I met with the guests in the green room before the show to explain the format and the process we used. We then walked into the studio just before taping was scheduled to start. We ran 30 minutes with no stops or commercial breaks. After the show, I usually raced out for class or appointments.*

*At the same time one of the counselors, Cynthia, was telling me she wanted to meet a nice Jewish boy and settle down. I said to her, "Have you met the new theater instructor? I think he's Jewish, and he's kind of cute." Cynthia asked, "Is he married?" I responded that I had no idea, but would find out.*

*The next day Les stopped by the Career Center to talk to me about the play he was planning to direct and some of the students he planned on asking to audition. During the conversation I managed to get in the married question and found out he was separated. I immediately reported back to Cynthia. But right after that Les asked me out and I turned him down. However, during the semester our work on the theater program continued to bring us together and I was enjoying his company. Several times he mentioned Ojai and how beautiful it was. When he suggested we take a drive up to Ojai, I accepted his offer.*

*His place was a picturesque, rustic ranch house with a patio surrounded by orange and avocado trees. We plucked oranges from the trees and talked until early afternoon. It was easy and light, and like nothing I had ever experienced before. Was it the setting, under the orange trees on the patio in Ojai? Maybe, but I was pretty sure it was this man. He was different. Ten minutes into the conversation we both felt this was something special.*

*In the afternoon we drove back to Ventura and had a late lunch at the Hungry Hunter restaurant. After a two-hour lunch, we drove back to my car. We sat in the car and talked until about 9:00 p.m. when we realized we had to actually end this day-long conversation. I drove away knowing that my life was in for a change.*

*He called me the next day and asked me to meet him at Charley Brown's, a local restaurant near the college. We met after work, and talked every day after that. It was intense, it was relentless, and it was crazy and magical at the same time. I don't act on impulse. I plan, I organize, and I think things through. But somehow, my life was now very different. Now I saw the world was different and now I felt different. I knew I could not continue on the path I was on.*

*A few days later I was talking with my Cousin Sheila. She knew how unhappy I had been, especially the last few years. I told her that after really thinking about it, I knew it was time to leave my marriage. Ted and I had been married for 10 years, but for the last five, at least, I knew that this was not the way I wanted to live the rest of my life. But up to now leaving was just too complicated. After all, we had "stuff" to divide up, we had a house together, we had a cat and it just seemed like too much work to make the move. Besides, where would I go? My husband was not a bad person—he didn't smoke or drink or gamble or hang out—but it was sort of like living with my brother, a very conservative brother. I never mentioned Les, just told Sheila that I thought I was finally ready to go. I told her I would save my money and make plans, and by next summer I could move out. Sheila said, "I have listened to you for the past five years. It will never take you that long to leave." How did she know?*

*Soon after, Ted and I went to dinner, and I broached the subject of my unhappiness. I was too much of a coward to mention that I had met someone who had made me realize how a relationship could feel, that the meeting had inspired my decision to leave. Ted listened but clearly did not truly understand how serious I was. I got the sense that he felt this was something that would blow over in a short time.*

*Sheila had been correct. Within a few weeks I had packed and moved out. It was surprising how quickly I made the move. No long-range plan, no setting aside some money, no worrying about "stuff," I needed to go. While my husband was on a business trip to Washington, D.C., my "prized" possessions were loaded into a van and moved to my girlfriend's garage. Fearful I might not get back into the house, I took my sewing machine, my favorite records, my books, my grandmother's china and my clothes. Everything else stayed. It is surprising how unimportant "stuff" is when you make up your mind to move. When Ted returned from his trip, I was out. He was very surprised that I had actually left, and I was relieved.*

*Luckily I was scheduled to leave on a trip to Europe with the college in a few weeks. It would give me some much-needed distance. We were scheduled to visit 13 countries in 30 days. Ted was not interested in going so I had booked the trip for myself. Between the time I booked the trip and the day it was to start, I had met Les.*

*I had always wanted to travel but it was not something in which Ted* had an interest. We did take a few driving trips to San Francisco and Las Vegas. We went to Chicago to visit my Cousin Ron and his wife Sheila. That was my first plane trip and I was 24 years old.

From Chicago we rode a train down to St. Louis to visit Ted's relatives. I enjoyed the train ride and meeting the older black men who worked as porters and dining room attendants. It was like seeing a living part of Black History. Once we took a trip to Hawaii. Unfortunately, the trip was not much fun. I was ready to explore everything. Ted wasn't feeling as adventurous. The highlight of the trip for me was that one evening I went by myself to a Don Ho show, was invited backstage by one of the band members and had a great time.

Les and I spent the evening together before I was to leave and had a goodbye dinner. The next morning Les dropped me off at the airport. At 7:00 a.m. we walked up to the tour group from the college and it became quite clear to everyone that this was a new couple they were seeing. I boarded the plane and was off on my first trip to Europe.

I was just beginning to understand this new relationship. I was beginning to understand why Hallmark wrote those beautiful cards that spoke of lasting relationships and love. In the past I would pick up those cards, read them and put them back on the shelf. Now, I understood. As I looked out the window and saw the city getting smaller beneath me, I knew the life I would return to would be very different. It had all happened very fast.

Our first stop was London. After flying all night, the traveling advice was not to go to sleep but to keep moving. We dropped our luggage and headed out to see the city. By early afternoon we were at Westminster Abbey. We walked in and were astonished by the amazing interior... and then, all of a sudden, the jet lag hit me like a ton of bricks. My fellow travelers left me sitting in a pew near the back of the church and went off to experience the art of making rubbings on tombs in the crypt of the church.

I remember sitting there with my head bobbing up and down. Through my half-opened eyes, I noticed a priest watching me intently. After a few minutes he walked over to see what was up. I smiled and said, "Jet lag." He smiled, nodded and walked away. Meantime, a very solemn ceremony had started and my friends were not allowed back in the sanctuary to retrieve me. They had to wait outside until the ceremony ended. Happily I did get a chance to nap while the ceremony took place.

We spent four days seeing the sights of London. One night our tour leader took a few of us to the theater, I did not know what we were going to see but I was thrilled for my first time to see London theater. I mean, since I was seeing a theater director, how could I not go to the theater in

*London? We sat in the first row of a small theater, and a few minutes into the performance I was very surprised to see the transvestite extraordinaire of* The Rocky Horror Show. *What a scream!*

*The next day, when everyone took off to visit Windsor Castle, I took a solo trip to the theater to see James Earl Jones. I do not remember the play, but I was bold enough to go backstage and meet him and get a photo of the two of us talking. The conversation was about my name Tyree and how he was reminded that Ben Johnson played a character, Sgt. Tyree, in the western movie* She Wore a Yellow Ribbon *starring John Wayne. I was amazed that I could just walk backstage and he was so inviting and friendly. What a treat for me.*

*Our next stop was Paris. No grass grew under our feet; we saw all the sights in Paris. We continued on to Dijon, then to Lausanne, and Lucerne, followed by Innsbruck and Salzburg.*

*Our next stop was in Munich, where we were scheduled to visit Dachau, the concentration camp closest to the city.*

*The trip to Dachau was very meaningful to me and gave me a glimpse of the horrors that Jews suffered under the Nazi regime. I had just met and fallen hard for a Jewish man so I almost had a sense of obligation to see firsthand a place in history that had impacted the Jewish people.*

*The camp was about 10 miles outside of the city. Above the main gate was a sign written in German that read, "Work will set you free," indicating it was a labor camp instead of the death camp that it was. We learned that this camp served as a model for other concentration camps. I was astonished to learn that the camp was in operation for over 12 years, from 1933 till the camp was liberated in 1945.*

*Even though it was summer, the concrete buildings were cold and damp. As we toured, the statistics I heard were mind-boggling. I left the camp with a deep sadness at seeing man's inhumanity to man.*

*As we drove away I remembered something my grandfather had told me. He said that people may have put us in boats and brought us to America to be slaves, but they never tried to wipe us off the face of the earth as they tried to do with the Jewish people.*

*Before we left Munich I had a disturbing conversation with one of my fellow travelers. In talking about our trip to the concentration camp, she actually said, "Well, the Jews did kill Jesus." I was stunned and began to correct her, feeling I had to defend Jews, defend Les. How can you believe such a thing? Needless to say, we did not have much to say to each other for the rest of the trip.*

*The next day we left for Heidelberg, a city that provided me with an experience opposite of the experience I had in Munich. Heidelberg was a fairytale city with a beautiful castle on a hilltop. That night we saw an opera at the Castle that was marvelous. Even not understanding German it was wonderful. We ended the tour in Amsterdam and Brussels.*

*I returned home very glad I had gone, but I was anxious to see my grandmother and, of course, Les. I had written to him throughout the trip, sharing my experiences and letting him know how much I missed him. Our separation had been difficult.*

*As happy as I was to be with Les, I began some soul searching. In my passion for this man, had I lost my senses? If someone had told me six months before that I would leave my husband for someone else I would have told them they were crazy. Plus the fact that these two men were opposite in so many ways: black/white, engineer/theater director, Christian/ Jew, and they had exactly opposites personalities. This is when I learned never to say never.*

*I admit I was nervous about dating a white man. One of the first times we went out to a club downtown and I walked past a group of black males, I stiffened, waiting for them to make a negative comment. They didn't, and Les, noticing my tension, told me to relax, everything was okay. He was right; we actually rarely got any negative reaction for being a couple, at least not any we saw.*

*As it turned out, Les being Jewish was helpful. Being Jewish made up for the fact that he was not black. After all, blacks and Jews had something in common: we were both targets for the KKK. The large number of Jewish people who had marched in the Civil Rights movement was common knowledge. But moving into a Jewish world was moving into a predominately white world, and how would I deal with that?*

While Tyree was away in Europe I decided to move from Ojai to someplace closer to the college. The daily drive was killing me. It was over an hour each way without traffic. Also, I felt I needed a change of scenery. So I moved out of Ojai and found an apartment in Woodland Hills. Once again I was moving and my life was changing. I wasn't sure what was going to happen. I just knew I was in love and wanted to be with Tyree.

# CHAPTER 2

## Family Heritages:
## Families of Immigrants and Slaves

### THE WIEDERS

M y dad, James Simon Wieder, Jimmy to his friends, was born in a very small town in Hungary. Maromaros was its name. It was located south of the Carpathian Mountains, northeast of Budapest in northwest Transylvania. Dad used to say the town, really a village, was in Transylvania and that we were descendants of Count Dracula, but he was only joking when he said it. I think. Anyhow, it was a little village that no longer exists in modern Hungary.

According to Dad, he was the youngest of 21 children. Yes, that number is correct… 21. My grandmother, Regina Wieder, had 21 children. Two sets of triplets, three sets of twins and nine single births. 20 years of giving birth to children! It's unbelievable really, but Dad said it was true. Several of the children died at childbirth, not an uncommon occurrence during that time. What happened to the others remains a mystery. Dad couldn't remember their names, just the ones who eventually immigrated to America: Isidor, Sam, Magda, Yola, and Joan.

My grandfather Lepot Wieder and grandmother Regina Wieder were married in 1888. Regina was 18 and Lepot was 23. Their first child, Isidor, was born in 1889, and their last child, James Simon (Jimmy) Wieder, my dad, was born in 1909.

Many people, when they hear my grandmother had 21 children, ask how old was she when she died. And when I tell them that Grandma Wieder lived to be over 80, everyone marvels at her strength. Then I tell them

Grandpa Wieder died when he was 55... of exhaustion.

The family moved to Budapest in 1910 where Lepot, a tailor by trade, opened a haberdashery. He became very successful. According to Dad, in those days if you had money you could pay a foster family to take your baby and raise the infant until it was two years old. Then the child would be returned to the family. This allowed big families not to have babies around with diapers, feedings, etc.

Dad remembers his foster family... he said they lived on a farm and that the farmer walked with a limp. He never said anything else about living on the farm.

In school Dad enjoyed playing sports. He was particularly good at soccer and long-distance running. He became a champion youth distance runner in his teens. After graduating high school, he went on to gymnasium (college).

In 1914 Hungary became involved in World War I (1914–1918), fighting on the losing side. During the war, Lepot's business began to suffer. By the end of the war, things had become very difficult for Jews in Hungary. Then in 1920 during the White Terror, a violent time of anti-Semitism in the country, he lost his business and all his money. Soon after he became ill and died.

Left without a husband and with a large family to support, my grandmother organized her children into a Dickens-type family. Each morning each child was given an assignment to go out into the city and obtain anything they could to help keep the family going. My dad's assignment was to follow the coal wagon, and whenever pieces of coal fell off, he was to pick them up and put them in the bucket he carried with him. By the end of the day he usually returned home with enough coal for Grandma Wieder to heat the stove for cooking. Of course he wasn't the only kid running after the coal truck and so he had to be able to run fast just to keep up. Dad could do that very well. He also had to be able to use his fists if and when the time came to hold onto his coal. Though not a big person, Dad wasn't afraid to use his fists to keep his coal bucket full and there were plenty of days when he'd come home with a black eye or a cut lip to prove it.

A year after Grandpa Wieder died, the family decided it was time to get out of Hungary. As Hungarian Jews, they had already felt the sting of anti-Semitism in Budapest. So in 1921, Isidor and Magda left for New York in hopes of making enough money to bring the rest of the family to the United States. Upon their arrival they went to live with Uncle Herman Harkowitz, Grandma Regina Wieder's brother, who was living in Brooklyn. In 1924, Sam immigrated to New York, followed by Grandma

Wieder in 1926, Yola in 1927, James (my dad) in 1929 and finally Joan (Jenka) in 1933. The Wieders were now in America.

Dad settled in New York and went to work as an assistant furrier, helping stitch pelts together to make fur coats, a job Sam had lined up for him. Dad's passport indicated that he was a "Pelletier" (furrier) by trade.

The work was hard, but he was happy because he was in America, had a job and was with his brothers. The only thing he was unhappy about, he told me, was the food he was eating every day at lunchtime. It all had to do with his lack of skill with the English language.

Dad was embarrassed that the only English words he knew that had to do with food were "ham and eggs." So every day, for the first three months, he went to lunch at the local cafeteria and ordered the same thing, "Ham and eggs." Then, one day, while waiting to order his usual meal, he heard one of the servers say to her companion in Hungarian, "Here comes that dope that always orders ham and eggs." Shocked to hear Hungarian being spoken, Dad immediately said back in Hungarian, "My God, you speak Hungarian! I am so sick of ham and eggs." From that time on Dad never had any problems ordering food.

Life was looking up for Dad. He had a job, a place to live and was learning to speak English. The only thing missing was soccer. He'd been an excellent young soccer player in Hungary and was looking for a team to play on in the States. When he learned a local Hungarian-American team was having try-outs, he tried out and made the team. Now, he felt he had everything. He was very happy.

## THE COUNTEES

NELSON *Countee, my great-great-great-grandfather, was born in 1816 in Virginia. To my great surprise I discovered that in the 1850 US census he was listed as a "Free Inhabitant." His occupation was listed as a "cooper," a maker of wooden, staved vessels—a skilled trade. His wife, Sophia Countee, was also listed as a "Free Inhabitant."*

*Prior to 1865 there were few ways that blacks could become free: either they were runaways, bought their freedom, or were the children of plantation owners and taught a skilled trade, such as being a cooper. My guess is that Nelson fit that last category. Census records for 1830 show a plantation in Westmoreland, Virginia, owned by Philip A. L. Countee. Slaves on the plantation included a 14-year-old male born in 1816.*

*It's important to note that as children our grandfather, Arthur Lorenzo Countee, had always told us that his great-great-great-grandfather was a fiddle player from Madagascar. As the story goes, he was placed on*

*a slave ship and ordered to play the fiddle so the captured slaves would
dance and exercise. Somehow he was kept on the ship, sent to Virginia
and upon arrival sold as a slave.*

*Was the fiddle player sold to the Countee plantation? Did he have a
daughter who might have been the mother of Nelson and whose father
might have been Phillip A. L. Countee, the plantation owner? My search
continues for additional records so that I can answer these questions.*

*According to the 1850 census 34-year-old Nelson Countee and his
wife Sophia were living as "freedmen" in Niagara, New York; but between 1844 and 1849 they were living in Canada where their first two
children, Robert Nelson (my great-great-grandfather) and his brother
William, were born. In 1860 Nelson and William lived in a boardinghouse
in Buffalo, New York, and worked as a cooper and laborer respectively.*

*In 1861, just before the start of the Civil War, Nelson moved the fami-
ly back to Canada and settled in St. Catherines, Ontario. Even though he
was a freedman, he must have felt the need to ensure his family's safety
by taking them out of the United States. This was a town of sanctuary and
rest for refugee slaves from the United States, one of the final stops on the
Underground Railroad.*

*Years later Robert was living in Memphis, Tennessee. Records from
the Freedman's Bank show that on March 9, 1871 he opened a bank account in Memphis with his wife Melissa Thompson and his mother Sophia
Ann as co-signers.*

*In Memphis, Robert was known as one of the leaders of the black
community. He held positions as both an attorney and a reverend. He
founded two prestigious black churches. One, the Beale Street Baptist
Church, was visited by former president Ulysses S. Grant in 1880 where
he expressed the hope that blacks would receive full equality in due time.
Reverend Countee said the visit was "an epoch in the history of our race."*

*He also worked with the civil rights activist, Ida B. Wells, giving her
a start in journalism by hiring her to write for his church newspaper,* The
Living Way.

*In the early 1890s, lynching black men in Memphis was becoming
more and more common. Whole congregations debated leaving the city.
Reverend Countee and Ms. Wells encouraged blacks to stay. But it soon
became too dangerous so Reverend Countee moved his family to Kansas
City, Missouri.*

*I was fascinated to find such detailed records of his history, and very
proud of his accomplishments.*

*Robert and Melissa had two sons, Charles Henry Countee (my
great-grandfather) and his brother Walter Benjamin. The brothers worked*

*side by side as owners of the Countee Brothers Undertaking and Funeral Directing Home, the oldest colored undertaking firm in Kansas City, Missouri. Charles and his wife Rebecca had two children, my grandfather Arthur Lorenzo Countee and a daughter Sadie Eulalia Countee who died of typhoid fever at the age of eight. As the local mortician, Charles Henry Countee completed her death certificate. My grandparents always spoke about him with a sense of pride. He was a black man who owned his own business and was very successful. They said he was a fine-looking man and a dapper dresser. His wife, Rebecca, was a schoolteacher and pianist. She taught Arthur to play classical music when he was a child and he carried those musical skills throughout his life. Of course, he added jazz, blues and popular tunes as he got older.*

*Arthur, my grandfather, was a good academic student as well as a musician. His academic and musical talents landed him at the New England Conservatory of Music in Boston, founded in 1867 and one of the first conservatories to grant admission to African Americans and women. This is the same conservatory where Coretta Scott King studied voice and music education in the early 1950s.*

*He told us he was allowed to attend classes but usually sat in the back of the classroom, and could work in, but did not have the resources to eat in, the cafeteria. Yet, his experience there was very positive. While he felt some of his teachers treated him more harshly than they did the white students he was able to overcome their biases and won them over with his talent. On June 25, 1918, he received a Certificate for the Public School Music Course. He told us that it was at the Conservatory that he learned how important it is to work to be the best at what you do. He stressed to us that people could take some things away from you, but never your education.*

*World War I halted his academic endeavors when he served in the infantry. While in France the ladies asked to see his tail because the white soldiers had told them that the black soldiers had tails like monkeys. Even that experience did not turn him into a bitter black man.*

*When he came home from the war he secured a job teaching at the St. John's Industrial Institute in Austin, Texas, a school for black orphans. The philosophy of the school was to lay a solid academic foundation, math being one of the most important subjects.*

*Arthur's skills in math were valued at the school. He enjoyed teaching and later carried that joy to teaching the piano. He married a fellow schoolteacher, Anoise Lofton, and had one son, Noyal, but the marriage ended after two years, and he moved to Kansas City, Missouri, where he met Ethel Rubey, my grandmother. She was a divorced mother of one*

*young son, Clarence Anthony, who my grandfather later adopted so he
also carried the name Countee. They married and had five more children,
Rubey Eulalia, Oneida (my mother), Charles Henry, Patricia and Beverly. In Kansas, Arthur secured a position with the US Postal Service,
one of the first black men to do so. However, early on that dream job hit
a snag.*

*When I was in the fourth grade my teacher was talking about an
upcoming election and wanted to know if our parents were Democrats or
Republicans and if we understood the difference. I went home and asked
my grandfather, was he a Democrat or Republican?*

*My grandfather told me that when he was working in the post office
in Kansas City, he lost his job for reasons he felt were based on discrimination. There were very few Negros in the post office at that time, and
often those working suffered veiled discrimination. As this was a federal
job, my grandfather wrote to President Truman and Truman sent an in-
vestigator to the post office in Kansas City who found the accusations
against my grandfather to be false and he was reinstated to his position.
Once his position was secured, he let them know that he did not care to
continue working with men who had falsely accused him of wrongdoing,
but he still wanted to remain with the post office. He was offered a transfer to California and the family moved with him, including his married
daughters, Oneida and Rubey, and their families. And thus, a few years
later, I was born in Los Angeles. My grandfather felt that Truman's response to his problem with the post office was so positive that he was
committed to the Democratic Party.*

*My grandfather was always willing to go to the authorities when he
saw something that needed an elected official's attention. For instance,
the traffic median in front of our house was full of weeds and not cared
for by the county. One day he took me to the County Supervisor's Office
when he went to request that our median be cared for as they did in white
neighborhoods. I remember sitting in the hallway while he went in to talk
with the County Supervisor. In a few months the gardeners came and
planted the median with trees and grass. Another lesson taught: Don't
be afraid to speak up for what is right. I was so proud of how he always
seemed to be able to take care of whatever needed to be done.*

*He continued teaching, only now it was piano students in the eve-
nings after his work at the post office. I was also one of his pupils. He
would listen to my lessons as he ate dinner after working at the post office
and giving piano lessons. I was always amazed that he knew, without
looking, which piano key I had incorrectly hit. How lucky I was to have
had free piano lessons, something I really appreciated.*

*Ethel Rubey, my grandmother, was the daughter of Rose Ellis Rubey, a schoolteacher in New York. However, we never knew much about her father's identity because my grandmother was an illegitimate child, something I did not learn until well into my adult years. When her mother, Rose Ellis Rubey, became pregnant she was sent to live with her brother, Clarence Rubey, in Kansas City, Missouri. Having an illegitimate child would cause her to lose her job as a schoolteacher, so after the birth of her daughter, my great-grandmother returned to New York without her baby, my grandmother, Ethel. Ethel stayed with her uncle and aunt in Kansas, and her mother visited her when she could, which was not often.*

*As a child Ethel had to work to earn her keep. Throughout her youth, she was the housekeeper in a boarding house owned by her aunt and uncle. There is one family rumor that says it was actually a brothel, but there is no evidence to support that report. Each morning her job was to clean the chamber pots in the guests' rooms before she went to school. Furniture received the white glove treatment from her aunt, and a price was paid if the glove found dust. It was a hard childhood.*

*When I heard the stories of her childhood, one in which she was a servant more than a child, where punishment was frequent and offered at the slightest provocation, I felt compassion for her and the hard life she had lived.*

*My childhood was much different. My grandparents' home was strictly run, we had chores and responsibilities, but nothing like the childhood my grandmother had to endure. She felt it was important for us to have a safe, clean home and therefore we all learned to assist her in that endeavor. "There is a place for everything and everything has a place." It was our job to ensure the house met those standards. My brothers learned to sew along with their outside chores, and I learned to do yard work. When my brother, Robert, went into the service, he made a bundle because none of the other soldiers could sew, and he was paid to attach their various badges and hem their pants. We were taught to be independent and self-sufficient, traits that I have carried with me and that have benefited me in my personal life and my career.*

*My grandmother was a very active woman. She belonged to several social clubs and often hosted them at our home; therefore we were put into service assisting with cooking, serving and clean-up. Her friends were always so impressed with how everything was set up and the delicious meals she prepared. But when they sat in the living room and said, "Ethel, this is so lovely, we don't know how you do this?" The "servants" in the kitchen, busily washing dishes and putting away food, said, but not too loudly, "We know how she does it, she has us." When we were adults and had moved into our own homes, she would call and say, "Well, my club is coming this Sunday," long pause. And we would each say, "Of course I will be there." We understood very clearly where our place was, there to help her with her hosting responsibilities. These were wonderful skills that have stayed with me as I host dinners and entertain today.*

*She was a fine seamstress and made many of our school clothes and taught me to sew as well. She did have one minor problem as she grew older, arthritis. She kept a pint of gin filled with plump raisins in the kitchen cupboard. When she felt pain in her joints she would take a swig of the iron-filled liquid, saying the gin mixed with the raisins was very helpful to her joints. My grandparents had other home remedies for many ailments. The one we hated the most was castor oil. At the first sign of a cold, a dose of castor oil was mandatory. It was truly vile tasting stuff but they swore it would keep us healthy.*

*In addition to keeping us healthy, my grandparents wanted to be sure we were good citizens. One of my childhood experiences that made me very proud of them and demonstrated to me a way that the average citizen could make a difference was what they did on Election Day.*

*At every election our den was transformed into a polling place. On Election Day I would run home from school because everyone in the neighborhood came to our house to vote. My grandmother often made a big pot of chili or spaghetti that sat on the stove for the neighbors. After voting, our neighbors would stop in the kitchen, grab a bowl and sit in the backyard talking to my grandfather as grandmother and her friends worked the polls. Because of that connection I always enjoyed the experience of going to a polling place instead of absentee voting.*

*In addition to raising the family, my grandparents enjoyed their music. Ethel had a beautiful soprano voice and was known as "The Nightingale of Kansas City." Arthur served as her accompanist. The two of them performed not only at their church but also at community events. He would compose songs for us and she would sing. I sat at her knee and listened while she brushed my hair. My favorite was, "His Eye is on the Sparrow"; to this day that song can bring me to tears.*

## THE GOLDBERGERS

Leopold and Eleanor Goldberger immigrated to New York City from Hungary on February 8, 1908 and married on February 29, 1908 (leap year). Hilda Goldberger, my mother, was born five weeks later on April 8, 1908. She was an "early" arrival.

The family first lived on New York's Lower East Side then moved uptown to the Bronx where they had an apartment on the Grand Concourse. Grandpa Leopold Goldberger worked as a journalist for the *Daily Worker*, the communist newspaper in New York.

Eleanor Goldberger was a housewife who had six children. Hilda (Mom) was the oldest, followed by Sylvia, Joe, Henry, Eddie and Florence. My grandmother was the typical Eastern European Jewish mother... loving, giving, nurturing and a great cook. For her, family was everything.

From the time my Mom was a little girl she looked and acted older. At a young age she was told to speak her mind. Something she continued to do throughout her life. The older she got the more independent she became.

In 1923 when she was 15 she quit school to work for her Uncle Marcus in his doll factory. She was a fast worker and made very good money. Her money gave her independence. She bought her own clothes, paid her own way, and provided money to the household.

In 1927 Grandpa Leopold died in a motorcycle accident. He was 42 years old. His sudden death left the family in deep financial difficulty. It was now the job of the children to bring money into the house. Hilda, 19, was already working at the doll factory, and contributing. Sylvia, 17, was also working at the factory and so they were now the major breadwinners in the household. Joe, 13, and Henry, 10, sold newspapers. Eddie, 8, and Florence, 5, were too young to work. Ma even took in laundry to help bring a few more dollars into the family.

In April 1927, Hilda married a man named Emanuel Eckstein, and on February 12, 1930, gave birth to a baby girl she named Marian. Not long after giving birth Hilda separated from Mr. Eckstein and returned with Marian to live with her family in the Bronx. Soon after she was granted a divorce.

Her life now had changed. Now she had a baby to consider so she was more particular about any man she met. Years later she told me if she were going to get married again, it would be with someone who had money and could take care of her and her daughter.

## THE WARRENS

*CLARENCE Nokomis Warren Sr., my father, was born in Newport, Arkansas. He was the second son of John Herman Warren and Bessie Day. My great-grandfather, William Henry Wilson Warren, was an Irishman, a fact I learned after I received my DNA results. I actually sent the information in to test the location in Africa where my ancestors might have* come from. To my surprise my results came back 22% Ireland. When I called my father's cousin she told me, "Oh yes, Grandpa William was an Irishman." He was born a Wilson but went to live with Mr. Warren and took his name.

The family worked the land on a cotton plantation. William had eight children. The oldest son, Joseph, did not want his children raised in Arkansas, so in 1940 he brought his wife Bertha Mae and his 11 children to Santa Monica, California. The next year the 12th child, a son, was born. My grandfather, John Herman, elected to stay in Newport, Arkansas. He married Bessie in 1924 and had two sons, my Uncle John born in 1925, and my father Clarence born in 1926. By 1930 my grandfather had separated from Bessie and had returned home to live with his parents. Bessie took custody of the two boys and in 1930 married Sampson Lee. They raised the two boys along with their four children.

Family legend is that John Herman was a looker and a ladies man. The 1930 census mentions that John was "crippled." Apparently one of the reasons for his separation from Bessie was because of a liaison he had with a young woman. When the woman's father confronted John he shot him in the leg, causing a life-long limp.

In 1942 John married Burble Wisdom and together they opened the Warren Burial Association, a mortuary and cemetery in Newport, Arkansas. After our mother died, Burble wrote to us and sent school clothes.

I did finally meet my paternal grandfather in 1966 when I was attending Compton College. He came to California to visit the Santa Monica Warrens and wanted to see his three grandchildren. Clarence, my oldest brother, was anxious to meet him, and I was indifferent. Robert was angry and said he had no interest in meeting him. "Our grandfather has known all these years where we lived and we never heard from him." My grandmother encouraged Robert to go and meet his grandfather, and after a long discussion with her, he agreed. As I recall the meeting was pleasant, but for whatever reason there was never any follow-up. I never saw him again.

## JIMMY AND HILDA WIEDER

THE early years of the Depression were very difficult for everyone in America. Jobs were hard to come by as millions of people were out of work. There were breadlines in every American city.

In late 1932 Jimmy met Hilda. They met at a Hungarian nightclub in New York City. Right away he liked her sassy, brash manner. She, however, didn't like him at all. Too short, too thin, and he had no money. Not the guy for her. No way was she going to date this Hungarian immigrant. But he was persistent and finally she said yes to one date. Soon after she started going to watch him play soccer.

Mom once told me, "Your father was very persistent about taking me out. He would show up at the clubs I would go to. He was there and he'd ask me to have a drink and dance with him. I liked dancing but I didn't want anything to do with him. I thought he was a little too slow for me. When we did dance I was surprised to find out he was pretty good. And he was fun to talk to. But he didn't have much money. What finally got me interested in him was agreeing to go and watch him play soccer. He was a very good soccer player."

In November, 1933, Mom and her younger brother Henry, everyone called him Hank, went out to Long Island to see Dad play. The weather was freezing. Everyone in the stands was drinking. Suddenly, a fight broke out on the field. My Uncle Hank recollects the following...

> There was a fight on the field and everyone in the stands went crazy. People were yelling and screaming. I looked out and saw this big guy running after Jimmy trying to catch him and hit him. I started to laugh. It was pretty funny seeing this huge lumbering ox trying to catch Jimmy who was small and thin and could run like a deer all day long. So I'm laughing and I turn to see if Hilda has seen it too but she's not beside me. I look up and see her running onto the field with her shoe in hand going after the guy who's running after Jimmy. As soon as I see that I take off and run down onto the field and grab her just as she is about to bop the guy in the head with her three-inch heel. If I hadn't grabbed her she would have killed the bastard. So I grab her and run off the field and all the while she's yelling and screaming and calling this guy names because he was going to hit "her" Jimmy. That's when I knew my sister really liked him.

In 1934 Dad accepted an offer to play soccer in Chicago. The owner of the team offered to pay him $15 a week to work in his garment factory *and* play soccer for the company team. He also promised Dad a chicken every week from the chicken ranch he also owned. Mom used to say the best thing about that job was you always knew you'd have a chicken for Shabbos every week.

After telling Mom about the offer he asked her if she'd come with him to Chicago.

"I told him I'd go with him but only if we were married," she said. He agreed. Then Dad asked, "What about Marian?"

"What about Marian?" Mom asked.

"If Marian could stay with Ma until we got settled it would be a big help."

So Mom went to Grandma and asked her if Marian could stay with her until she and Dad got settled in Chicago. Ma said yes, so in late May, 1934, Jimmy and Hilda moved to Chicago. On June 2, right after moving there, they got married.

Times were hard in Chicago. It was the height of the Depression and for most folks having enough money for food and the rent was a constant struggle. Mom remembered that block parties were held every week so food could be shared with neighbors. However, even though times were tough, she always spoke about their time in Chicago with great affection.

A little over a year after moving to Chicago, Dad got a call from his future brother-in-law, Jack Jortner, who was the manager of a coat factory in New Britain, Connecticut. Jack told Dad he was looking for an assistant manager to help run the factory. Would he be interested in the job?

That night Dad told Mom about the offer. They'd be able to have Marian come live with them if they moved. Mom readily agreed once she learned Marian could live with them. So in 1935, Dad and Mom left Chicago and moved to New Britain, Connecticut, which was just a short 90-minute drive via the Merritt Parkway from New York.

Dad got right into life in New Britain. He loved playing poker and was very good at it. He told me he had a head for remembering numbers, which helped him when he played.

From 1935 until 1940 Dad worked as the Assistant Manager of the New Britain factory. Then in 1940 he was made Manager after Jack left to work in California. By then Mom and Dad had settled into life in New Britain. They made friends, had an active social life and joined the local Orthodox Jewish Synagogue... not because they were very religious but because the Rabbi was one of Dad's poker playing buddies. Dad, a poor Hungarian immigrant, had worked hard and had become successful in America. The only thing he did not have was a son.

In 1941 Mom gave birth to a baby boy who lived just a few days. Mom and Dad were both devastated by the baby's death. They decided to try again for another child. In May of 1942 she became pregnant. It was a difficult pregnancy because she was weak and bedridden a great deal of the time, and she also had to deal with depression.

Then on January 17, 1943 at around five in the morning Mom told Dad it was time so he packed her into the car and drove to New Britain General Hospital. On the way he got lost going through New Britain Park, a place he'd driven through hundreds of times. Years later Mom told me Dad was so nervous he forgot the way and they drove around in circles for 10 minutes until he found his way out. She thought it was pretty funny but at the time she wasn't laughing.

They arrived in just enough time. At 6:30 a.m., Mom gave birth to a baby boy. Dad was overjoyed. He had a son. They named the baby Leslie. And so... my life began.

# CHAPTER 3

## *Childhood: Two Different Worlds*
### *1943–1956*

I WAS born in 1943 in the middle of World War II. It was a time of great urgency in the country. When the war ended I was two years old.

My early childhood years I spent growing up in Connecticut. I was my Dad's pride and joy. When I was little he would take me around town and show me off to all his friends. "This is my son," he'd tell his buddies and I'd smile at them and stick out my little hand to shake. The men would laugh and shake hands with me. They all called me "Little Jimmy." Early on "Little Jimmy" became one of the boys.

For the first six years of my life we lived on the ground floor at 154 Lyons Street in New Britain. Above us lived the Dairys with their two sons. Noel, the youngest, taught me how to ride a bike, and Jean-Paul, the oldest, taught me how to fight.

Out back was a small yard with a couple of trees and a clothesline. In the far corner of the yard was our garage, an old wooden building that had two front doors that swung out to open. Dad never parked his car inside because that's where he set up my Lionel Electric Trains. We constructed an entire town on a large wooden table and my electric trains ran around and through the buildings. The table took up most of the floor space inside the garage. I wish I still had that train set. It was very cool.

Besides the fun stuff I also had chores. I had to take care of my clothes, keep my room clean (my mom was an Old World neat person) and help sweep the snow from the front and back steps.

The war years (1941–1945) were good years for Dad. Before the war Dad's factory made ladies suits and coats. During the war they made

Army uniforms. Dad, however, still made some ladies coats that he sold on the side.

He was excused from serving in the military because his factory made military uniforms so his job was deemed essential to the war effort. He was also deaf in one ear, an old soccer injury, thus making him ineligible for the draft.

By 1943 he was running the third largest business in New Britain, the first being Stanley Tools and the second Colt Firearms.

He employed 200 people. They took up the entire second and third floors of a three-story building at 191 Arch Street. The first floor was occupied by the town's Buick dealership.

The owner of the dealership and Dad were friends. All during the war, Dad would give the man coats to give to his girlfriends. In return Dad got extra gas coupons. Those extra coupons allowed us to drive to New York almost every weekend to see Mom's and Dad's families.

One of the more vivid memories I have of those trips to Manhattan is going with the family to the Hungarian Gardens Restaurant, an Old World European-style establishment where the waiters wore long sleeve white shirts, black pants, black bow ties and long white aprons. I remember they used to come out of the kitchen balancing six plates of food on one arm. The restaurant had a Hungarian band that played Gypsy music and there was lots of drinking and dancing. I also remember the place was filled with cigarette smoke. Back then everyone smoked.

My first clear memory of Grandma Wieder was at my Dad's sister Aunt Joan's apartment in Manhattan. I was four years old and by then she was in her late 70s. I remember she had an Old World air about her, almost regal. She was seated wearing a long black dress. Her gray hair was done up in a bun. She had high cheekbones, and a slight Slavic cast to her eyes.

I remember she held out her hands and spoke English with a thick Hungarian accent. "Leslie, come to me," she said. I walked over and she put her hand on my cheek. She looked at me and gently stroked my hair. "Are you a good boy?" she asked. I nodded yes. She nodded back and said, "Good. Good." Then she leaned over, kissed me on my cheek, held my face in her hands and said, "You be a good boy for your father. A good boy." Then she patted me on the head and I was dismissed. I remember that one visit very clearly but I don't remember any others with her. She passed away when I was still very young.

In 1947 I started kindergarten and walked to school with my friends. I liked school but I was also always getting into mischief. Nothing bad, just kid stuff.

The first and second grades are a bit vague but I remember some things. One time I said something under my breath about a teacher who heard me and told me I was being disrespectful, then told me to come to the front of the class where she proceeded to take out a ruler and crack me across the knuckles. Hurt like hell but I didn't cry.

Then there was the time I wanted to be in the school orchestra but I didn't play an instrument so they gave me the triangle to play. Everyone thought I'd be upset about playing the triangle, but I wasn't because every time I struck it all the other instruments stopped playing.

When Dad bought the first television set for our home on Lyons Street, my young life changed. Immediately I was glued to the wonders of TV. Watching TV was such a strange new thing that I'd get up early on Saturday just to watch the Indian test pattern. Cartoons and old westerns made up most of the schedule on Saturday mornings. Very soon my living room was the place to be on Saturday mornings for all the neighborhood kids.

The other thing we did on Saturdays was go to the movies. Dad would drive my friends and me into town and let us off at the Strand Theatre. We'd sit from nine until three in the afternoon watching cartoons, serials and sometimes a Disney feature or a western, all the while eating loads of popcorn, candy and soda. Great fun.

Now Mom, she loved to go to the movies. Dad, however, wasn't a big movie guy, especially during the week because it took him away from his poker games. But occasionally we'd all go see a film on a Saturday night.

In the summer of 1944 and for the next four years my dad rented a cottage at Crescent Beach, Connecticut, right on Long Island Sound. We'd go for three months to get away from the heat and humidity that covered most of New England during the summer.

Mom, Marian and I stayed at the cottage. Dad stayed in New Britain during the week but would come down on weekends. From the start my Aunt Sylvia (Mom's sister) and her daughter (my Cousin Susan, a year younger than me) shared the cottage with us when her husband (Uncle Sydney, an officer in the Army) was sent overseas. We shared the cottage with them for several summers. Mom liked it better being at the beach when Aunt Sylvia and Susan joined us. Mom and Sylvia were very close and it was good for Sylvia to be with Mom while Sydney was overseas.

Crescent Beach is a small beach town on Long Island Sound, not far from Niantic. Our cottage was one of a group of three that sat just across a small road leading to the beach.

Every morning the vegetable man came around in his old truck selling fresh vegetables and fruit while the ice cream truck arrived daily at three. To this day I still remember how the vegetables and fruit smelled when I went with Mom to buy what we needed.

Our little Crescent Beach community was close knit. Families like ours rented all the surrounding beach cottages throughout the summer. Some stayed for three months like we did, others for a week or two. No matter the length of time, everyone was made to feel welcome. Crescent Beach was what you'd call a workingman's summer beach town.

I loved being at the beach. I was in the water every day. I have photographs of me at Crescent Beach with white blond hair from being out in the salt water so much.

I loved to play in the waves and had a great time building sand castles as well as running along the beach. As a kid I never tired of the sun, the water or the sand and that has not changed over the years.

*I was born in my grandparent's tract house in the unincorporated part of Los Angeles that sat between the areas known as Watts and Compton. It was 1946 and for some reason my mother could not go to the hospital so the doctors came to her.*

*On a Sunday afternoon two doctors from County General were sitting in the dining room waiting for the birth. When the labor pains grew closer my grandmother went into action. By the time the doctors had washed their hands and donned their gowns, I had arrived. I of course do not recall this incident but the shared memories of that event have been told to me on numerous occasions by my aunties. I was named Tyree (after my father's first cousin) Oneida (after my mother). The location of my birth was intriguing because two years later I would come to live in that house permanently upon the death of my mother.*

*In 1949, my mother, Oneida, went to the hospital to give birth to what would have been her fourth child. Neither of them came home. She and the baby died of amniotic fluid embolism, a very rare condition found in labor and childbirth. The shock of losing my mother, Ethel Oneida Countee Warren, and her baby was a devastating blow to the family and, as I learned later in life, to my father, Clarence Sr. His grief and despair led him to place my two brothers with his Uncle Joseph in Santa Monica, and me with our maternal grandparents, Arthur and Ethel Countee.*

*At the time of my mother's passing we lived on 118ᵗʰ St. in Los Angeles. My father, Clarence Sr., and my Uncle Noyal, my mother's half-brother, painted cars in the vacant yard next to our house after they finished their respective day jobs. Our father would sometimes play hooky from work to detail cars. He and Uncle Noyal also painted houses when work was slow.*

*Later that year my grandparents told our father that his children needed to be together so Arthur put my father in the car and drove him to Santa Monica to retrieve my brothers. After that I never saw him again.*

*For most of my life I thought he left because he did not want to raise three small children. Somehow I never asked my family specifically why he left and no one ever thought to explain.*

*Years later when I was an adult my Cousin Erni and I were visiting our Uncle Chuck, my mother's younger brother. He, my Aunt Rubey and my mother often went out together. My father came up in our conversation that afternoon, and to my surprise my uncle told me that our father left because he was so in love with my mother that her death had devastated him. Uncle Chuck told me that one evening, when they were out to dinner, my father was so distraught over my mother's death that he put his fist through a wall at a restaurant. It was shortly after that that he left town. "Yes, your father loved him some Oneida," was how Uncle Chuck put it.*

*How could I have not known that? Suddenly I felt sorry for my father. How horrible it must have been for him to lose his wife and baby so suddenly. But I also wondered why that kept him from coming back for us as he told my brother Clarence that he would.*

*Strangely enough he was never a true absence in my life. He was this person who existed in title, nothing more. As I grew older my only concern was that one day he would return and want to claim me and I would not want to go with him. Like I said, I never saw him, but occasionally he'd call.*

*As a child, I do remember his calls, usually late at night. Our grandparents would wake us and march us into their bedroom where the phone was located. We lined up and spoke to him each one in turn. As I recall the conversation was always the same: "Tyree, don't you remember me? I'm your daddy. I used to sit you on my knee and read you stories," he'd say slurring his words. My response: "No, I don't." As I grew older I realized the alcohol he had consumed to gather the strength to call us caused the slur in his voice.*

*My brothers, Clarence Nokomis Warren Jr. and Robert Nelson Warren, and I came to live with our maternal grandparents when we were six, five and two years of age respectively. Having raised their own seven children they took on the responsibility of three very young grandchildren. It was a huge undertaking on their part. Their youngest child, my Aunt Beverly, was only two years older than Clarence. After we moved in, because of the closeness in age, she became our "sister," not our aunt.*

*The age at which a parent disappears impacts children differently. Clarence Jr. as the oldest remembered our father and continued to long for a reconnection with him, which never happened. When Clarence Sr. did call the phone numbers he left were never correct. In 1961, Clarence received a letter from our father stating that he was living in Kankakee, Illinois, had remarried and had a daughter, Joanne. It was the last letter Clarence received. He continued to attempt to find our father and finally in early 2000, by using his social security number, found that our father had died in 1990.*

*Robert, the middle child, was hurt, confused and resentful of our loss. During those first few months in Santa Monica, when Aunt Rubey and Aunt Pat would go visit, they found Robert crying and asking for our mother.*

*As for me, being the baby, too young to remember, I was able to transfer the role of mom and dad to my grandparents. It often confused people when I called my grandparents mama and daddy but it was a puzzlement quickly explained.*

*The home our grandparents provided was a joyful place. It's a funny thing about space. The home I live in now is three times the size of the home where I grew up. Now I have four bedrooms, three baths. The house supported three people: husband, wife and daughter. My grandparents' home had two bedrooms and one bathroom and supported six people, yet never once as a child did I feel it wasn't big enough. Let's not even talk about closet space. The reality is we had a lot less of everything and still felt as though we had more than enough of what was really important— unconditional love. We had each other and a home that was filled with music, games, books and laughter.*

*Our grandparents took pride in their home, the first house purchased when the tract went up for sale in 1944. Years after Ethel sold the house in 1968, the neighbors continued to refer it to as the "Countee house." It always had a neatly mowed lawn (work accomplished by my brothers) with neatly trimmed flowerbeds and was the showplace of the neighborhood. In the backyard we had a wonderful covered patio, where daddy built a barbecue pit. We had an orange tree, a large, plentiful lemon tree, and an apricot tree that provided preserves during the winter. We hung tin pie plates in the branches to frighten the birds away from the apricots, but they often sat on the branches playing with the shiny objects.*

*In the back of the garage, mother planted a small vegetable garden. Unfortunately it was often inhabited by insects which I didn't like, but which my brothers did. Robert took pleasure in capturing large green caterpillars and performing various experiments I chose not to watch. But the garden provided lettuce, collard greens, tomatoes and melons. For many years we had an incinerator where we burned the weekly trash until the city banned the practice.*

*The living room held a brocade sofa in rose tones, four occasional chairs, a coffee table with matching end tables, and a pedestal desk where Arthur would sit and write checks for the monthly bills. They transformed the small dining area to allow for a baby grand piano where daddy would sit and write songs, give piano lessons, and provide the family with frequent piano concerts. They expanded the front window to a "picture" window to bring in more light and show off the piano. It was a treasured space where I would often lie under the piano to read.*

*They knocked out the back wall of the house to build a den, our family room, which opened on one side to the dining room. The other three walls held large windows, again for light. This is where we spent most of our indoor time; the living room was for company.*

*The den had a green vinyl couch that opened to a double bed where the boys slept after we outgrew the practice of two kids in each twin bed in the kids' room. Beverly and I got the twin beds and Clarence and Robert moved to the den every night to make up their bed on the sofa. A small television sat on one corner and on the other sat our prized fish aquarium.*

*We had guppies that bred, well, like guppies, angelfish that were beautiful but fragile, neons that cost 10¢ each and a catfish that was with us for a very long time. When he died we put him in a matchbox and buried him in the backyard with a serious funeral and a plaque, "Here lies Catty, our catfish." I loved that aquarium and could sit for long stretches of time watching the fish. Sometimes we were lucky enough to see the fish give birth. The little fish would squirt out and immediately hide in the water plants.*

*A long low bookcase was filled with books, classic literature and today what would be called Black History books. My grandfather made a wonderful scrapbook with clippings from* Life *and* Look *magazines with articles about slavery in America. It was truly our "family" room. We played Canasta and Chinese Checkers and gathered together to watch television. I loved our home. It was a place where people felt welcome and I felt safe and secure.*

For years Dad's factory had been very profitable for his New York bosses. So every year he'd ask for a raise but they kept putting him off. "Next year," they would say, then give him a check for a few hundred dollars to keep him happy. But in 1949 he knew the factory was making big money so he went to see them in New York to ask for a raise.

His bosses agreed Dad deserved a raise so they offered to raise his salary by $15 a month. Dad countered and asked for $25. They said no, $15 was all they could afford. Dad left the meeting very disappointed.

Shortly after returning from New York, Dad got a call from his brother Sam. Sam was now living in Miami, and made my father a business offer. He wanted to form a coat factory called Wieder of California (in Florida, but the word California had more cachet). Dad would handle the production work and Sam would handle sales. Sam would put up half the money they needed to start, and Dad would put up the other half. Miami was the place to be, Sam told Dad. There was cheap labor and the weather was great all year round. The more Sam talked, the more Dad was interested. But of course, he still had to talk to Mom. I remember they argued about the move.

"I don't want to live in Miami. It's too far from New York, and you know how I feel about your family." Mom thought Dad's sisters were snobbish towards her. "Besides, who do we know in Miami?" she asked.

"You know Yola and Magda and Jack and Isador and Sam and Elsie and…"

"Those are your family, Jimmy. Not mine," said Mom.

"Hilda… I'll be my own boss."

"I don't want to go, Jimmy."

But Dad wanted out of New Britain. He'd been working for Bernstein and Shapiro for over 12 years and their refusal to offer him a substantial raise made him realize it was time to move on. So Dad went to the bank, wired most of his life savings to Sam in Miami and Wieder of California was born.

In the summer of 1949 we moved to Miami. Dad was happy, Mom… not so much.

Driving down to Miami was an eye-opening experience for all of us. I'd never been in the south and I know Mom hadn't been either. I was seven years old and it was the first time I'd ever been anywhere where there were separate facilities for black and white people. It was the first time I came face to face with segregation. I'd seen news reports on television about such things but it didn't seem real to me. It wasn't something I personally witnessed in my day-to-day life. It wasn't something that took place in my world. So when I saw it for real, it surprised me. Suddenly I was witnessing for the very first time what segregation looked like. Even at a young age I remember it made me very uncomfortable.

I'll never forget the first time I saw separate signs for white and black water fountains, toilets, and separate seating sections at restaurants. Living in Florida, I realized, was going to be a lot different than living in Connecticut. My folks didn't like segregation and said so many times while we lived in Connecticut. The whole time we lived in Florida we never got used to it.

Years later I remember thinking about those signs when I sat down to write my play, *Voices*. I thought about them as I listened to the recorded voices of African American men and women talk about their lives as slaves during the Civil War. My memory of those signs is still vivid as is the angry feeling I got when I first saw them.

I grew up in a family that had relatives murdered in the Holocaust. Relatives who were rounded up and taken in box cars to concentration camps where they were separated then taken to the gas chambers to be killed. I had been educated to understand the terrible consequences of separating races.

We were in Miami Beach for four years. For the first two years life was good. Dad rented a house on 86th Street and Mom started to adjust to living in Florida. She wasn't thrilled but she figured out a way to maintain.

Because the summer weather was so hot and humid Dad rented a cabana at the Sagamore Hotel for us so we could use the pool and keep cool during the day.

I loved going to the Sagamore. Mom and I would get up in the morning and after breakfast we'd take the bus to the hotel. There we'd hang out all day. I'd go swimming in the huge pool and Mom would play canasta with friends.

I loved my time at the pool. I made friends with the lifeguards and enjoyed the run of the place. I swam in the ocean and learned how to dive off of the 10-meter diving board. I was in the water all day long and thus my swimming improved.

During those first two years we took lots of driving trips throughout the state. We visited the Everglades, Silver Springs, and Key West and really enjoyed ourselves seeing all the attractions the state had to offer. Dad took me to the racetrack and dog track and we even went to the Jai alai games. Life was fun.

Then in the third year things began to change. The business began to flounder. Dad said Sam wasn't selling enough to make the business successful. Money got tight and that caused a strain in the house. Mom and Dad began to argue. Mom kept after Dad to leave the business before he lost everything but Dad wasn't ready to give up. Things got worse and finally one night Dad and Mom had a fight that resulted in Dad choking Mom in a fit of anger. Before anything more happened he ran out of the house and was gone for three days. When he came home he was greatly distressed about his behavior and soon after that he told us we were leaving Miami and moving to Los Angeles where he'd found a new job managing a factory in Oxnard, California.

That first summer in Los Angeles was tough for both Mom and me. I didn't have any friends and Mom didn't drive so she was stuck in the house. Every morning Dad took the car and drove to Oxnard, a 90-minute drive. Very soon that drive became a real burden. Four hours on the road every day will do that to you. Plus, the job wasn't working out for him. He wasn't getting the money that his new boss had agreed to pay him so Dad started looking for a new job again. Then one day in August he came home and told us he was going back to work for his old bosses in New Britain and would be leaving at the end of the month to return to Connecticut. Since I was just getting ready to start school Mom and I would have to stay in California until next summer. Mom was stunned and so was I. He said he'd be back for the holidays and then return next June to move us back to Connecticut.

Mom got very upset. She didn't want to go back to New Britain. She didn't want to go back to snow and cold weather. She liked being close to her family, and by then her mother and her brother Henry had moved to Burbank, only 10 minutes from where we were living. Then she realized if Dad were gone, who would drive her around to get food or go to the stores? He told her she'd have to get a driver's license and begin to drive herself.

Right after Dad left Mom began her driving lessons. She took instruction twice a week and within a month got her license. She was very excited about it. She could go anywhere she wanted by herself. Suddenly she was independent. It was to be a most interesting year.

Not long after getting her license Mom told me to get into the car. We were going to Hollywood to see a movie. I think it was *Hondo* with John Wayne. It was the first time she would drive from our North Hollywood house to Hollywood via the 101 Freeway. It was a big adventure.

I remember that drive clearly. Mom drove very carefully and very slowly. At first she was nervous and didn't say a word. But once we got off the freeway in Hollywood, Mom was suddenly very talkative. We made our way to the parking lot next to Grauman's Chinese Theatre. She parked, we got out and she gave me a big hug. She had made it to Hollywood on her own. She could drive the LA freeways and go anywhere she wanted. It was a liberating feeling for her.

Mom loved going to the movies and now that she could drive we started going to the movies twice a week. It was from Mom that I got my love of movies.

Around Christmas, Dad returned. Mom was glad to see him. He didn't say much about the New Britain job, just that it wasn't the same as it used to be. But the money was good and he said he'd found a nice house for us in Hartford. Mom wasn't thrilled about returning to Connecticut but she had a driver's license so she'd be able to get around on her own.

After New Year's Day, Dad flew back to New York. The first half of 1954 went by pretty fast. We left North Hollywood in June of 1954 and drove straight across the middle of the country to Connecticut, arriving in Hartford seven days later.

Our new home was on Cumberland Street in southwest Hartford. It was a nice neighborhood made up primarily of Irish Catholics with some Greeks and a few Italian families thrown in. We were the only Jews on the street. Our house was a two-story brick structure with green and white window shutters and a sun deck on top of the garage. It had a traditional New England look to it.

At our first Christmas we learned our street was known for the beautiful Christmas decorations that adorned every home. However, since we were Jewish, we didn't put any up. So that first year every house in the neighborhood except ours was decorated with beautiful Christmas lights. Our house looked very out of place. It was as if we had a big sign on our front lawn that read, "Jews Live Here."

So the next year we went all out and joined in the Christmas festivities. We decorated our house in green and white lights and had a giant Christmas tree in the living room that everyone could see through our living room picture window. We also had a small menorah in the window as well. That year our house took third prize for best decorations on the street. Mom was very pleased with that.

In the fall of 1955 I joined the Hartford YMCA swim team. I was a very good swimmer and won swim events in record fashion in my age group (11 to 12-year-olds) all over the state. I swam freestyle sprints. Over the next two years I won YMCA, AAU, and New England championships. My swimming exploits were written up in the local newspapers. The *Hartford Courant* did an article on Dad and me emphasizing that Dad was a former professional soccer player and Hungarian running star. He was very proud of that article.

I also joined the local Boy Scout troop. That gave me the opportunity to attend the World Jamboree of Scouts at Valley Forge, Pennsylvania the summer of 1955. While I was at the Jamboree I wrote a series of "letters" about the Jamboree that were published every day on the front page of the *Hartford Courant*. I got that assignment after winning a writing contest sponsored by the newspaper. I was really happy about winning the writing contest, not just because my "letters" would appear in the paper but because I was also being paid for every article that appeared. My professional writing career had begun.

As much as joining the Boy Scouts and the YMCA swim team was exciting, the most memorable event that took place while I was in Junior High was my first sexual encounter. When I was 12 I lost my virginity in a pretty bizarre way. The mother of one of my friends seduced me. At the time it was a frightening experience. I wasn't prepared.

After it was over I was very confused and afraid. I was afraid of what I'd done because of whom I'd done it with, my friend's mom. That really bothered me. Somehow I felt if anyone found out, *I* would be punished. But in regards to the actual act of intercourse? That's another story. Let's just say I found that part… enjoyable.

Not long after that encounter my friend and his mom moved away and I never saw him or his mom again. I never told my parents about it. I didn't think it was something I could share with my folks.

In the spring of 1955 my dad reminded me my Bar Mitzvah was next year. We weren't what you'd call religious Jews. We were High Holy Day Jews. That meant we usually attended High Holy Days services.

So, with my Bar Mitzvah looming on the horizon, Dad took me to see the Rabbi, and one, two, three I am enrolled in Hebrew classes to prepare for my Bar Mitzvah.

I meet once a week with the Cantor who attempts to teach me my section of the Torah. It's a struggle but we press on. The one good thing I have going for me is a good singing voice. He asks if I have ever thought about being a Cantor. Me? Never. (I'm just trying to learn my Bar Mitzvah and he's trying to recruit me to the Yeshiva.)

Dad hires a tutor to help me learn the Hebrew. We meet twice a week. It's slow going but I plunge ahead until finally Bar Mitzvah day arrives. Inside the synagogue I sit on the Bema and look out to a packed sanctuary. I look up to the balcony where the ladies sit and see Mom with my grandmother along with my aunts and female cousins all sitting in the center of the first row looking down at me. Downstairs sit all the men. Dad sits with my uncles front row center.

The service begins. When it comes time for my part, my chanting in Hebrew actually comes off sounding pretty good. I get through the prayers without any trouble. Torah reading is next. I start chanting and after a few minutes make it through without any problems. Now all that's left is my speech. Thanks Mom. Thanks Dad. Thanks for coming everyone. Today I am a man. Yada, yada, yada. My folks love the speech. Then it's time to celebrate.

The party is held at our house. It lasts all day and night. I am given handsome monetary gifts along with the obligatory fountain pens and wristwatches. The money I receive is immediately placed into a bank account for my future education. The party finally breaks up early Sunday morning. In the end my folks were very proud of my accomplishment. So now I was a man.

In June 1956 I graduated Junior High. Next stop Buckley High School. I was ready.

*When you live in a segregated community you don't encounter overt racial issues because everyone you encounter is also black. The covert racism touched me indirectly because it impacted our neighborhood in subtle ways. My grandmother shopped for groceries in the white neighborhoods because she said they brought the old meat and produce to the stores closest to us. Every Friday she and my grandfather would travel to the markets just outside the Compton border for their weekly food shopping. They subscribed to the* Los Angeles Times, *but also to the black-owned* Sentinel *newspaper in order to get the information on issues in our community. They subscribed to* Look *and* Life *magazines, but also to* Jet *and* Ebony *to get the stories on black celebrities and politicians. Almost every adult conversation included the topic of being black in America, not in a negative way, but as a fact of life. When I was older and became involved in the Jewish community I was surprised to learn that Jews as a minority also talked about being Jewish as much as blacks talked about being black. I had to chuckle to myself when I realized that such self-consciousness was common among members of minority groups.*

*There were gangs when I was growing up, but none of the drive-by shootings and level of violence that began in the 1980s when crack cocaine and guns were introduced to our community. In the 1950s we all pretty much knew who the gang members were and they pretty much left non-gang members alone. There was no fear of walking into someone's territory if you were not a gang member, no fear of wearing the wrong color. But still it was important to know where trouble spots might be, and as a little girl I instinctively knew to be cautious and watchful of my surroundings. My brother Clarence was once beaten up by a group of thugs when he was walking home from high school with a girlfriend. He hadn't strayed onto the wrong street, he was on a main boulevard, but he was told the beating was an initiation activity. He came home with a broken nose and was pretty bloody; the young lady was not bothered at all. Even though in our immediate neighborhood there was no gang activity, after that incident my grandparents encouraged us to be more vigilant when we were out and about.*

*So even though there was some gang activity in the community at large my grandparents were comforted to a degree by the neighborliness of where we lived. People knew each other and looked out for each other. For example one evening my brothers were coming home from choir practice and decided to stop at the local drug store and for reasons far beyond my comprehension decided to shoplift a candy bar. The store clerk caught them and instead of calling the police, as is often done today, he kept Clarence at the store and sent Robert home to fetch our grandfather. My grandfather returned to the store with Robert to get Clarence and meet with the store clerk. Beverly and I stayed home anxiously awaiting their return. When they returned my grandparents sat us all down and talked about what the boys had done. No spankings this time, but a stern discussion about doing what is right. Their disappointment and the embarrassment the boys suffered turned into a life lesson.*

*There was a fervent respect for older blacks in the community and the church carried significant weight. Pastors were respected and listened to (within reason). Certain places, churches, schools and libraries were off limits to graffiti.*

*Other subtle messages came to me as a kid. For years into my adulthood, I reacted to anyone with a Southern accent with immediate apprehension. I never said anything overtly but gauged my acceptance of them by first assessing their potential for prejudice. Southern food was wonderful, but all else Southern was to be viewed with suspicion until I knew better. No one ever said to me people with Southern accents were bad, I just instinctively knew to be wary.*

*But there is always the yin and the yang of life; there were laughs as well when it came to being black in South Central. When we were kids, outdoors playing or engaged in a board game, we had to stop what we were doing and run into the room with the television because there was "a black person on TV." No matter whose house you were at, there was mandatory running to the television to see the black person on TV. Unfortunately the sightings were often quick and by the time we got to the television the vision had vanished and it was all for naught. As kids we thought it was hilarious and would return to our games yelling, out of earshot of our parents, "Come quick, there is a black person on TV." Of course to our parents, who really thought it was an American breakthrough, it was really important.*

*Then there were "flesh-colored" Band-Aids. Yes, Johnson & Johnson actually made flesh-colored Band-Aids. We would put them on and laugh and laugh about whose flesh they matched. Clearly not ours.*

*The other fun item was greeting cards. All the faces were white, or even worse, white and blond. So sometimes we would buy them and color in the faces. But we had to be careful which crayon we chose, because in that crayon box was a "flesh"-colored crayon.*

*Because times have changed we no longer have "flesh-colored" Band-Aids and Hallmark has realized there is a market to be made from ethnic cards. However, because I'm in an interracial marriage, I still can't find cards that fit our situation, so I sometimes buy a card and color in the female. My daughter gets a kick out of that bit of artistic work.*

*Holidays at the Countee house were always fun and filled with family. To provide a sense of our celebrations, Memorial Day is a great example. The day always began with the aroma of meat on the grill. Daddy was always up early on holidays to start cooking. He would fire the barbecue pit so all the grilling would be done by early afternoon. The smell of spare ribs came floating through our open bedroom window and we woke up smiling because we knew a feast awaited us that afternoon.*

*We dressed quickly and headed to the kitchen where Beverly was making our usual breakfast, oatmeal. After breakfast, the chores had to be done, sweeping and dusting, setting up folding tables and chairs in anticipation of the family that would be arriving soon. My chore was to set out the red-checkered picnic tablecloths and put all the board games on the table. By 10 or 11 the aunts, uncles and cousins would arrive. I could hardly wait for my cousins to race into the backyard so we could begin a full day of board games, cards, hide and seek, jump rope, and jacks. But first after everyone had arrived we had a trip to make.*

*It was Memorial Day weekend and we had to take the time to honor my late mother, Oneida. With one of my uncles staying behind to tend the barbecue grill, we loaded the cars and went to the cemetery, about a 15-minute drive. Stopping at the gate we purchased flowers to go along with the few we had taken from my grandparents' garden. There was a ritual with this. The aunts led the way with my grandparents coming next, then the uncles, and finally the kids walked in order to my mother's gravesite. My brothers and I had been told that when a person dies, after they are buried, their souls rise slowly to heaven. For many years, as a very young child, I would look at the area above my mother's grave and squint to see if I could see her spirit rising, but I never could. It was not a sad trip to the cemetery, it was a time that we went to say hello and let her know that we were thinking about her. We didn't stay very long, but long enough to hold hands and say a prayer. My grandmother would give an update on the three of us, the three my mother had left behind, and boy did I want those reports to be good. For the weeks leading up to Memorial Day I was on my best behavior to ensure a favorable report. With the grave dressed, our prayer finished and the report given, in reverse order we loaded into the cars and returned to the house.*

*By then my grandfather's friends had arrived at our house, his co-workers and buddies from the Post Office. His Cousins Odell and Marcus also arrived with their families. I so enjoyed watching these senior citizens, these older black men who had lived what I thought were fascinating lives. Several of them were musicians and I listened to their stories of Friday night dinners when they all came together to eat catfish and play in rousing jam sessions. They talked about the clubs they used to go to and how they danced all night. They sat around the table while daddy finished cooking the meat, ribs and chicken, hot dogs and hot links. Even though it was a bit early in the day, they had brought their friends with them, Jim Beam and Johnnie Walker. They nibbled on chips and sipped their whisky. My grandfather would sit at the head of the table while we ran around, as kids do, and I would hear him tell his friends that this was the life, having his family around him and being with his friends. It made him proud and I felt so happy that he was happy.*

*By early afternoon the grilling was complete and the rest of the feast was brought outside from the kitchen. Collard greens, corn on the cob, hot corn bread, coleslaw, baked beans and ice-cold lemonade. The lemonade was made with the lemons from our tree, so to me it was really special because I had helped to squeeze the lemons the day before. We sat around the tables and laughed and ate, and ate and ate. Then dessert was brought out from the kitchen, peach cobbler, served with homemade vanilla ice cream. My world was complete.*

*After cleaning the dishes, the games continued. Each table hosted a different set of games. The older men always played dominoes, slamming down their pieces and calling out their points so loudly that the neighbors across the street could probably hear them. I learned early on that you couldn't play dominoes unless you could slam the dominoes and yell out your points; and clearly girls were not allowed at the table.*

*As the sun was starting to set it was time for the aunts and uncles to call my cousins to their cars. The final rounds of "last tag" back and forth between all the children continued, arms reaching through the car windows until the cars pulled away from the curb. My grandmother would call the four of us in for our baths and to get ready for bed. Being the youngest, I was usually first. After a hot bath and clean pajamas I was ready to crawl under the covers. My siblings followed and we talked about our day and how much fun we had with our cousins.*

*Holidays were joyful times, my grandparents beaming and happy that the family had come together. This ritual was repeated throughout the year. I looked forward to the Fourth of July, Labor Day, Thanksgiving, Christmas, Easter, birthdays and anniversaries. Each national holiday our family celebration was an opportunity for us to come together. These events taught me the importance of family and the importance of sharing happiness. Coming together was a foundation of the Countee household and it is a tradition that continues in our family.*

*Growing up with my brothers and Beverly was always an adventure. During our playtime we not only played games, but also made them up. One game, "Your Favorite Time in History," was played frequently. We had to state a time and place and tell about why we wanted to live then and there. As the youngest, I did not have as much material to work with, but I did my best to keep up with the older kids. One day I selected the "Old South." I wanted to live in one of those big plantation houses and wear one of those big white dresses like Scarlett O'Hara. With a wide grin and a laugh, my sister, Beverly, informed me that if I lived then and there, I would not be wearing one of those big white dresses, nor would I be living in the house, I would be in the field in a burlap sack picking cotton—a dream shattered.*

*Another of our favorite games was to travel around the house on safari, which meant we went around the house not touching the floor, jumping from one piece of furniture to the next, losing points each time a foot hit the ground; obviously a game played when my grandparents were not home.*

*As all children did, we had a bedtime curfew, but when my grandparents were not home we never made that curfew. Our dog, Rusty, would start to bark when the family car was making the turn from Central Ave. onto our street. This gave us time to turn off the TV and dive into bed. Why we thought my grandfather was not very smart I will never know. He would come in, touch the top of the TV then head to the bedroom belt in hand. We lay in bed pretending to snore like we had been asleep for hours. He laughed and would spank us over the covers until we started to laugh and give ourselves away.*

*Oh yes, those stories about choosing your own switch from the tree are true. Ours was the big apricot tree out back, and yes, you had to come back with a decent switch or daddy would get a bigger one. I hated the thought of the switch, so I was always a good girl. My brothers were the troublemakers. Robert seemed to get in trouble the most.*

*In those days it was perfectly acceptable to get "a keen switch." Never was sure what that meant, but my grandmother always said it, and "just hit the back of those little legs." That was in the toddler phase. As you got bigger, the belt came off.*

*Being the youngest had advantages and disadvantages. On the plus side, Robert included me in his hobbies. I assisted with the building of his model airplanes and read spelling words as he studied for upcoming tests. When he was in the cadet corps I served as his "company" as he marched me around the backyard to practice his cadence calls. He was always quick to try to teach me new things, how to ride a bike or how to fix my skates. The first time I had to shave under my arms I was afraid I would cut myself, so he took the razor and did it for me. At night he would brush my hair because in the movie* Little Women, *the sisters were always brushing their hair. Clarence, being a bit older, always saw himself as my protector, and when he could provide it I would find an extra nickel or quarter in my pocket. My brothers were my champions, my caretakers. I was the little sister and I loved the role.*

*Beverly, our "big sister," was a terror. She ruled the house, especially when our grandparents were gone. She was the baby in her house until the three of us arrived so at first we were somewhat of an imposition. She was bossy and "knew everything." But she was also our caretaker when my grandparents were not home and enjoyed having the role of big sister. She would lock us out of the house and not let us back in until just before they were scheduled to return. She also enjoyed the roll of dictator. Once she broke a vase, blamed it on Robert and dared him not to tell that she had done it. She and Clarence would get into real fights, screaming and throwing things. Robert and I would watch and wait for the dust to settle, which it always did. The altercations ended just as fast as they started and sometimes ended in laughter. I grew up thinking that all older brothers and sisters fought, especially when they were so close in age. Today of course they are very close and no one would ever know they fought all those years. For a long time Beverly never fessed up to the fact that she was such a terror, but now as we are all getting older, she admits she was pretty bad. But in spite of the overreaching bad behavior, she was our big sister, and we knew we could count on her when needed.*

*Spiders were my big downfall; they frightened me terribly. One day grandmother was washing grapes from the neighbor's yard to make jelly. The grapes were in the sink when the phone rang. She asked me to watch the sink to be sure none of the ants crawled out of the water onto the counter. I proceeded to stick my arm in the water and play with the grapes. All of a sudden I looked down and the biggest spider in America was crawling up my arm. I screamed so loud that my brothers who were working in the yard raced into the house. Mother dropped the phone and charged back into the kitchen. When they found out it was a spider they all laughed at me. Grandmother was really upset because now they had* no idea where the spider was because I had flung it somewhere. I received no sympathy for my plight of the spider attack and sat in the corner of the den crying until daddy came home. At least from him I got some sympathy. If I saw a spider, they would lock me in a room until I killed the creepy crawling thing, crying through the whole ordeal. Today, I still hate those creepy crawly things.

It seems that I was always providing my siblings with some reason to laugh at me. One day I was sitting on the curb in front of the house watching my siblings play ball with the neighborhood kids. Suddenly the dog from next door came up to me and licked me in the mouth. Because my grandmother was a bit of a clean freak and always warned us about germs, when the dog licked me in the mouth I truly thought I was going to die. I screamed, jumped up and ran into the house, grabbed a bar of Ivory soap and proceeded to wash out my mouth, of course crying the whole time. The soap tasted terrible. The siblings and friends followed me into the house trying to find out what had happened. When I explained through the tears and gagging on the Ivory soap that the dog had licked me in the mouth and I was going to die, they literally rolled on the floor laughing

I entered kindergarten at George Washington Carver Elementary. My memories of Carver are very positive. We had teachers who cared for their students and worked hard to give us not only "book" learning, but talked to us about life and surviving in a world that might not be too friendly to us. We were black children in a white world and there were things we needed to understand.

We were taught that we had to navigate the world differently than white children, that restrictions would be placed on us for some of the things we wanted to do. I specifically remember being told that going to college was not going to be easy, we would have to work twice as hard as white children to succeed. I was not exactly sure what that meant, but it kept me on the working-hard-to-succeed path.

But we also were taught to enjoy what we had. We danced the May Pole, had square dancing classes, and bank day on Thursdays to learn about savings (I think there may be some money left in an old Security Pacific Bank account somewhere). We learned to draw and play music; I played the recorder, a small flute-like instrument, and my brother, Robert, learned to play the cello. We acted in holiday plays and sang in spring concerts. My grandmother participated in the PTA and made cookies for the bake sales. She sewed costumes for various programs. I was so proud that she was always there to help.

One wonderful mentor from elementary school was Mrs. Nance. She *worked in the principal's office and remains a friend to this day. Now in her 90s she lives in a retirement complex in Long Beach. Her daughter, Collette, and I were best friends. When I was married Mrs. Nance hosted a lingerie shower for me and invited all of my elementary school teachers. To my surprise, all seven of them attended. Well up in age, they came smiling, laughing and happy to see me; and to my embarrassment brought some of the frilliest nighties. When Collette and I saw gray haired Mrs. Hall walking up the driveway we were astonished. We thought she was 80 when she was our third grade teacher 15 years earlier and here she was coming up the driveway with a bounce in her step. Actually the yellow and green nightie she brought was the skimpiest. I remember being a bit embarrassed when I held it up. These were women who cared about their students, and their attendance at my shower was a testament to their continued caring well beyond my time in their classroom.*

*Before I left elementary school I received my Social Security card. I was in the third grade. Somehow, the children in the family—my siblings, Aunt Rubey's kids, and I—were signed up as extras in the movies. Beverly and Clarence were extras in* Pinky, *the 1949 drama about a light-skinned black woman passing for white. Clarence and Robert accounted for 20 of the 5,000* Fingers of Dr. T *in the 1953 movie about a young boy who doesn't enjoy his piano lessons. They also had scenes in* Show Boat *and* I Remember Mama. *My claim to fame was in one* Amos 'n' Andy *Christmas show. I was one of the children standing in line waiting to sit on Andy's knee as he played Santa Claus. As I recall, I earned $12, and my grandmother let me go with her to the store to select clothes with my earnings. However, I never got as much work as the others.*

*One day I was in the studio waiting for the others to finish a scene. I was standing next to my grandmother with one of the studio men. I asked him why I couldn't be in the scene with the others. The studio man, who I recall was very tall, leaned over and told me it was because I bit my fingernails. I thought that was pretty odd because how could the camera see my fingernails? But in those days, children my age did not contradict grown-ups, so I didn't say anything. It was not until I was a bit older that I realized that being the "high yella" girl in the family, I was not dark enough to show up as a "colored" girl on film. So my film career was limited to the back of the line in that* Amos 'n' Andy *Christmas show. My Cousin Erni actually got to sit on Andy's lap. Even though I did not work as much as the others did, I still was able to go to the studio with them. We spent the day playing in the parking lot when they were not on call. All in all it was a unique experience and another bonding time for the Countee kids.*

My grandmother was a soloist in the church choir and would sing
hymns at home. My grandfather was always composing songs and hymns
like "When Life Crumbles, What Then?", songs for friends' weddings
like "Blessed be the Tie That Binds," songs that spoke to the struggle
of the black man in America like "When?" (the lyrics began, "When
oh when will my brother be a true loving brother to me? When I was in
bondage I could not read, I could not write, but now I am free and he
does not treat me right") and arranging orchestrations. He was featured
on a Tommy Dorsey album, A Swinging String of Pearls. He also wrote
fun songs for us to sing that had a boogie-woogie beat like, "Me, My
Baby, and My Double Bubble Gum," and "Grandma Loved Her Coffee."
He always sent his compositions to the Library of Congress Copyright
Office. He said it was important to be sure no one took his music for their
own, another lesson for me about being smart in life.

It gave me such joy to experience my grandparents' music and hear
their stories about the old days when they performed around town. My
grandmother sang as a soloist in New York with W. C. Handy, the father of the blues, and for a short time my grandfather played with Count
Basie. Their talent always moved me.

Our time at the studios ended just about the time I was ready to go
to junior high school. Compared to my experience at Carver, my junior
high school was unruly. I was surprised that many students showed little
respect for teachers and would talk in class and joke around. No one, it
seemed, listened to what the teachers said.

I think I received good grades in English because I sat at the front
of the class and was polite. Our math teacher made up games to help us
learn math but it was clear to me the students did not appreciate his efforts. They made fun of him because he was old and stooped over when he
walked. But in Social Studies, Ms. Carr, one of the few African American
teachers, was a strict disciplinarian, and all the students knew you did
not mess with her.

After junior high my grandparents decided it was time for me to move
to Whittier, where there were better schools, to live with Aunt Rubey and
Uncle Herbert and my cousins. I left junior high as one of the top students
in the school, but when I entered high school I soon learned I did not have
the skills that matched those grades. The summer before my entry into
high school, I had an experience that would stay with me for many years.

I had joined the Girl Scouts in elementary school and had great experiences with my troop. Our leaders were wonderful women I looked up
to. I worked hard to earn merit badges, badges I still have tucked away in
my dresser. The summer before I moved to Whittier, I had the opportunity

*to attend an away Girl Scout camp on Catalina Island.*

*My grandparents could not afford to send me, but our troop received one scholarship to the camp. The troop leaders gave it to me. I was thrilled. It was an amazing opportunity. Robert helped me pack my clothes for camp. He had some Boy Scout items he let me borrow, a mess kit and poncho. Then the most wonderful thing happened just as I was ready to get in the car to go to the pier. My grandfather came into the bedroom with a small box with a red bow. Now he never bought gifts, that was my grandmother's responsibility. Sure he took her to the store and probably provided the money, but she made the choices. This time it was something he picked out just for me. I opened the box and was ecstatic to see an official Girl Scout knife and compass. I had never had real Girl Scout logo items, only secondhand items from the Salvation Army Store, or from my brothers. My grandfather had gone to the store to get this just for me. Wow, what a send-off to camp. Today I still have both.*

*When we arrived at the camp, I was assigned to a cabin with 11 other girls. I was the only black girl in the group, which was a new experience for me, but I was anxious to meet new friends. We had some time before dinner, so we stowed our duffel bags and introductions were made around the cabin. Someone suggested we go outside to play before the dinner bell. One of the girls suggested a race to a rock that was just up the road.*

*We lined up and she said, "Okay, last one to the rock is a nigger." Everyone took off at a gallop, except me. My feet froze and my mind said, "Did she really say that?" I stood there dumbfounded and was still trying to process what had just occurred when two of the girls stopped running and returned to me. Realizing what had just happened, they all came back and asked if I was all right? I did not answer, just looked at them, because I wasn't sure if I was or not. By then the others returned laughing and, seeing me in somewhat of a stupor, remembered the fate of the loser, to be a "nigger." Now a deafening silence took over. I was still a bit numb and they appeared to be embarrassed, especially the instigator of the travesty.*

*I turned and walked into the cabin and sat on my bunk. My two initial rescuers came and sat next to me, wanting me to say something, but I really had nothing to say. I was trying to decide if I was going to stay at camp or not. Sleeping with these 11 girls might not be what I wanted to do for the next seven nights. Then the rest of the girls entered the cabin and the apologies began. I listened, accepted the apology, but now the thrill of camp on Catalina had lost its luster. Understand, I was not angry, more dumbfounded that someone would actually say such a thing with me standing right there.*

*I finished the week, but kept wondering about my cabin mates. Of course the rest of the week they were model Girl Scouts, outwardly at least. But part of Scouting is learning life lessons and on Catalina I learned to be suspicious. I learned that what people say to your face might not be what is in their heart. It taught me a level of distrust, especially in racial issues, that has stayed with me, although tempered as I get older. Fortunately that last experience did not take away the positive experience I had with Scouting. My involvement in Scouting provided me with many positive life lessons, good friends, caring leaders and learning opportunities.*

# CHAPTER 4

## *Meeting Family*

1978. Early Fall. Tyree has returned from her European trip. By then we'd been together about four months. It's early morning. My place. Phone rings. I pick up. It's my mother calling from Las Vegas telling me while on vacation Dad has had a heart attack and is in the hospital. She says he's going to be all right but he'll have to stay for a week. Dad wants me to come to Las Vegas, pick up his car and drive it back to Los Angeles. The doctor won't let him drive across the desert but feels in a week he should be well enough to fly home.

I remember asking all the questions, "Is he okay? How bad was it? Is he awake?"

"Everything is fine, just come get the car and see your father," mom replies.

I tell her, "I'll be there as soon as I get a flight."

I hang up the phone and turn to Tyree. "What's going on?" she asks.

I tell her about Dad and that I have to fly to Las Vegas. Then I say, "Hey, why don't you come with me? This will be a chance to meet my folks and I won't have to drive back across the desert alone."

Tyree looks at me and says, "That's the dumbest idea I have ever heard."

"Why?" I ask.

"Think about it, Leslie," she says. "Your father just had a heart attack. He's never met me. He's in the hospital right now recovering. I walk into the room, a strange black woman. You introduce me, 'Hi Dad, this is my girlfriend Tyree,' he takes a look at me, grabs his chest and drops dead.

Bad idea, Leslie!"

But I'm not thinking straight and tell her it will be fine. I tell her I need her to come with me. I keep after her. Reluctantly she agrees but continues to tell me how dumb my idea is all during the flight to Las Vegas.

At the time I'd been waiting for just the right moment to tell my folks about Tyree. To me this seemed like the right time. Tyree wasn't convinced.

Arriving in Las Vegas we grab a cab to the hospital. We enter the lobby. Mom is there waiting. I go to her, give her a big hug and start to say something but notice she's not looking at me. Instead she's staring at this black woman standing beside me. I recover, "Mom, this is my... friend... Tyree." Mom looks at Tyree, arches an eyebrow and says, "Friend?"

Tyree steps in and gives Mom a hug and tells her how concerned we are about Dad. Mom looks at Tyree and then at me and shakes her head. Then she says, "Let's go see your father." She takes Tyree's arm and leads us to the elevator.

Third floor, my dad's room in ICU. I move towards the door but Mom stops me and says, "Let me go in first... to see if he's sleeping." She slips into the room leaving us standing in the hall. Tyree turns to me and says, "Friend?" Before I can respond the door opens and Mom motions for us to enter. Mom takes my hand and walks me over next to Dad's hospital bed. He is hooked up to beeping machines and oxygen. His eyes are closed. Mom moves to his side and touches his hand. I move to the other side of the bed and lean over and kiss his cheek. He looks pretty good considering he's had a heart attack. A mild one I'm told but nonetheless a heart attack.

As I kiss his cheek he opens his eyes and sees Tyree standing at the foot of the bed. I motion for her to come up and stand beside me. She does and I say, "Dad, this is my friend, Tyree." She leans over and takes his hand and says she hopes he feels better and asks if there's anything she can do to help. Dad smiles and says, "Take Hilda to eat. She's been here since yesterday and hasn't had breakfast." Just then the nurse comes in and tells us we all have to leave. "Too many people in the room," she says. So the three of us leave.

As Tyree and I step into the corridor Mom says, "I forgot something. I'll be right there." She turns and walks back into the room.

Outside in the corridor as we wait, I turn to Tyree. "See, that wasn't so bad was it?" Tyree just shakes her head, amazed at what's transpired. Before she can reply Mom comes out of Dad's room. "Come on," she says, "let's go have breakfast and you can tell me all about your new friend." Then she winks at Tyree, takes her arm and marches towards the elevator with me scrambling behind trying to keep up.

Years later Mom told me what was said in the hospital room as Tyree and I waited in the hall to take her to breakfast.

THE SCENE:

Dad's Hospital Room

FADE IN:

Dad lying in his hospital bed hooked up to machines and oxygen. Mom enters and moves to his side. His eyes are closed. She takes his hand.

> MOM:
> So, Jimmy, what do you think?

He opens his eyes and looks at her.

> DAD:
> (softly)
> Hilda, is she Mexican?

She shakes her head and pats his hand.

> MOM:
> No, Jimmy. Go back to sleep. Rest.

FADE OUT.

And that's how Tyree met my parents. Great timing... right?

*Our relationship was continuing and it was positive and strong. I am so close with my family and I knew it was time to bring the new guy around. There was no need to be coy about what was happening with us; I knew this relationship was permanent. We had both been around the block, so we understood relationships and how this was so tremendously different for both of us.*

*When word got out that I had left my marriage, my family was supportive. Apparently for a long time my family had felt I was not myself in the marriage. My ex was conservative in many ways and the family felt my personality had been stifled. They were correct. Les provided me with a sense of freedom I had not felt for a long time.*

*As the "model wife" for my ex I had certain characteristics to fulfill: be thin, have long hair, wear makeup. I was the accompaniment to the Pierre Cardin suits he wore and the Porsche he drove.*

*The first time Les and I went away for the weekend, I started to pack my rollers and makeup. Les wanted to know what I was doing. He told me I did not need that, we were going for a casual, relaxing weekend. I was astonished. My ex had insisted I wear false eyelashes to the drive-in. Once I went for a hair trim and the beautician cut my hair much shorter then I had intended. On the way home I purchased a wig to wear so I would not get grief over my hair being short. Les' acceptance of my natural self was so refreshing.*

*The family knew about my separation and now it was time for them to know about Les. I had told my Cousins Erni and Sheila about Les just after I met him but swore each of them to secrecy, making each think they were the only person who knew about my new love. I am not even sure why I did that, but I did.*

*When I got back from Europe and Les was my constant companion, I finally fessed up and told them that they had both been told about my new beau. They were furious. They had both kept my secret and were a bit upset, telling me they could have been talking about this affair with each other all this time. Somehow I wanted to feel them out about this new relationship with, yes, a white guy. I set up a meeting at the Hamburger Hamlet in Hollywood. Les and I walked in and Erni and Sheila were sitting in a booth waiting for us. Of course the meeting was great. They both saw how happy I was so they were happy for me.*

*When I told my sister Beverly I had met someone and that, well, he was Jewish. Her response, "Well, that's okay, we both come from slavery. That makes a connection." My brother Clarence just wanted to know if he was a nice guy and if he made me happy. Clearly no one was upset that I had left my ex. Next I called my grandmother to let her know I had met someone and assured her I was very happy and I would bring him to meet her very soon.*

*A more immediate concern for me was finding a place to live and move my belongings from my friend's garage. I found an apartment and was surprised at how high the rent was; it was comparable to my house payment. I got settled and was planning a time for my grandmother to meet Les. A few days later at the start of the fall semester I was sitting at my desk at Moorpark College when I received a call from Sheila that my grandmother had been rushed to the hospital. I left work and hit the road for the drive to Los Angeles.*

*My grandmother was 81 and in fairly good health, but did have a long-suffering problem with emphysema and had arthritis in her shoulders. As a family we scheduled daily visits to her hospital, each of us taking specific times to be with her. I went as often as I could, although Tuesday night was my assigned time.*

*One Tuesday I took Les with me to meet her. She looked so frail in her hospital bed. When I introduced Les to her she looked up and smiled. I told her he was my new friend, and she nodded politely. When he turned to leave, she looked at me again and said, "Who is that?" I smiled and told her again, he was my new friend. Aunt Rubey and Aunt Patricia were at the hospital that night and also met him. It was ironic that I first met Les' parents when his dad was in the hospital and he met my grandmother for the first time when she was in the hospital. She may not have truly understood who he was, but I was grateful that she had at least met him.*

*The next opportunity for Les to meet my family was at the annual Thanksgiving potluck at my Cousins Ron and Sheila's house. The attendance usually totaled 50 to 75 people. An all-day open house, one was sure to see relatives who lived on the other side of town, spend the day catching up and meet new friends. It was always a joyous occasion. So bringing Les to this event would give everyone the opportunity to get the meeting over with at one time.*

*Les met everyone and was his usual charming self. He immediately became part of the group and I could see that they all saw what I saw in him: an easygoing person, friendly and comfortable with who he was. My family has always been an open and accepting group of people. They welcomed Les and were very happy to see me in such a good space. My Cousin Countee told me that he was so glad to see me so happy and my brother-in-law Tommy told me Les had a lot of "soul" and seemed very much the right person for me.*

By November of '78 Tyree and I were a couple but we were still attempting to be discreet about it at work. Mom and Dad were the only ones on my side of the family who knew about us. But when it came to her family, I soon learned nothing was a secret from "the cousins." Tyree has a lot of cousins but her two closest were Sheila and Ernestine, whom everyone called Erni. So before meeting the entire family I had to meet Cousin Sheila and Cousin Erni.

It's a Friday afternoon in early fall. Tyree and I are seated in a corner booth inside the Hamburger Hamlet Restaurant on Hollywood Blvd. with Cousin Sheila and Cousin Ernestine. Both women are attractive, funny, intelligent and sharp.

Its obvious Tyree and I are in love. We sit close, holding hands under the table. Every so often she leans in and presses herself against my shoulder. We smile at each other all the time.

We eat and drink and before we know it a couple of hours have gone by. I've told them about my childhood, schools, family and anything else they ask me about. I'm at my charming best.

Then it's time to go and both cousins give me a hug and a kiss. We leave the restaurant together. On the street we split up to go to our respective cars. Tyree holds my hand as we walk away. I smile at her and say, "Went well, didn't it?" She smiles at me.

"I knew they'd love you," she says. "You're a charmer."

I smile and nod my head. "Works every time," I reply.

Right after meeting Sheila and Erni, Tyree invites me to the family Thanksgiving potluck dinner. It's time she says for me to meet her whole family. I wasn't sure what that meant but I was okay with it. I mean, how many family members could there be? I figured maybe 20 folks.

Tyree told me her brothers and cousins would all be there waiting to meet me. Oh joy, I thought. Now I get to meet "the guys."

That year Thanksgiving dinner was held at Cousins Ron and Sheila's home in Redondo Beach, California. When we arrive we walk in and the first room I see is the den. We stop in the doorway and I look in and see 20 to 25 black men seated around the room watching a football game on TV. Everyone, it seems, is shouting at the game on the TV. However, as soon as Tyree and I stand in the doorway, all talk immediately ceases and everyone turns to look at the short Jewish white guy with Tyree.

It stayed that way for about an hour or at least that's what it seemed to me… in reality it was only a few seconds. Suddenly Clarence, Tyree's older brother, appears and starts leading me outside to the patio. "Don't worry, Tyree," he says, "he'll be fine. We'll take good care of him." Tyree smiles, kisses me on the cheek and leaves to go upstairs. As I'm escorted through the room, everyone, it seems, is eyeing me.

Outside on the patio Clarence introduces me to Robert, Tyree's other brother, along with Cousins Ronald, Count and Willie. I shake hands with each one and they all greet me with either, "Hey, how you doing?" or just "Hey," until I get to Cousin Willie who shakes my hand and says in his deep bass voice, "Good morning," a phrase I will learn is his standard greeting line to everyone no matter the time of day.

"Want a beer?" asks Cousin Ronald. "Sure," I reply. Count tosses me a cold beer. I see everyone already has one. I raise my bottle, look around, smile and say, "To the family." Smiles all around. "Family," they all say. We clink bottles and drink.

Just then Tyree appears at the patio door. "You boys having a good time?" she asks. Everyone laughs. "I have to take him away so he can meet the Aunties and the rest of the family upstairs." I wave goodbye and as I'm leaving Cousin Count says to Tyree, "He's a real cool guy, he'll be good for you."

Six months after we'd begun seeing each other, everyone in our respective families knew about us. Happily both families were very accepting of us, showing us much love and affection. So once that was out of the way the serious business of creating a relationship began. Both of us began moving into new worlds. For Tyree, this meant not only being involved with a white guy in his world but also being involved with and learning about the Jewish faith and about Jews. For me it was time to experience black culture firsthand.

*While we had two separate places, Les made sure he was at my place almost every night. One night as I was setting up my apartment he actually criticized the pictures I was putting above my bed. Apparently he thought that dainty butterflies would not do it for him. I had to pause and remind him that this was actually my apartment. He quickly realized his mistake and declined to make further comments about my decorating. Smart move on his part.*

*So now we are a couple. We had met each other's family and are ready to begin getting to know each other, really know each other. Wow, I thought, I have really done this. I never dated in high school, and I married one of the first men I dated in college, and that was 10 years ago. So now at age 32 I am getting to know a new person and he comes from a world very different from mine. There is no doubt about the passion of this relationship, it is over the moon, but now there is the day-to-day living, across racial and religious lines, an unfamiliar new world for both of us. For example there were the issues of music, food and hair.*

*Our musical tastes had a clear division of black and white, though admittedly he actually had black artists in his world. I had a very limited repertoire of music, strictly R&B, some smooth jazz and light classical. I was a Motown girl who loved Gladys, Dionne, Teddy Pendergrass, Earth Wind and Fire, etc. I knew no white artists except The Beatles, Sinatra and Tony Bennett. Somehow Ms. Streisand managed to get into my collection; she was the only white artist I owned. So Les, whenever a white artist came on the radio or a singer on the TV, had to tell me who they were: Jefferson Airplane, Guns and Roses, Joe Cocker, The Eagles, etc. I had no clue. He had a much larger musical repertoire and his included black artists. He was a big fan of Marvin Gaye, Jimi Hendrix, Teddy Pendergrass, and Bob Marley.*

*Then there was that whole kosher issue. Thank goodness Les' family was not kosher so I would not have to deal with separate dishes and diet restrictions. Les assured me he was perfectly okay with my continuing to cook barbecue spare ribs. He also grew an appreciation for our New Year's tradition of collard greens (to ensure money for the new year) and black-eyed peas (to ensure good luck). I had the challenge of learning to cook Hungarian dishes and Jewish delights. Chopped liver and matzo ball soup became favorites of my family with my sister and cousins making sure they had the recipes.*

*Then there was the issue of hair. When we first met Les' hair was curly, what I would call a white boy 'fro, and my hair had what is known as a reverse perm that straightened my natural curls. So his hair was looking like a "natural" and mine was straight. A few months into our relationship I learned that he actually went to a hairdresser to have his hair permed on those little rods to give it that curly 'fro look. Conversely he learned that my hair was not naturally straight, but that I went to the hairdresser to have mine straightened.*

*So I'm with this white guy who now gets to learn about black hair. His lessons included learning about pressing combs, the chemical reverse perm, and the "kitchen."*

*First the pressing comb. A heavy iron comb, it was heated on the stove and used to straighten my locks. You had to be careful with the pressing comb to make sure it did not get too hot or you could burn your hair. As a little girl, there was the need to hold your ear down so the person pressing your hair would not burn your ear. After years of pressing my hair, I began to use a reverse perm. The reverse perm process involved a chemical cream that was put on for 10-15 minutes, and then washed out with conditioners to soften the results of the chemicals. Getting your hair permed at the beauty shop cost a few bucks but you could also do it at home. That's when Les stepped in, putting on latex gloves, and became "Mr. Les, Stylist." It was much easier to have him apply the perm, especially in the back. He took great delight in the process.*

*Finally, if you are a white man married to a black woman, you will hear about the "kitchen," that place at the nape of her neck. If you have a short hairstyle you might ask the beautician to trim the "kitchen." It's something that was often said back in the day, but you still hear it.*

*Of course he asked me why it was called the "kitchen" and of course I had no idea, we just always called it the "kitchen." So now I have to go and find out why. Asking around, I found several answers: because it's at the back of your head, like the kitchen is in the back of the house; because the kitchen is where things are cooked, like your hair cooks with a hot comb.*

*Taking care of my hair was time consuming and caused me lots of grief trying to get a style that was easy to work with and that I liked. Years later we planned a trip to Italy and I was concerned about taking my flat iron, curling iron, rollers, etc. My hairstylist said I should just let the chemicals grow out and wear my hair in a natural, so I did. A few days into the trip Les said to me, "You know what I haven't heard on this trip?" "No," was my reply. He said, "I haven't had to hear about issues with your hair. This is wonderful."*

*Les' styles have changed over the years as well, mostly with his hair getting thinner, and his beard getting gray. He actually decided to color his beard once and burned his chin. After that he decided gray was distinguished, and I told him it looked good, so he went with natural as well.*

*These were the fun things we could laugh about. We knew that on the important values of family, social justice, and politics we were in sync.*

Then there's food. I am an adventurous eater. I'll try anything and everything. Tyree? Not so much.

For me eating soul food was a wonderful adventure. I mean who doesn't like barbecue ribs, hot links and fried chicken? It was easy for me to enjoy the taste of collard greens and black-eyed peas with a piece of hot buttered cornbread, one of my favorites. And I really enjoyed the wonders of peach cobbler. For Tyree it was a little different. For her it was learning to like both Hungarian and Jewish food. Hungarian goulash was easy for her to enjoy as was chicken paprikash and stuffed cabbage, apparently both our grandmothers made that dish. On the Jewish side she loved matzo ball soup, but who doesn't like that? And of course chopped liver and potato latkes (potato pancakes) are Jewish soul foods. However, she wasn't very keen on gefilte fish, but then who is? Learning to enjoy each other's food was a positive thing and we both embraced it wholeheartedly.

On a much more serious note there was the issue of being a black and white couple. Now, I never had any problems going to events where there were more black people than whites attending. Usually I was excited to go and meet new people. Many times we went to social functions and I would be the only white person there. It never bothered me. Of course I was with Tyree, and usually some of the cousins, so I was always introduced as a member of the family. I'm sure that helped.

However Tyree told me she was always aware of often being the only black person in the room in both social and work settings. It was something she said you grew up with... being aware of your surroundings, especially if you are black in a white world.

Being an interracial couple was never an issue for us and I think it was because we were older, established in our careers and had accepting families. We weren't kids just starting out trying to make it. Also, someone once told me that we projected an image of being Les and Tyree, never "white Les" and "black Tyree." Yes, we were a black and white couple but we never presented ourselves that way. We always presented ourselves as Les and Tyree and that's how everyone saw us.

# CHAPTER 5

## *High School and College*
## *1956–1966*

I WAS excited about going to high school at Buckley, one of four high schools in Hartford. Besides my school there was: Hartford High, where most of the students were black and usually had the best basketball team; East Hartford High where most of the immigrant families lived and had good football teams; and West Hartford High, where the Jews lived and had lousy athletic teams. Buckley High was mostly Irish and Italian... very Catholic. There were about a thousand students enrolled. The school itself looked like a poster for an Ivy League school.

Classes were more interesting than in junior high. As I remember I did especially well in English and History. My language class was pretty good but I only did okay in Math and Science. Even though classes were harder and more demanding I ended up with a B average my freshman year.

I made the varsity swim team my first year swimming the sprints. Halfway through my freshman year an article appeared in the *Hartford Courant* regarding our team's chances for a state championship. I'm mentioned as one of the reasons the team has a chance to win the title. The paper called me the "Freshman Flash." I took a lot of ribbing for that nickname.

By mid-season the senior athletes began to notice my swimming accomplishments. I realized this after a Saturday football game when a senior varsity player invited me to a team party. That was a big deal for a freshman.

As my freshman year moved along, my swimming exploits continued with greater scrutiny by the local papers. When it came time for the state swimming finals I won four gold medals and our team won the state title in our division.

Upon returning from the state meet, I found that my locker assignment had been changed, moved from the third floor, where all freshmen had their lockers, down to the first where the senior athletes had theirs. I was now in Jock-Ville heaven and riding high.

At the end of the school year I was awarded a letter in swimming and bought a letterman's jacket. The jacket was a badge of honor, and since I was the only freshman who received a varsity letter that year, I wore it with great pride.

One day in the fall of my sophomore year after swimming practice my coach called me into his office and told me Springfield College had been scouting me and had talked to him about my going there on a swimming scholarship. He told me I'd be majoring in Physical Education and with that degree I could become a coach. He told me I should talk to my folks about the opportunity. I went home with the news and told my parents. Suddenly my future is all laid out in front of me and I'm very excited about the prospect of going off to college to become a coach.

Then in December, without any warning, Dad announced he'd been offered a new job in California for twice his current salary and had accepted. It seemed things hadn't worked out the way he thought they would since we moved back to Connecticut.

We're leaving Hartford in June, he tells us. We're moving back to North Hollywood. I am crushed. My entire life exists around Buckley High School, my swimming, my athletic scholarship to Springfield College, all my friends. I feel my life is ruined. I mean, it's tough enough to uproot any kid from their school, but in the middle of high school? That's really hard.

Mom, however, is elated by the news. She's very happy to leave the cold weather and get back to warm, sunny Southern California and be closer to her family. Grandma Goldberger, Uncle Henry, Aunt Florence, Uncle Dick and my two cousins are all living in Burbank a few minutes away.

I ask if I can stay with any of my friends for a year so I can graduate from Buckley but Dad won't let me. We are going and that's it, end of discussion. Pack your bags, it's moving time.

June arrives and once again we are packing for a move across country. In the last eight years we'd moved four times across country. I remember that I was in a lousy mood the whole way. My life in Hartford had been fun and exciting. Now all of that was gone.

We move into a small house in North Hollywood, and immediately I am alone. I mean I don't know anyone on the street or the neighborhood. No one. I stay home a lot and make up sports games for imaginary sports leagues. I have a good imagination, and this time it saves me.

That summer I talk to Dad about college. I tell him I want to go away to school. He nods his head and smiles and says, "We'll see."

"We'll see" isn't the response I am looking for. "We'll see" doesn't mean, "Yes, you can go." But that's how he leaves it. Right away Mom tells me not to worry. When the time comes I'll be able to go. Somehow that didn't make me feel better.

In September I start attending North Hollywood High School and boy is it different from Buckley. The place has a glow to it. Everyone smiles a lot and looks very healthy. The lifestyle out in LA was about sun, surf, the Beach Boys music and fun. There were no freezing winter days where I had to get up at six in the morning and shovel snow off the driveway and sidewalk. In LA it was always sunny and there were palm trees and lots of interesting places to see. Also, things were much more liberal in LA. It was a lifestyle I quickly related to and one that would have a great influence on my life.

I figure the best way to meet people was to get involved in sports, so I try out for both the swim and football teams. When the football coach asks what position I play, I say running back. Big mistake.

At the first practice I'm surprised at the size of the football players. Compared to the players in Connecticut, the North Hollywood guys are huge. They're also very fast. At the first practice I line up in the backfield and get ready to take the handoff from the quarterback. The play starts and the entire defensive team immediately crushes me. I lie on the ground hurt and unable to see or think straight. I stagger to the sidelines and realize football isn't for me. I'm too small and too slow to play running back on the varsity team, so I'm shipped to the "B" team. That's Junior Varsity in California speak, where I can play linebacker at 140 lbs. It doesn't take long, however, before my body starts saying things to me like, "Get the hell away from football!"

The "B" team played their games before the varsity so I was always in the stands for the varsity game. And it was lots of fun because we had a really good varsity team the two years I was at North Hollywood High. But what I was really amazed and excited about were the yell leaders who were down on the field leading the cheers. I noticed the Head Yell Leader was constantly talking on the PA system to the crowd. He was like a stand-up comedian. I thought, leading yells is a lot more fun than getting crushed on the football field, so I decided to run for Head Yell Leader at the next school election. Now I just needed to learn the cheers.

I didn't give up athletics. I made the swim team and, even though all the swimmers were bigger and faster than anyone I knew on my Buckley teams, I did pretty well my first year, winning two gold medals in the city championships.

At the end of the semester school elections are held. I'm on the ballot with two other guys running for Head Yell Leader. At the election assembly all the candidates say why you should vote for them. When it's my turn I get up and do cartwheels across the auditorium stage ending by leading the students in the yell, "Go Huskies!" The other two guys just led a cheer. I win the election. Everyone said they loved my cartwheels.

My social life at North Hollywood High started out slow but once I became Head Yell Leader it picked up steam. Every weekend there were two or three parties to attend. It was at one of those parties I met Karen.

Karen was tall and slender with shoulder-length dark brown hair and large brown eyes. She was pretty and very, very smart. She was also Jewish. We started dating and pretty soon we were a couple. Karen was serious about politics, the law and social action. I was interested in sports, parties, and having a good time. Not a good fit, but in the beginning, who knew?

Senior year was filled with lots of activities as well as trying to get high grades so I could get into UC Berkeley. I wanted to go away to college in the worst way. I was feeling very constricted living at home. I felt I was ready to move out.

That summer I applied for a job as a lifeguard. There were so many applicants that I didn't get selected, so Dad hired me to work in his coat factory. I thought, okay, I'll work with the cutters. Those are the men who cut the cloth from paper patterns. In the past every time I visited Dad at his factory I would always go and watch the cutters work. But Dad had a different idea. He made me the janitor.

Every day I cleaned toilets, swept the factory floor and took out the garbage. To top it off the factory wasn't air-conditioned and the place was really hot. I also almost got fired my first day on the job.

At the end of the day I was sweeping up all the cloth remnants around the sewing machines into the trash cans when Dad walked over to me.

"Stop! What are you doing?"

"I'm sweeping up like you told me," I reply.

"Come with me," he says and leads me to a door at the back of the factory. "Open the door," he says.

I open the door. He turns on the light and I see the room is filled from the floor to the ceiling with remnants.

"Those pieces of material, those rags, are worth a lot of money. Never throw them away. The ragman comes around four times a year and I sell all those pieces to him. When you make a coat you never throw away the rags. Now go back and finish cleaning the toilets."

I came away that summer with a deep respect for the men and women who are janitors and custodians. I learned firsthand it's a very tough job. That summer job was a real character builder for me.

Later when I became the head of the Moorpark College Performing Arts Center I always made it a point to give the men and women who worked as custodians in the building free tickets to all Performing Arts events. I learned early on that if a building isn't clean everyone notices. I appreciated what they did.

Fall semester of my senior year, I sign up for choir to fill out my schedule. It was an elective, and since I was a pretty good singer, and the choir was always looking for men, I thought it would be an easy "A."

The first day of class the teacher tells everyone they have to audition. Not to get in to the class but to know what part you would be singing. You know, bass, tenor, alto or soprano.

I had been in a singing group back in Hartford and really enjoyed performing, so I figured this would be easy. And since my last name begins with a W, I knew I wouldn't be called the first day.

Auditions begin. The first student who gets up to sing is amazing. She has a great voice and everyone loves her. The next is just as good and the next and the next. It soon becomes apparent the class is loaded with talent.

Next up is Pam, a cute redhead. I sit and watch this red-headed ball of fire do a song-and-dance routine that just blows everyone away. She is awesome. She is easily the best female talent in the class. She is funny and smart and cute and... and... yeah, I am infatuated. I admit it. First time I saw her perform I was a goner. Never mind I already had a girlfriend... Pam was the girl for me. She just didn't know it yet. As for Karen, well, I'd think of something.

At the next class I'm called to audition. I had a strong singing voice. I was a baritone. When I finish I think I've done pretty well and get a nice round of applause.

Every spring the music department produced a Broadway musical. My senior year the musical chosen was *Brigadoon*. I auditioned for the show and was cast as the male lead opposite... guess who? Pam. Wow! This meant I'd be seeing her every night for the next three months. Great! Then it hit me... I'm going to be the lead in a musical. I'd never done anything like that in my life.

At first Pam and I are buddies. She laughs at my stories and I laugh at hers. We have a similar sense of humor, but she isn't interested in me, romantically. Me? I was the pursuer, my usual role when it came to women. I went after her and never thought much about Karen. I figured I could handle it. Boy, I was wrong about that.

The 10 weeks of rehearsals seem to fly by and suddenly it's show-time! It's a life-changing experience for me. All the shows sell out. The audiences love the production. Cheers and standing ovations every performance.

Taking curtain call bows in a high school auditorium filled with your classmates, family and friends all standing and cheering is really heady stuff. It's like scoring the winning touchdown in the championship football game. In high school that becomes legend. With *Brigadoon*, however, we didn't get that just one night, we got it for six nights in a row.

I made a lot of new friends as a result of being in *Brigadoon*. Many I learned were already show business veterans.

Hanging with these new friends I got my first taste of what show business was really like. The lifestyle they introduced me too was very different from anything I had experienced in Connecticut. My life in the theater was beginning, and I was fascinated by all of it.

The show ends and my world returned too normal. I start getting ready for finals, then graduation, then summer vacation and, in the fall, out of the house and off to Berkeley.

But first there is the senior prom and I've got a problem. I'd asked Karen at the beginning of the semester to be my date but that was before I started working on *Brigadoon* and got involved with Pam. Karen knows I don't want to take her but she's not going to give me up and have no date for the prom. And I don't have the balls to tell her I want to take Pam instead. Big problem.

The prom is held in the school gym. While Karen stands watching, throwing daggers with her eyes into me, I dance with Pam. The prom ends and Karen and I are off to the Coconut Grove nightclub at the Ambassador Hotel where we will dance some more and watch the great Nat King Cole perform.

The evening ends and I take Karen home. Standing on her front porch she tells me she never wants to see me again and slams the front door in my face. My romance with Karen is over.

The week before graduation the program is printed. Inside below the picture of each graduating senior is listed the college or university they will be attending. I check my picture and below it is listed University of California, Berkeley.

That night at dinner I show the program to my folks. Dad reads it then gives it to Mom, who reads it then puts it down and looks at him. I remember for the longest time they just looked at one another. It was as if an entire conversation was taking place between them without a word being said. I look at them and then Mom says to Dad, "Tell him."

Dad looks at me and says, "We don't have money for you to go to Berkeley."

"What?" I say.

"I don't have any money to send you there, Leslie. There is no money for that."

"What about my college fund?"

"I had to use the money to keep the business going," he replies. "You'll have to go to a local college."

I get angry and say some dumb things and storm out. Later, I sit in my room upset at the sudden change in my life. Well, at least I have Pam, I tell myself.

The next day I go see her and she tells me, "I can't see you anymore."

"Why?" I ask.

"Because my folks don't want me to date anyone who is Jewish."

"What? What are you saying?" I stammer.

"My folks don't want me to get serious about you. I'm sorry."

Then without saying another word she turns and walks away. That really shakes me. We had been going out most of the year and she never said my being Jewish was a problem.

When I get home I go straight to my room. I sit on my bed feeling as if my life is over when there's a soft knock at my door. It opens and Mom walks in.

She walks over and sits down next to me. I tell her about Pam and what she told me. I have never felt like this in my life. Mom takes my hand and says, "I know this hurts, Leslie, but it's better to find this out now than later. Believe me, there will be other girls." Then she kisses me on the cheek, gets up and quietly walks out. I sit in silence after she's gone. I'm angry, hurt and frustrated. For the first time in my life I feel the sting of anti-Semitism.

June arrives and graduation looms. My high school years are ending. It's been quite a ride. I loved high school. Going to two different schools actually turned out to be a positive thing for me. At Buckley I was known as an athlete. At North Hollywood I was known as a performer.

June 1960 I graduate high school. I am 17 years old. In the fall I enroll at San Fernando Valley State College in Northridge, a 15-minute drive from my home. Not where I planned on going for my college career.

Nonetheless I was going to college.

*In 1960 at the end of the summer I moved to Whittier to live with my Uncle Herbert Troupe and Aunt Rubey Troupe, my mother's older sister.*

*When our mother died, Aunt Rubey did everything she could to help our grandparents raise the three of us. When my aunt and uncle moved to Whittier the family consensus was that Whittier was a "good" school and I would benefit from attending high school there.*

*What was the difference between the two schools? I can best sum it up this way. At our local high school a student might be asked, "Are you going to go to college?" At Whittier High School, the question was, "Which college will you be attending?"*

*It was a matter of expectations and the school mandated necessary preparation for students in college prep classes.*

*With the exception of my three cousins and me, Whittier High School was practically an all-white school. At least, we were the only African Americans on campus. I was a bit concerned about attending an all-white school but the excitement of getting to live with my cousins outweighed any trepidation I had.*

*Moving to Whittier was a pioneer action on the part of my aunt and uncle. Before I joined them for high school, they lived for a few years on the grounds of the Fred C. Nelles School for Boys, a residential facility for juvenile delinquents. My Uncle Herbert was a supervisor at the school and all the supervisors lived on the grounds in cottages with their families.*

*The complex was entirely surrounded by a large fence topped with barbed wire. Just on the other side of the fence were large eucalyptus trees, basically designed to hide the fencing. Nelles was located right next to a residential neighborhood.*

*All the cottages were named for presidents and the Troupe family lived in Hoover Cottage. The grounds between the cottages were like a massive playground. On Friday nights the school showed movies at the common hall and the families were able to attend. During the summers my brothers and I often stayed with my cousins at Nelles; I think it was to give our grandparents a bit of a break.*

*At some point, though I do not recall why, the families were asked to move off the grounds. My aunt and uncle bought a home exactly one block away from where they had been living for over five years. But some of their new neighbors were not prepared for a black family to move into their neighborhood. The Troupes were the first black family to move into Whittier.*

*My aunt and uncle had a white friend negotiate the purchase of the house; it was 1957. The day they moved in half the neighbors put up "For Sale" signs, including the minister who lived next door; the other half brought over cake.*

*Early on there were trials for the family. Once when they returned from an outing, someone had put a garden hose through the mail slot in the front door and flooded the house. One of the local boys would throw rocks at Cousin Ernestine on her way to school; she was in the 7ᵗʰ grade. She never told anyone, but a neighbor observed the action and told my Uncle Herbert. He and my aunt were so furious that after they talked to the police they called the local news station. Bill Stout and the Channel 5 News crew arrived to tell the story. For the next few days, Cousin Ernestine was escorted to junior high school in a police car. She says it was more embarrassing to show up at junior high in a police car than to put up with the rock throwing. Cynthia, the baby of the family, was in elementary school and suffered being spat upon and cursed at when she was in kindergarten and first grade.*

*Many were appalled by the bad behavior of their neighbors. The Troupes joined Plymouth Congregational Church and received positive support even though they found out early on some members did not want to be involved with the new arrivals. The church became a great social outlet for the children.*

*Uncle Herbert was well respected at Nelles and my cousins were star students at the high school and the boys were active in track and field. All of this helped the negative activity quickly disappear. My Cousin Ernestine was elected as one of the song leaders, a big deal indeed, and Cousin Ronald was a Cardinal Key recipient, the highest all-around honor given to only 20 seniors each year.*

*However, my male cousins did experience a bit of a problem being the first black residents to walk the streets of Whittier. The town was obviously not used to seeing young black males out and about, so my cousins were picked up several times by the local police thinking they were runaways from Nelles School. My uncle went to the police station, spoke to the Chief and explained that he did not dress his sons in blue jeans and white t-shirts, the uniform the boys serving time wore. They were his children. After that meeting the police just drove by without stopping Ronald, Elverse and Countee when they saw them out walking.*

*When I moved to Whittier, Uncle Herbert took me to the high school to enroll. The admissions counselor looked at the records from my junior high school and told us he would schedule me for honors classes. I told him that even though I had all A's and B's I was not sure I had learned* much. Both he and my uncle ignored my comments and scheduled me for what they thought were the appropriate classes.

On my first day in English class my suspicions held true. I was a bit nervous, first because I did not know anyone in the class, and second because I was concerned about my placement in the honors track. Then it happened. As a refresher, the teacher asked one of the students to diagram a sentence on the blackboard, and then another student did the same. It was clear to me that everyone in class understood the process. I sat horrified that the teacher would ask me to do the same, and I had never seen a sentence diagramed, had no clue what they were doing, and this was a refresher for them. I recalled how my English teacher in junior high spent so much time trying to maintain order; no sentences were diagrammed in his class.

I went home that night in tears and told my aunt and uncle that I wanted to go home. I did not want to go to the new school. I did not want to fail. They dried my tears and told me that everything would be fine. They had faith in me. Well, clearly they were not going to take me back home, so I had to stick it out. I went from being one of the three smartest girls in my junior high to having to work very hard to make B and C grades.

Another problem for me at Whittier High School was the mandatory freshman swimming class. I didn't know how to swim and now had to learn to do so in an Olympic-sized swimming pool. I was excited and frightened, but I made it through and learned enough to pass the class. I excelled in speech and most of the social sciences. English was very difficult for me because of the very poor experience I had in junior high.

Drill team my junior year was the most fun. The school had a championship drill team headed by Mrs. Withrow. She was a tyrant, but a lovable tyrant. She was determined to have a championship squad every year and that is exactly what she got. Competition to get on the squad was fierce. Tryouts were held in the gym and watched by everyone. I was very nervous, but held my own and was selected. We performed at all of the Friday night football games in immaculate red and white uniforms, polished white boots and red and white pom-poms. We made them from crepe paper, and fluffed them in the household dryer. The squad was entered into numerous competitions, usually on the weekends. It was almost a military operation. Once at inspection, we lost a competition because my good friend Sally had a bobby pin out of place. The competition was that tough.

I saw my first theatrical performance at the Whittier High School auditorium, Paint Your Wagon, a very impressive production. Because of *that show, I wanted to participate in the theater program. So for the next two years I was part of the continuity act for the annual student variety show. We would come out and sing a song or perform a short comical skit, ending with the announcement of the next act that was going to perform. The faculty was marvelous at making sure everyone had a chance to participate. It was great fun.*

*After my earlier experience at Girl Scout camp I was concerned about possible racial prejudice at school, but my cousins had been attending school in Whittier for a while, and while they had some issues in the very beginning, by the time I got there things were fine. During my four years at Whittier I did not experience overt racial problems. Rather issues were under the surface and indirect. If students had an issue with my cousins or me, they did not confront us directly.*

*However, I realized early on that I would live with one disadvantage: I knew early on that dating was simply not going to happen. There would be no prom for me, no Friday night dates, but I wasn't much into boys so it wasn't a major deal. I realized dating was just something I would do later. That isn't to say there were no boys I thought were cute, but I was black and going to an all-white school, and in the early '60's interracial dating was not in the cards, not in that community. The only date I recall was the Girls' League Dance where I asked a classmate if he would like to attend with me. He said yes. It was a formal affair. I wore Beverly's debutant dress, long white gloves and a wonderful updo. He wore a white dinner jacket and bought me a lovely corsage. This was my first high school date and my last. It was fun and I was glad I had the courage to do the asking.*

*So other than the high school dating scene, I did enjoy the other activities the school had to offer. I was active in clubs, pledged for one of the off-campus clubs, held several student body offices and served on the student council. My academic skills were coming along, but I had to work at it: lots of reading and study time.*

*I really appreciated living with the Troupe family. The house was always bustling with activity. My aunt and uncle were very busy with their jobs and numerous social activities. Aunt Rubey was constantly attempting to win the LA Times crossword puzzle contest and she had all of us kids helping her fill in the puzzles. She was determined to win the cash prize. We never did, but we worked at it all the time. Money was a bit scarce, so at the end of the month we often had waffles for dinner: just flour, eggs, milk and sugar. Inexpensive, right? We had a waffle maker and it was put to use often. Our other cheap dinner was biscuits—10¢ a carton—and hot dogs.*

*Then Aunt Rubey got into using a pressure cooker for dinner. One evening she was on the phone and the boys were grumbling about wanting to eat. I took it upon myself to go into the kitchen and get dinner on the table. Unfortunately I did not know that you were supposed to let the pressure out of the pressure cooker before you take the top off. The explosion was pretty loud and our dinner ended up on the ceiling, walls, floor and unfortunately much of it on me. Second and third degree burns followed so Aunt Rubey rushed me to the doctor. I had third degree burns on my forehead and right hand, and second degree burns on my chest. I was going through puberty and was very embarrassed that the doctor had to remove my blouse and treat the burns on my budding chest. When we returned from the doctor's office the boys were not happy since they were busy cleaning up the explosion and trying to figure out what they could have for dinner since the planned meal was being cleaned off the ceiling.*

*We never had a lot of money so we were constantly dreaming up ways to save a few bucks here and there. Once Ernestine and I wanted to go to the movies, but had no money for popcorn and sodas. So we made hamburgers, cooked frozen corn and took potato chips. We wrapped the hamburgers in foil, put the corn in a small jar and thought we would eat during the movie. But when we actually got in the theater, we were too embarrassed to open our little packages, so we sat through the movie not eating.*

*Aunt Rubey was a loving individual and would give anyone her last nickel or the shirt (or blouse) off her back if they needed it. During this time she worked at Metropolitan State Hospital, a facility for the mentally ill. On occasion she would come home with someone who had just been released but had nowhere to go. She offered her home for "just a few days" until they could get on their feet. So sometimes we had newly released patients sleeping on the sofa. As kids we thought it was a bit crazy and I slept with one eye open while our visitors were there. Luckily we never had any incidents with her guests, but that was my Aunt Rubey, generous to a fault.*

*The Troupes had a wide social circle and I found the people we were with to be very generous. Plymouth Congregational Church had a weeklong camp for the youth group that was held during spring break. I had wanted to attend but didn't want my grandparents to spend the money, so I told them I really didn't want to go. When I was saying goodbye to my cousins who were going to attend the camp, my grandfather arrived to take me home for the weekend. By the time we reached the house at 123rd St. my Aunt Rubey had called. One of the kids who had been scheduled to attend the camp had come down with the flu and could not attend so they called my Aunt Rubey to offer me the slot. My grandfather immediately turned the car around to take me back to Whittier in time to catch the bus with the rest of the kids.*

*But sometimes people were not always what they seemed. I had one friend in high school whose family took me along when they went to theater and concerts, events I would never be able to attend on my own. I was even a bridesmaid at her wedding. Several years after graduation I ran into a mutual friend of ours and we got to talking about high school and how the three of us often hung out together. After we'd had a few cocktails, the woman mentioned that our friend's mother was such a bigot that she didn't want me to be in the wedding and had said she wouldn't be there if my friend insisted I keep my role as a bridesmaid. I was stunned to hear that. I know if the mutual friend hadn't been tipsy she would never have told me that story. This was something that had happened 10 years before. I then realized that I had fond memories of our friend's father; he was the one that actually used to take us to concerts and theater. And I became conscious of the fact that I had no memory of her mother. Now I figured out why. Her mom obviously made herself scarce whenever I was around. Needless to say, I was in the wedding, so even though mom had warned her, my friend went through with having me participate and never told me about the issue with her mom. Another life lesson, you never know what is truly going on behind the scenes.*

*While in high school I worked at several different jobs. I began with housecleaning after school, ironing for neighbors and of course babysitting.*

*By my junior year I was able to work at the downtown Bullocks department store for Christmas, spring break and some hours during summer. While I did not mind the house-cleaning job, I did have to walk home—after dark past a small cemetery. Creepy. Luckily, that was only for one semester.*

*My senior year held many memorable events. In November of 1963 while sitting in my morning English class the loudspeaker came on and we were able to hear the news about what had happened to President Kennedy in Dallas. I remember the morning well. We sat in stone silence as the school kept the radio report on all morning. As the announcer gave the details of his passing, many in the room began to cry. We, as well as the rest of the nation, were shocked by what had happened. That weekend I went home and was glued to the television watching the funeral. The nation was truly in mourning.*

*I remember sitting in the den the night John F. Kennedy was nominated. I tallied the votes of each state until the final votes were called that gave him the Democratic nomination. I was too young to vote for him but closely followed the process that led up to his election.*

*My final memory of high school was being selected to give one of the two student speeches at commencement. My grandparents were so proud that I had been selected. They came with Aunt Rubey and Uncle Herb and my sister Beverly with her husband Tommy. Beverly said I began and ended my speech with a great big smile. It was a wonderful memory to close my high school experience.*

September 1960. My first day at San Fernando Valley State College and I am clueless regarding how to sign up for classes. How do I get classes? What classes should I take? How do I get a counselor? What is a unit? What do you mean I have to run for classes?

All the initial information I get about how to enroll in classes, what classes to attend and how to read the class schedule, I get from other students. And yes, I have to run for classes. Running from building to building to get to a certain classroom in time to find a seat. Otherwise you line up outside the classroom door hoping someone will actually get up and leave because they are in the wrong place.

At the end of my first day at college I have filled out my class schedule. I declare I'm a pre-med major. Why pre-med? I'm not sure. Maybe it's because every Jewish family wants their son to be a doctor or a lawyer. Or maybe I just wanted to impress my folks. I really don't know why I did it.

I've signed up for classes in chemistry, biology, math, English and Introduction to Theater. The latter being an elective I've chosen to fill out my schedule. Oh, and I sign up to play water polo to fulfill my Physical Education requirement. I think playing water polo will be fun. Silly me.

Water polo is not what I expected. Not at all. I don't know why on earth I ever thought I could play college water polo without ever playing it before. I thought, foolishly: I was a champion swimmer… how tough could it be? Answer: Pretty friggin' tough.

First day of practice we're lined up waiting to play the varsity and it hits home that I don't know how to play and I don't know the rules.

Coach blows his whistle, throws the ball into the center of the pool and suddenly everyone is diving into the water and racing to get the ball.

I dive in. Fast swimmer that I am, I get to the ball first and put my hand on it when suddenly something yanks my swim trunks down to my knees. When I stop to pull them up I'm belted in the face by an elbow and next thing I know I'm being helped to the side of the pool spitting up water and blood. Welcome to water polo.

For the next couple of weeks I learn the game and get my ass kicked every day by my "teammates." Needless to say I didn't play much that first season.

When the semester ends the season also ends and I know two things. One, water polo is a tough sport that takes lots of strength and endurance. And two, after getting a couple of bloody noses along with bruised ribs I decide water polo isn't for me. I never played again.

I have to admit when it came time for me to go to college I thought I was ready. I thought I could handle myself pretty much the way I got through my years in high school. But I was wrong. I don't understand anything in chemistry, biology or math. English, I'm holding my own. The only class I'm doing well in is Introduction to Theater.

By the end of my first semester it's obvious I'm not cut out for pre-med. My grade point average is 1.6. I'm placed on academic probation. So I decide to switch my major from pre-med to Political Science.

When I tell my dad I'm changing my major to Political Science he doesn't understand. "Study politics? Who studies politics? You just vote for the person who says what you want to hear." That was my dad's thinking. He couldn't understand what I would do with a degree in Political Science.

"Maybe you could teach science in high school?" he says.

My mom just smiles, "Why don't you become a teacher?"

"Me, a teacher? No way. Never," I answer.

Then I learn I have to take my math class over. I'd gotten an F. I'm not happy.

It looks like I am going to have to put a lot more effort into actually going to classes and cut out everything else during my second semester or I will flunk out of college. That hits me hard. The fear of failure really came over me. I didn't want to be disgraced. The only thing that was going good for me was the Theater Arts Department.

The Theater Department was an interesting place. First there were the students who were a strange lot. The theater has always embraced the strange. Then there was the faculty, an interesting mixture of men and women. Some were brilliant artists while others were great technicians. A few were drunks and horrible teachers, but they all loved the theater. It meant more to them than anything else. They were committed to the art form.

Everything about theater was interesting to me because I felt I belonged. I felt at home. So even though I'd switched my major to Political Science, I began to think… maybe I should become a Theater major instead.

But I wasn't ready to tell my folks because I wasn't sure what I wanted to do in the theater. Act, direct... maybe write? I really didn't know. I also didn't have a clue about how to get into that industry. Maybe, I thought, I could get some help from my Hollywood friends.

I managed to get through the second semester and finish with an A in theater, three C's, and a D. Ugh. I am still on academic probation.

I start my second year of college under a great strain. Being on academic probation is a pain in the ass. It weighs on you all the time. You have no margin for error. You know if you screw up in class and your grade point average drops below a certain level you will be kicked out of school. No one is going to come rushing to help you.

By midterms I'm still having problems with my classes, all except my theater class, where I'm doing very well. But if I don't get off probation I'll be kicked out of school.

The theater becomes my outlet and my therapy. I loved acting class. Loved it and was good at it. When we started doing scenes I'd help other students with the staging. I was directing but didn't know it. I got good grades and spent all my spare time in the theater building. Like I said, I felt at home, comfortable with the environment. It was when I was outside the building and away from the theater that I felt conflicted and lost.

The school year ends. My grades come out. I get an A in my theater class but don't do as well in the others. Then I'm told my counselor wants to see me. I have a feeling my time is up. I have flunked out. I wasn't happy.

I go see my mentor, the Theater Department Chairman, Dr. Bill, a big man standing maybe 6'5" with a booming voice. I remember the first time he came to my Introduction to Theater class and said, "My name is Dr. Bill and that's spelled G-O-D!" That got everyone's attention.

He was big, loud, and very tough but a great teacher. I really liked him but I wasn't happy about seeing him right then. I go to his office and knock on his door. Dr. Bill's booming voice bellows, "Come in, Wieder!"

I open the door, skulk in and sit down in the chair opposite his desk. We sit silently for a long time, me with my head down and him silently staring at me. After what seemed like 10 minutes but was most likely 30 seconds he says, "Wieder, it's time you get your ass out of here and get your life together. You're going in too many different directions trying to please too many people. And, outside of theater, you're terrible in all your classes. So here's some advice. Suck it up and leave. I know you're on your way to see your counselor, who's going to tell you you're no longer academically eligible to remain in school, and then he'll tell you that you're being dismissed. I've seen your grades."

I looked at him but said nothing. At that moment I felt like a total failure. God, I felt like shit.

"So," he continues, "here's my advice. Tell your counselor you want to transfer to a Junior College and get your grades right. Then reapply for enrollment here as a junior. You need to get away from here, Les. You need to go somewhere and find out how to be a student and find out what you really want to do. Keep in touch with me. I think you've got a lot of talent but you just aren't clear about what you want to do. Remember, you can't please everyone, and ultimately if you're gonna be happy you better please yourself first. Understand?"

"Yeah, I understand," I mumble. "Look, Dr. Bill... I want to thank..." I start choking up.

"Get the hell out of here, Wieder!" he bellows.

I take his advice and face the facts. I failed at college on my first attempt. I wouldn't fail again.

In the fall of 1962 I enrolled at Los Angeles Valley College as a Theater Arts major. When I first got to Valley I was still wounded from my prior failure and was determined to do better. I was looking for redemption. I was looking for a direction. I was looking for a purpose in my life... something that would inspire me.

I knew I didn't want to do what my father did, be in the schmata (garment) business. I knew I didn't want to work in a factory. I wanted to do something different.

I found everything I was looking for in the theater. I loved the diversity of the people and the energy that theater students brought to the program, I felt comfortable in the liberal lifestyle that went with being a theater student. Growing up in the 1950s in Connecticut I wasn't a *Leave It to Beaver* kid, yet I grew up in a home that reflected a lot of what Beaver stood for. So when the social rebellion of the '60s started I bought into it hook, line and sinker. And the theater was a place where a lot of that rebellion was coming from.

For me being "in" the theater was different. And different was always what I wanted. So it was at Valley College where my real feelings about theater began to take shape.

During my first semester at Valley I got the opportunity to direct my first play. That opportunity changed my life. I selected *The Zoo Story* by Edward Albee. I had a good time in rehearsals. I found out early on I could easily communicate with actors. Also I had a good eye for staging and movement. My directing instructor said I was a natural. I also liked being in charge. I liked everything about directing including the pressure. When it came time for the play to be performed the audiences gave it a standing ovation. What a rush!

I felt more comfortable directing than acting. I knew deep down that as an actor I'd never make it, but directing… that was different. I liked the whole process, of figuring out a script, directing actors, working on the sets and lights and costumes. For the first time in years I was feeling pretty good about school.

One day my dad asked me, "What does a director do?"

"Well," I said, "it's just like you remembering every single thing that goes into making ladies coats. You know all the details on how to make it and can make it yourself if need be. That's what directing a play is like. I have to know a lot about many things and be able to tell lots of people what I want them to do so that in the end the show comes out the way I envision it. A theater director needs to know about acting, lighting, set design, costumes and sound. Everything that takes place on the stage is the responsibility of the director."

"And you like all that?" he asked.

"Yes," I replied. "I like the responsibility of directing. I like creating something that moves people. I like the energy of rehearsals and the excitement of performances and I like being the boss. That's why I love to direct."

I buckled down and began enjoying classes and learning all I could about the art and craft of being a theater director. When I finished my first year at Valley, my grades were up. I was happy.

November 22, 1963. 10:30 a.m. I am walking across the campus headed for the Quad. Suddenly, people start running every which way. Some are crying. Some are shouting, "Kennedy got shot! Kennedy got shot! President Kennedy has been shot in Dallas." I turn and run to the theater building feeling numb.

The theater building's corridors are filled with students. I edge my way inside where a TV set is showing the news. Walter Cronkite on CBS News is reporting about the shooting. The place is silent. Then Cronkite announces that President Kennedy is dead and everything gets very still. Then the crying starts.

JFK was a young man and his assassination took the joy out of life for many people. Looking back I can see it was the start of a long period of unrest and upheaval in our country: JFK is assassinated, Martin Luther King is assassinated, Robert Kennedy is assassinated, racial conflict in the south, the Vietnam War protests. I was deeply affected by all the turmoil in the country.

After two years I return to San Fernando Valley State College as a junior and a Theater Arts major.

This time around I do much better at Valley State. I've learned to organize my life. As a full-time student I'm taking a full load of theater classes. My first year back I pass all of my classes with a B+ average. Then in the fall of 1965 I became concerned about my draft status. The Vietnam war was heating up and I had lots of misgiving about fighting in a war I didn't believe in, but I also knew if I was drafted I'd serve.

I'd been exempt from the draft while I was a full-time student but I'd be graduating in June of 1966 and knew once that happened I'd be a prime candidate. The Army would take one look at me and think, "College graduate. Check. Single. Check. Age 22. Check. Sounds like officer material to us. Drafted!" Once that happened my next stop would be Vietnam and I knew the life expectancy of a Second Lieutenant in Vietnam was pretty crappy.

In the spring of 1966 I receive my draft notice. Not long after, I begin having severe stomach pains. I go see our family doctor and after examining me he informs me I have a stomach ulcer. I tell him about my draft notice and my upcoming physical so he writes a short note explaining my condition along with what medication I'll be taking, hands it to me and says, "Good luck."

My physical takes place at the Selective Service building in downtown Los Angeles. I hear my name called and walk over to where a doctor is seated. After enduring a 10-minute probing examination I place my physician's note in front of him. He reads it then looks up at me and asks, "What medicine do you take for your ulcer?" I answer and he nods then marks my paperwork. I look down and watch him check the box that reads, UNFIT FOR MILITARY SERVICE. Then he writes two words under it, stomach ulcer. A few weeks later I receive a letter from Selective Service officially informing me I am 4F.

Twenty years later new research shows that my ulcer is a virus that can be treated with new anti-virus medicine. I take the treatment and after four weeks my ulcer disappears. Twenty years of pain suddenly gone.

While at San Fernando Valley State College I pursue my directing studies with lots of energy. In June I graduate with a BA in Theater Arts. My mentor, Dr. Bill, is all smiles at the ceremony and says to me, "See Wieder, I told you you could do it. I'm proud of you."

Even though my parents aren't sure what I'm going to do with a degree in Theater Arts they are both very proud of me too.

*After graduation from Whittier High School, I returned to my home on 123rd St. to live with my grandparents, ready to attend Compton College. I had been offered a one-semester scholarship to Chapman College, and while I was grateful for the opportunity, I had no idea how I would secure the funds after one semester to be able to continue to attend there. I did not understand at the time that once at the college, I might be able to find additional resources.*

*My grandparents were alone at the house. My grandfather had recently retired from the Post Office and I felt I should be with them. Besides I knew I could handle the financial demands of a community college.*

*A few weeks after I returned home, Mrs. Nance, the mother of my best friend from grammar school, Collette, took me to meet a friend of hers. I do not recall her name, only her face and her hands, and especially her act of kindness.*

*When we met, she was seated in a rocking chair with a plaid blanket across her lap. She asked me about school and said Mrs. Nance had told her I wanted to go to college. She asked me what I wanted to do when I graduated, and I told her maybe teaching, but I was not sure yet as I wanted to explore options. When we finished our visit (I was still a bit curious as to why we had come but was too polite to ask), the woman took my hand and wished me good luck. As I stood to leave, she handed me an envelope and said it was a little something to help me on my journey. I thanked her without opening the envelope but as soon as we were in the car I did and found $25. Mrs. Nance had told her my resources were limited and this lady whom I never met before wanted to help me. The $25 was deposited in the Security Pacific Bank on the corner of Rosecrans and Central Avenue, the beginning of my college fund. Clearly $25 was not going to get me through college, but it was such a generous, thoughtful gift to a young girl with a dream of participating in higher education.*

*Since then I pay that gift forward by supporting college scholarships for community college students. I have told this story often to let others know that acts of kindness, no matter how small, can have a lasting impact. I have seen the gratitude that community college students display when they receive scholarship funds. The fact that others recognized their efforts was as important as the dollars they received, often more important.*

*That summer I secured a job at J. J. Newberry's, a local department store. On my first day on the job, I was placed in the hardware section. Interesting, until all the staff decided to go to lunch and leave me alone in hardware! A few customers came in and asked questions for which I had no answers, but I still managed to help them find what they were looking for. How do you leave a 17 year-old girl alone, on her first day, in the hardware section? I survived the day but it was traumatic.*

*Shortly after I was hired, at the store, my sister suggested I take a civil service test for the State of California Employment Department, which is where she worked. I got myself downtown to the State Offices and signed up for the test. I passed the Clerk Typist test and started working Monday through Friday at the Compton Office while keeping my job at Newberry's on the weekend.*

*A few weeks later I headed to Compton College to enroll in my classes. I really didn't know much about the registration process and found myself frustrated as I kept selecting classes that were already filled. A very unsympathetic lady behind the counter with a lovely red pencil kept lining out my selections and sending me back to the list of posted classes. At one point I was close to tears, it was so harsh. If she pulled out that red pencil one more time I was going to lose it. I stepped behind a pillar, took a deep breath and went back to try again. Finally I came up with a list that was not greeted with the red pencil. I persevered and at the end of the day I had my classes. I was ready to be a college student.*

*In the fall when my college classes started, my supervisor at the Employment Development Department suggested I could work part-time through the school year. I snapped at the chance and began going to school, working at EDD in the afternoon and Newberry's on the weekend. I really thought I was superwoman. After three months, I realized it was impossible. Working seven days a week and attending college left little time for study and sleep. I reluctantly quit the Newberry's job.*

*I liked Compton College; the teachers were committed and caring. I joined a few clubs, pledged for Usherettes (we ushered at all college events), and began life as a college student. I was not much for dating but was asked out by a young African American man who was the former student body president. He was a few years older because he had gone into the service, then returned to college. He was an engineering major. We dated a few times and soon were going "steady" as we called it back then. Ted was a serious person, ambitious and driven. In a very short time we were engaged and had set a wedding date.*

*During my time at Compton I purchased my first car. I was really tired of riding the bus to work and school so I saved as much as I could to buy it. My grandfather went with me to the dealership and when I had selected my car he was there to cosign the loan. However since he was retired they would not let him be a co-signer. I checked my savings and realized I could buy the car outright, $750 for a 1954 Ford Falcon, light blue with a white top. My grandfather had me call his insurance agent to be sure I was covered before I drove it off the lot.*

*The only problem I had with the car was that it had a Confederate flag decal in the back window. How could I buy that car? Grandfather*

*said it was a good car. I could scrape out the decal and the car would
have a deserving owner.*

*Now I had a certain amount of independence and I could go where
I needed to without waiting for a ride or the bus. As usual, my brothers
were there to offer guidance. Clarence taught me how to check the oil and
the air in my tires, told me to get it serviced regularly, and to always keep
a half tank of gas. Robert told me Ford stood for Fix Or Repair Daily but
he would be around to help with repairs if needed.*

*Fortunately I never had any trouble with the car, only human trou-
ble. Once when it was time for servicing I took the car to a friend of my
Aunt Pat who owned a nearby gas station. I left the car overnight so they
could change my spark plugs, the oil and other services. I picked up the
car the next day and paid $40. When I got the car home, Clarence came
by and was looking in the engine. He told me that they did not change the
spark plugs, that those plugs were the ones he had put in the last time he
worked on the car. He drove with me back to the station to get my money
back. The owner said he thought the other guy at the station had done the
work and the other guy said he thought the owner had. Well, my money
was returned and I learned my first lesson about service repair: check the
work and don't be so trusting, even if it is a "friend."*

*Later that year, I was able to work extra hours at my job. I had a
pretty nice check so I gave my grandmother five extra dollars on my $25 a
month rent. Around the holidays, my hours were cut so I assumed I would
not have to pay my $30 rent. My grandmother assumed differently and
asked me for the payment. I explained that my hours had been cut so I did
not have the money that month. She opened my dresser drawer, picked
up my bank savings book and reminded me I had money in the bank. She
explained that when you're out in the world, your landlord wouldn't let
you slide on your rent. I was stunned and hurt. I dutifully went to the bank
and got the $30 for the rent. After that I called my brother Clarence and
moved in with him and his wife and new baby. I told my grandparents
it was because they lived closer to the college, but I was just mad that I
had been asked for rent when my grandparents knew my funds were low.
One afternoon they came to visit me at Clarence's and when I saw them
walking up the steps I felt so bad that I had moved out. I went home the
next day. The other lesson I learned was that my grandparents were more
precious to me than a silly issue over rent.*

*In the summer of 1965 I had finished my first year of college and
was continuing my work at the EDD office in Compton. The summer was
hot and dissatisfaction with unemployment and the police was high. One
afternoon, a routine traffic stop erupted into what was later called the*

*Watts Riots.*

*For the next few days it sickened me to watch the destruction, looting and burning of the city on television. The fires were in our neighborhood. Why would you burn down the stores of your community? It was a case of intense anger and little rational thought. I understood the frustration of those out of work, those who had been harassed by the police, but burning your neighborhood stores, putting your neighbors out of work, made little sense to me.*

*For six days, the community was on fire, businesses were looted. 14,000 National Guard troops were called in and curfews were established. When it ended, 4,000 people were arrested, 1,000 were injured and 34 people had died. One evening I stood on the corner of 123rd St. and Central Ave. and watched the grocery store on the corner of 120th St. and Central Ave. burn to the ground. It was our local grocery and drug store. It was years before it was rebuilt.*

*Martin Luther King Jr. came to Los Angeles during the riots to try to calm the neighborhood and explain to the LA powers, the Police Chief and the Mayor, why people were so frustrated. He did not condone the violence and urged the community to stop the violence. We were grateful for his intervention and I think it helped. The most dramatic aftermath of the riots was the introduction of numerous poverty programs designed to provide some relief from the intense poverty and unemployment. Since I was working at the Employment Office I became involved with the implementation of the first projects. Were they effective? Over time there was some improvement, but it would be years, decades before the community began to show signs of recovery.*

*Working at EDD was a great experience. I had a good supervisor and great coworkers. I was the youngest in the office so I had lots of "mothers." One day I was working on an assignment but was not quite finished at the end of the day. I told my supervisor that I would finish it as soon as I came in the next day. She looked at me and quietly said, "No one promised you tomorrow." I learned something that day. I sat back down and finished.*

*I worked at the Department of Employment in Compton for two years and then was transferred to the Watts Service Center. The office had expanded after the riots with new programs to counter the poverty in the community. I finished Compton College in two years with 56 transferable units, enough to transfer, but not enough to graduate. Since my goal was a four-year degree, I thought it was more important to move on to Cal State Long Beach. In hindsight I should have made sure I had those extra four units and completed my Associate Degree. It would have been a good marker of my academic progress. At the end of four years, two at Compton and two at Long Beach, I was still fifteen units short of my BA degree.*

*My life while attending Cal State Long Beach was very busy so I fought to get the classes I needed with the schedule I needed: 15 units between eight and 12, five days a week. I was due at work at 1:00, left the office at 5:00 p.m., then headed home. At 6:00 p.m. I went down the street to babysit for my cousins, Guy and Lisa, while my Aunt Pat worked the night shift. I helped them with their homework, made sure they had dinner, put them to bed and, when she came home at midnight, headed back up the block to my house. I had that routine for the two years I was at Cal State Long Beach.*

*My fiancé, Ted, and I both transferred to Cal State Long Beach, but he was a year ahead of me. We were still a couple and had planned a June wedding, which would be after my second year at Long Beach and his graduation.*

*My grandfather had worked in the Post Office for over 35 years and retired February 3, 1961. When he retired he began working at a piano store near the Crenshaw Center. The owner encouraged him to give piano lessons at the store after closing. He also continued to give lessons at home. He enjoyed being retired and having more time to enjoy teaching and composing.*

*One day I heard him talking to my grandmother about finances. He told her that he had set everything up so that she would be okay if something happened to him. His pension would be enough to cover her expenses until she decided to sell the house. I remember understanding how important it was for him to do that and how proud I was of him for thinking about it and realizing it was so important for my grandmother to be able to live comfortably. His planning for her was one of the things that made me realize the importance of planning for the future.*

*A few years after his retirement he became ill, his kidneys began to fail and he ended up in the hospital. The family, children and grandchildren were there daily to be with him. The hospital wanted us to limit our number of visitors and we explained that would not be possible so we worked out a compromise: We would limit the number of family in his room and hallway, and the rest of us would stay in the room provided for family visitors. It was a bit crowded but we managed. After several weeks of being in and out of the hospital, he died on September 8, 1967 at the age of 70.*

*I received the call when I was at work at the Watts Service Center. I knew he was very ill so I was not shocked by the call, but it shook me to my core. I was shaking and crying at the same time. One of my co-workers walked me to my car, offering to drive me home. I assured him I could make the drive. When I got to my house I saw all the cars and could not go in. I was devastated by my grandfather's death and I knew I wasn't ready to face the people gathered there. I continue driving to Uncle Noyal and Aunt Josephine's. I just needed some time. After a short time with them to settle myself I drove home. When I arrived at the house I was actually very happy to see all those family and friends there. I knew when they left later that night I would be alone with my grandmother and I was not looking forward to being alone with her in her time of grief.*

*The afternoon was very surreal for me. I continued to breathe, people were sitting around talking, cars were going down the street but my grandfather was dead. That evening when Walter Cronkite came on TV with the news I fully expected him to say at the end of his broadcast that "Arthur Lorenzo Countee passed away this afternoon." I was 21 years old and a college student, but still expected that announcement on the TV. I sort of knew it was not going to happen, but listened for it anyway.*

*The next morning when I opened the front door I saw cars driving on Central Avenue, the newspaper was on the front porch, the Helms Bakery truck delivered bread and the mail came. It was disconcerting; how could everything go on as though nothing had happened? It was then that I realized that when people died, the world paused briefly, took a breath and then continued on. This was part of the circle of life.*

*I ached at the loss of my grandfather. I could not bring myself to attend the viewing, and Aunt Pat and Aunt Rubey gave me a very hard time because I refused. Even at the funeral I sat as the full row of mourners stumbled past me on their way up to the casket. I was in a daze through much of the service.*

*Among several jobs he had, my Uncle Chuck served as a motorcycle officer who covered funeral processions. He had insisted on accompanying the funeral procession. I sat in the limo and watched him race by from intersection to intersection to stop traffic as the procession passed.*

*I was so touched by the number of people who attended my grandfather's funeral. This was a man who was loved and respected. The line of cars continued for blocks.*

*Losing Arthur Lorenzo Countee was very traumatic for me and I struggled to continue attending classes, working and looking after my grandmother. Following a death there is a lot of paperwork to deal with and I recall taking my grandmother to various offices to fill out forms to get all of his affairs in order. I was glad for the work because it kept me busy while dealing with my grief.*

*A few weeks later, Ted and I were at the drive-in watching the movie* Hawaii. *At the end of the movie the main character stumbles through his home looking for his wife, who had died several years before. For some reason that scene resonated with me, and all the tears I had not yet shed for my grandfather spilled from my heart. I cried uncontrollably. It was truly a cathartic release.*

*After that my grandmother and I settled into our routine. She was so strong when it came to dealing with our loss. She had lived a long life and had suffered the loss of friends, two of her children and now her husband of 47 years. She understood the circle of life and accepted its inevitability. I know her strength helped me cope. She continued with her church club and began to take a few trips with the local senior citizen groups. She went on a Caribbean cruise and took a few bus trips to Las Vegas. I was so happy that she had her companions to spend time with her.*

*That spring she began to make plans to sell the house and move closer to Beverly and her family. I was also starting to finalize plans for a June wedding and she was helping me. One afternoon, while she and I were relaxing in the den discussing wedding plans, the phone rang and it was a call from Clarence Warren Sr., my father. We had not heard from him in years. My grandmother chatted with him for a while then told him I was to be married in a few months and he should come out to California to walk me down the aisle. I was horrified, what, walk me down the aisle? I did not know this man. Uncle Herbert, who I had lived with while attending Whittier High School, was to do that. My grandmother handed me the phone to talk to my father. I shuddered at the thought of even talking to my father but dutifully took the phone from her. I engaged in some small talk, and then told him Uncle Herbert was going to walk me down the aisle. I am sure he was relieved. After all he had not seen me in over 20 years and it was a bit late to forge a daddy-daughter relationship at this point. But that was my grandmother, always trying to be positive. He elected not to come to California and I never heard from him again.*

During my junior year in college I began to look for a job in Hollywood. Since I had no family in show business I needed to find something to get a foot in the door. A friend who worked as a Page at CBS Television told me about a job opening. Was I interested? Yes, I told him, I was very interested, so he gave me the name of his supervisor. I called and got an interview.

The interview goes well and when it's over the supervisor tells me I'm hired and to come in the next day for orientation and just like that I'm a Page at CBS. I'm in Show Biz!

For the first two months my job is to lead tours around the studio. After doing that for a couple of months I'm moved into the regular schedule and begin working on shows, taking phone messages for the staff. This was before everyone had a cell phone.

At first most of the shows I work on are game shows. Eventually I start working on big variety shows. The two that stand out for me are *The Red Skeleton Show* and *The Danny Kaye Show*.

I worked on the *Skeleton Show* for a year answering phones and taking messages. Working on his show was a great lesson in comedy. Red was very funny. He was a natural clown and an excellent mime and watching him perform was an education. Plus everyone loved working with him because of his kind and generous nature.

One thing that he did really impressed me. Before every taping Red would walk up to everyone, cast, crew and staff, and shake their hand and thank them personally for being on his show. That simple gesture spoke a lot about the character of Red Skeleton. In turn, everyone on his show loved him.

I remembered that gesture later in my life when I started directing and would do the same before every opening night performance. That gesture proved to be a wonderful bonding element for all my shows.

While Red played the clown and variations of that character type on his show, Mr. Danny Kaye played a wide variety of characters in his sketches, but it was in his singing and dancing and the production numbers where he really shined. He moved very gracefully and like Red had a great face which he used to great effect. He was also very, very intelligent and, unlike Red, Danny Kaye was very intense.

While Red would excuse a slight mistake during rehearsals and laugh it off, Mr. Kaye wasn't happy when someone other than he or his guest star screwed up. You didn't want to make mistakes with him. He was tough on all his writers and directors. In fact I remember one time he fired a director while the show was being taped. Everyone loved working on the show because even though Mr. Kaye could be a ballbuster, he was a world-class talent, he could deliver the goods.

# CHAPTER 6

## *Early Careers*
## *1966–1977*

AFTER my graduation I keep looking for a better job and finally the opportunity presents itself. I went to work for Barney McNulty who owned the cue card concession for most of the television shows in Hollywood. He started out with Bob Hope and very quickly became the king of cue cards. One day I asked Barney, whom I'd become friendly with when he worked on shows at CBS, if he had any openings. Surprisingly he did and I was hired. I was elated with my new job. For starters I would be paid substantially more working on cue cards. In fact I'd be paid the same rate as a prop man and those wages were a lot more than the minimum wage I was receiving as a Page. But the best thing about working for Barney was I'd finally be making enough money to get my own place. With my first month's paycheck I rented a small apartment in Sherman Oaks. I was finally on my own.

My first cue card assignment was printing and holding cards for the soap opera, *Days of Our Lives*. I worked on that show for several months before I started working on several others. The best were *The Dean Martin Show* and *The Hollywood Palace*. The worst was *any* game show. Games shows were boring, boring, boring.

On the *Dean Martin Show*, Dean always talked to whoever was holding his cards, cracking jokes and making the person part of the opening. You, however, were never allowed to say anything back to him and you never appeared on camera although sometimes he'd grab you by the arm and pull you in front of the camera for whatever reason. That was great because then you'd be paid extra. Otherwise you were his silent off-camera joke foil. It was fun.

Friday. Showtime. Dean arrives and we get set to tape the dress rehearsal for the first show of his second season. The audience lights dim, the studio lights come on, the announcer says, "Ladies and gentleman, Dean Martin!" Music! Applause!

Dean appears, a drink in hand, and moves to his mark. He looks up at the camera. I'm standing beside it holding his cue cards directly under the lens. The music fades. The applause dies down and Dean starts to read.

He reads the first card, hits the joke just right. I pull the card and hand it to Mike, my assistant. I wait for Dean to continue but he just stands there not saying a word. He takes a sip from his glass, smiles but still says nothing.

The stage manager rushes up to my side and looks at Dean who smiles and says, "The cards are wrong."

Dead silence.

I look at the card. Sure enough, the second and third cards are definitely out of order. I look behind me for Mike, whose responsibility it is to make sure the cards are in order, but he is nowhere to be found. Mike has skipped town.

The stage manager steps out in front of the camera and says, "Stop. Hold it. Director is coming down." The dress rehearsal comes to a halt. I'm thinking... I'm screwed.

I hear the director as he thunders down the hallway screaming, "I'll kill that kid! I'll fucking kill that kid!"

He bursts through the studio door, grabs the cards from my hands, throws them to the floor and then in front of 300 audience members, the cast and the entire crew starts to call me some pretty awful names which make me start to lose my temper. I'm about to say something when suddenly Barney rushes up, throws his arms around me and leads me out of the studio, all the while telling me, "Say nothing! Just keep walking!"

He escorts me back to the cue card room and tells me to stay put and not leave. I ask, "Am I fired?" Barney just shakes his head and leaves. I'm alone thinking, "WTF!"

I'm not fired. I remain on the show but I'm barred from the set and banished to the cue card room where I just print cue cards. It's humiliating.

Two weeks go by. I'm still in cue card hell when one day the director walks by the open door and sees me printing cards. He stops and looks at me. I stop printing and look at him. "You still here?" he asks. "Yes sir," I reply. He looks at me then nods his head and says, "Okay," and walks away.

The next day I'm back on the floor holding Dean Martin's cue cards. Of course when Dean sees me standing in front of him he can't help but make jokes about my ineptness. I take it in stride. It's good to be back on the set.

I got through that humiliation and vowed I'd never put myself in that position again. From then on I always double-checked to make sure my cards were in the correct order. Oh, and Mike, my cue card assistant? Never saw him again.

My second Dean Martin story starts with a bad joke he told at my expense while he rehearsed his opening monologue. I can't remember the actual "joke" but I remember at one point he called me a schmuck. That's a Yiddish word for prick. He said it as part of the joke but for some reason it struck me wrong and it must have shown on my face. Anyhow, he finishes the monologue then returns to his dressing room to talk about any changes he wanted. The producer, the head writer and the cue card boy Les all follow him.

I walk in the dressing room and take my usual place. As I start to pull the first cue card Dean stops everything, leans forward and says, "Hey, kid, I'm sorry if what I said earlier, calling you a schmuck... You know, I really didn't mean anything...."

"No. No, it's okay," I stutter but he waves me off.

"No, really, I'm sorry if I offended you. I mean it. I was just joking," he replies. "Sorry."

For a moment I can't say anything. I mean his remark did offend me and I guess my facial expression must have said it all. I remember after he apologized, the room got very still. Then I said, "Okay. Thanks." And that was it. We went back to working on the monologue. That gesture, Dean Martin apologizing to me for some offhand remark said a lot to me about the man. Dean Martin was a "mensch," a good person. He was a very decent man and a good guy. I loved working on his show.

*The Hollywood Palace* was a weekly variety show on ABC with a different host each week. I'm assigned to work the show that Milton Berle, Mr. Television, is hosting. I am his cue card boy for the week.

Rehearsals begin and every few minutes Milton blows a whistle and everything stops. He then proceeds to tell the director how to stage the scene being rehearsed, where to place the cameras and how fast or slow each cut needs to be made.

I once asked the cameramen who worked on the show, all veterans of early TV, why none of them got upset when Milton Berle stopped rehearsals and told everyone what to do. They looked at me as if I was crazy. Finally one veteran cameraman said to me. "Do you know why they call Milton Berle, Mr. Television?" I said I didn't and he replied, "Because he invented how to do all of this when TV first started."

I learned more about directing television from watching Milton Berle that week than I'd ever learned before in my life. It's all about timing and tempo Mr. Berle told me.

In the fall of 1967 I decide to go back to college and get my Master's degree in Theater Arts with an emphasis on directing. I apply to UCLA and am admitted for the winter quarter. I start classes in January 1968. Very soon after I start I'm placed in the graduate research program instead of the graduate production program. I want to direct but they see me going into theater research. I'm not interested in doing that so after two quarters I leave UCLA and apply to Valley State, now known as California State University, Northridge (CSUN), and am accepted into their MA Theater Arts production program.

When I return Dr. Bill, my theater mentor and department Chairman, asks for a favor. He wants to know if I'd be interested in directing a production of *Murder in the Cathedral* for the department's upcoming T. S. Eliot festival that he's producing. He tells me the faculty member scheduled to direct has taken ill and won't be available to stage the show and no one else on the staff is available to step in and take over. In return he'll make sure I get to direct a main stage production for my graduate thesis project. I agree and soon after I'm in pre-production for *Murder in the Cathedral*. I'm a happy guy.

In late fall the show opens. The run goes very well and the production is well received. As a result of helping him out Dr. Bill comes through for me and I get to direct a musical on the main stage as my graduate thesis project. But before all that happens I meet Peggy.

Peggy is an attractive talented actress who immediately caught my eye when she came to audition for *Murder in the Cathedral*. She had a strong audition so I cast her in the production. One evening after rehearsal we go out for coffee and she tells me about herself.

She tells me she'd recently left a Catholic convent in Indiana, where she was about to take her final vows to become a nun, and returned to California to be, of all things, an actress. Nun to actress, go figure.

It's very evident to me I am attracted to Peggy and begin spending more time with her after rehearsals. Pretty soon a romance begins.

The spring semester of 1969 was a pretty turbulent time at the university. In January the university makes the national news with the "student protests" that took place on campus. The news media called them, "student riots."

The protests happened at the Administration Building that was across campus from the theater building where I was in rehearsals. My reaction to it was mixed. I sided with the students but hated the idea that those who were responsible for the protest weren't there when things got out of hand. I was also upset that something like that was happening at "my school." But in reality I was much more concerned with directing my show than the riot.

In the spring of 1969 I direct the musical, *The Roar of the Greasepaint, the Smell of the Crowd* for my Master's Thesis Production. I am the first graduate student in the Master's directing program to be given the opportunity to direct a main-stage musical as a thesis project. Thanks again to Dr. Bill.

Everything goes well with the show and I receive an "A" grade for directing the production. When the show closes, all that's left for me to do is take my written exams. Once I pass them I'll be done with graduate school and have my Master's degree. So I take the tests and much to my embarrassment I get a C on one of them. Anything lower than a B grade means you have to re-take the test.

A couple of weeks later as I'm preparing to re-take the test I hear of a job opening at the Greek Theatre in Los Angeles. Built in 1929 the Greek Theatre is a 5,000-seat outdoor amphitheater located in Griffith Park. The theater is looking for an Assistant Production Manager for the coming summer season. As soon as I hear about the job opening I hustle to get an interview.

Jack, the Executive Producer and head of production, interviews me. The interview goes well and when it's over he asks me if I want the job. I immediately accept and ask when I'll be starting. I figure I have a couple of weeks before I have to begin. Wrong. He tells me to report the next day. So I place a hold on re-taking my exam. The next day I report to the Greek and at the age of 26 my real education in show business begins.

My first day on the job I arrive at 8:00 a.m. and report to Jack, who sits me down and proceeds to tell me the facts of life regarding my position.

"Okay, kid, this is the most important thing you have to know about the theater." Then he leans forward and says something that has stayed with me for the rest of my life.

"It's called show business NOT show art," he tells me.

Then he says I have four weeks before the first show opens and during that time I've got to learn all about union rules, budgets, contracts and the Teamsters... things I was never taught in college.

It's soon evident to me Jack knows everything about producing theater and he becomes a wonderful mentor for me.

A week after starting at the Greek, he introduces me to David Banks, the Production Manager at the Huntington Hartford Theatre in Hollywood. The Hartford is where the Greek Theatre Association produced its non-musical productions.

At our first meeting we immediately hit it off. During the season David and I go out after our respective shows close each night and hit the Hollywood clubs where it seems David knows everyone.

David seemed to know as much about running a theater as Jack did. After his time at the Greek he became the Production Manager for *The Rocky Horror Show* both in New York and Los Angeles. We had a close friendship that lasted for 40 years until his death in 2012.

During this time my relationship with Peggy had become serious so we decide to get married. Looking back I realize we should have just lived together.

I tell Jack our plans and immediately he offers us the use of his large Hollywood Hills home for the ceremony. He also offers to cater the entire affair, provide the music and have a friend design our wedding outfits. It is an overwhelmingly generous offer and we happily accept.

Wedding day. Jack's house is decorated like a Moroccan bordello. Peggy's dress is a long orange crushed-velvet Renaissance gown with sweeping sleeves. On her head is a garland of flowers. I wear an orange velvet medieval renaissance shirt with black pants. All the brides maids and the grooms men are outfitted like flower children. Everyone in the wedding party is barefoot. We love the clothes. The family? Not so much.

Presiding over the ceremony is a friend of ours, a Unitarian Minister who is also an astrologer, he wears his astrologer's gown with all the signs of the zodiac on it along with a cone-shaped hat. We love him. The family? Not so much.

The music starts and the ceremony begins. Bridesmaids and groomsmen enter and take up positions. The minister enters wearing his astrology gown and hat and takes his place. I walk in and take my place next to the minister. When I look at him I start laughing. To me he looks like Merlin, the magician. Peggy appears making a grand entrance in her fairy princess gown that weighs 30 lbs.

The minister begins and suddenly I hear crying. At the time I thought these must be tears of joy. Everyone is happy for us. Then I saw it was my mother, Peggy's mother and her grandmother who were crying. Later Mom told me they were crying because they knew we were making a mistake.

After the ceremony both families separate to different corners while Jack's friends and our wedding guests huddle together in the large living room. A few minutes go by before the wine comes out and people start drinking... the music starts playing... the chairs are removed and people start dancing and the party finally gets started. Then the food appears and everyone starts eating. Everything tastes wonderful, especially the marijuana-laced brownies. They are a big hit. Peggy's Italian grandmother eats several before passing out.

When the Greek season ends I'm once again out of a job. I loved working at the Greek and am offered the chance to return the following summer but in the meantime I need to find work.

I tell Jack my situation and he tells me to speak with Susan McKlay and Chris Burns. They own a music management company and are looking to hire someone for their office. The possibility of working in the music biz intrigues me. It isn't the theater or movie business but at that time the music biz was the hottest area in the entertainment world to work in.

The week after the Greek closes I go for my interview with Susan and Chris. I ask them about the job and they tell me they want someone to help them in the office with their search for new clients. We talk for about an hour and when the hour is up I'm hired and just like that I'm in the music business. Soon after starting work I begin going out every night to clubs with Chris and Susan on their never-ending search for new talent.

After making the rounds of clubs for a couple of weeks I am given a new assignment. I am going on the road as the road manager for a new singing group we'd just signed. Chris has booked 20 performances in California starting in San Diego and ending in San Francisco. I will be driving the van. I have no idea what a road manager does but I think it will be "fun." I'll be gone for two months. When I tell Peggy she hates the idea.

While I am on the road, my marriage begins to show signs of trouble. She starts saying things like maybe we've made a mistake getting married.

After two months on the road I come home exhausted. Right away Peggy and I begin to argue. Since I'm working so many extra hours she wants me to ask Chris and Susan for more money. She had a point. Even though I was enjoying my job I was doing a lot more than I expected. I knew I was working way over 40 hours a week and not getting paid any overtime. So I went and asked them for a raise. They said at the present time they couldn't pay me more but when they could they'd give me a substantial raise. I tell Peggy what they told me. She says I should look for a new job. Once again she mentions maybe our marriage was a mistake.

June 1970. The business begins to slow down and in late summer they miss a paycheck and right after that they fold up shop. My time in the music business is over and once again I'm out of a job. The Greek's season has already begun, so it's too late for me to return. I go back to working part-time doing cue cards but after a few weeks I'm laid off. I go on unemployment. Money becomes tight. I get depressed. I feel any dreams I have of directing are vanishing. There is no joy in the house.

In late October I come home and find the place empty. Peggy has moved out. I walk into the kitchen and see her wedding ring on the kitchen counter with a note next to it that reads, " I don't want this anymore." Soon after she files for divorce. The marriage is over.

Without Peggy's income from her part-time job as a secretary I don't have enough money to pay the rent so reluctantly I move back home. Dad says nothing about my job situation or the end of my marriage, but I can tell he's not happy about it. Mom is angry with Peggy for leaving me. Mom is always on my side.

A new year is looming. 1970 has been a roller coaster ride ending on a downward spiral. I hope 1971 will be better. I'm hustling every day hoping to find work but nothing is happening. Then I get a call from Billy, a writer friend, asking if I'd like to work on a project with him.

He tells me he has a deal to write a script for a children's TV show and is looking for a writing partner. In the past we'd written a script together but I'd never written anything for children. But, like always, I figured I could learn.

In four weeks we finish the script and hand it in. We think we've done a pretty good job and are looking forward to writing future episodes. Wrong. The script is rejected and that is that.

I'm 28 years old and have no job. My dreams of being a director seem very far away. Then Billy tells me he's going to San Francisco for some fun and wants to know if I'd like to join him. Sure, I say… anything to get out of town. So I tell my folks I'm going to San Francisco with Billy to do some more writing.

In San Francisco we drink, party hard and lead a very indulgent life. Then… I get sick. At first I'm tired. Then I catch a cold and that develops into a case of pneumonia. But that doesn't stop me from burning the candle at both ends. Finally, in early March, we are at a party and I suddenly get violently ill and begin throwing up blood. Billy rushes me to the hospital. Tests show I am bleeding internally. I begin getting blood transfusions. I'm told I will be hospitalized for at least a week. I have a ruptured ulcer and have lost a lot of blood. They tell me I'm in serious condition. When I hear serious condition I freak out. Right after giving them my home phone number I lose consciousness.

When I wake up my dad is sitting beside my bed in the hospital. When I see him I start to cry. He comes over and puts his arms around me and holds me. Dad isn't a hugger so his hugging me is a huge gesture on his part. He tells me he is taking me home where our family doctor will treat me. The San Francisco doctor tells him I shouldn't fly but Dad insists.

We are quiet the entire flight back. When we get off the plane I'm taken straight to the local hospital where I stay for a week, then go home to recuperate. Once back home Dad never says anything to me about my San Francisco experience.

June 1971. I feel my life has hit rock bottom. For the next month all I do is sleep, eat and read. Mom makes sure I eat well. I get lots of chicken soup during my recovery. It's times like these I'm lucky to have a Jewish mother.

After one month of recovery I grow restless. I begin thinking about finishing my Master's degree. I'm not sure why. All I know is that it will give me something to do.

*In the spring of 1968 the country suffered two tragic losses. First, on April 3rd, Martin Luther King Jr. was assassinated. It was a hateful act, something that many blacks had long feared would happen. Robert F. Kennedy rushed to the black communities in several cities to try to stop the unrest. He shared his pain of losing his brother just a few years before. I was horrified, and saddened. So much hate for a non-violent man. I grieved at his loss. My grandmother was so saddened by his assassination, we held hands and cried together as we watched yet another funeral procession of a beloved public figure.*

*Then a few months later, Robert Kennedy was assassinated in Los Angeles after winning the June primary in his bid for the presidency. The black community had welcomed him with open arms, excited that the Kennedy legacy would continue. Then just before midnight, right after he gave his victory speech and spoke of moving on to the Convention in Chicago, he was shot. I was helping my grandmother count ballots. Again, our home had been opened to our neighbors as a polling place. This would be the last time elections were held at our home. I was to be married in a few days and she would be putting the house up for sale.*

*I drove the ballots to the collection station, then hurried back home to watch the news. How much more could the Kennedy family take? I felt especially sad for Ethel, pregnant with her ninth child, and of course for her children and the rest of the Kennedy family. The nation mourned and once again grandmother and I held hands and shed tears. Within weeks*

*pictures of John, Martin and Robert began to appear in homes through-
out the community. Who else would stand up for us? Who else would
be willing to take up the standard for civil rights? Lyndon Johnson had
gotten the Civil Rights Act of '64 passed, but much work still needed to
be done.*

*In June of that year Ted and I were married at Bel-Vue Presbyterian
Church, which was just a block from where my parents lived at the time of
my mother's death. We had continued to attend both Bel-Vue and Neighborhood Community Church in Los Angeles where my grandparents often
performed. When I was a young girl, Bel-Vue sponsored my Girl Scout
troop. Years later when I was attending Compton College, I taught the
fourth grade Sunday school class. It was also the church where Beverly
and Tommy were married several years before.*

*Uncle Herb stood in as my surrogate father assigned to walk me
down the aisle. Clarence, Robert and three of Ted's friends served as
groom's men. For me, Cousin Erni served as maid of honor; Robert's
wife Faye, Ted's sister, Margie, Collette from elementary school, Shannon
from high school, and Nancy from Compton College were my attendants.
We had no children of the appropriate age in the family, so the flower girl
and ring bearer were children of coworkers.*

*The wedding was small, about 100 people, but just what I wanted. Be-
ing on a small budget, I wore Beverly's wedding dress, but did purchase
a new veil. For the reception Aunt Rubey roasted turkeys and everyone
pitched in to make sandwiches. Pounds of potato salad were also made
for the guests. The reception was held at the church social hall. Beverly's
reception had been held at our house on 123rd St., but with grandfather
gone, it would be too much for my grandmother to host. We chose the
social hall for another reason. Holding the reception at the church meant
we would not be serving champagne, a rather cost-effective decision.*

*We did not have much of a honeymoon. As we left the church, we had
car trouble, so instead of driving to Las Vegas as planned, we drove to
Robert and Fay's house because they were holding a post-wedding party.
Everyone was surprised when we drove up but happy to have the bride
and groom at the celebration. The next day, after car repairs, we headed
to Las Vegas for our delayed honeymoon.*

*Our first apartment was in Long Beach, but since I still had one more
year of work on my BA, in the fall we moved to an apartment in Reseda
so I could attend college in Northridge. Ted commuted to his engineering
job in Oxnard. I remember going door to door on Reseda Blvd. to find
an apartment. One manager actually said to me that she would check to
see if the other tenants minded if a "colored" couple moved in. This was*

*1968. Ouch. Obviously, I never returned to that building.*

Racial relations continued to be a problem in LA. In the fall of 1968 when I entered San Fernando Valley State College in Northridge, there was an influx of 150 black students, whereas the previous year there had only been 23 black and seven Latino students. I didn't realize I would be attending a campus where racial tensions between the students and the administration were on edge. That fall an agreement was reached to begin a Black Studies program.

In January 1969 another demonstration began at the administration building regarding the start of a Chicano Studies program. I was standing with others on the lawn in front of the administration building in support of the new program. We were advised to remove all jewelry, especially pierced earrings. I thought, "If this is a peaceful demonstration, why did we need...?" Before I could finish the thought, I hear glass breaking and screams. Some students had rushed the building and the police had responded.

The crowd turned to run, I was pushed down. Two students grabbed my arms, helped me up and got me to the edge of the crowd. My knees and hands were scraped and bruised. Someone walked me over to the health office, and of course, I was questioned as to what I had been doing. Now I was really nervous because just then a policeman walked in and took a look at my bandages. For some reason he moved on and chose not to question me any further. However, 14 other students were arrested that day. What disturbed me the most was that the leaders of the movement who had set up the demonstration that day were not even on campus, but others were arrested. The following day there was another demonstration and more arrests.

Things began to settle down during the spring semester and thankfully I graduated in June with my BA. In the fall I enrolled in a Master's degree program for Educational Psychology. I was determined to finish as soon as I could. I also started to work at the Employment Office in Pacoima.

The night I was to graduate with my MA was my grandmother's 75th birthday, June 13, 1971. I decided it was much more important to throw her a party than to go to that graduation. The whole family came to our apartment in Reseda to celebrate. She was so happy and loved having her children, grandchildren and great-grandchildren with her to share in the celebration. We played games, we ate, and we laughed and danced.

Not long after getting my MA degree Ted and I purchased our first home in Northridge. My grandmother would come and spend weekends and I so enjoyed having her. I actually wanted her to move to the condos *at the end of our block but realized with both of us at work most of the time she would be isolated from the rest of the family and her church friends.*

*We had a good social life, friends for Saturday night Bid Whist parties and dinner dates. Our most frequent partners were my Cousin Erni, her husband Bob and two college friends of hers, Jarvis and his wife Myra along with Lanny and his wife LaVonne. We found something to do every weekend. A lot of times we rotated homes to play cards, watch movies, and cook dinner, all relatively inexpensive forms of entertainment.*

*Ted had a lot of interests, and I began to participate in the activities he liked. He had spent some time learning to ice skate before he met me and wanted to go back to that, so we would travel into Culver City for his lessons.*

*He met with one of the few African American ice skating instructors. She was also the coach for professional ice skaters Tai Babylonia and Randy Gardner, so she knew her stuff. He really worked at it and as usual he was pretty successful. His tall lean physique lent itself to the sport and he was actually quite graceful. I on the other hand just bummed around on the ice. This was not a venue where blacks were commonly found. After a while, his demanding work schedule and the drive over the hill took us off the ice.*

*His other activity was karate, again with a great instructor, Chuck Norris, who was one of the nicest people I had ever met. He had a studio on Ventura Blvd. After Ted had been attending classes there for a few months I decided to join him, so one day I showed up with Ted and enrolled in the beginning classes. I stood there decked out in my karate gi with my white belt ready for class. A few minutes in I was ready to quit. I must have lasted a few classes, but this was tough stuff. Ted, who always succeeded in everything he attempted, of course made it to his black belt.*

*After I quit my silly attempt to run up the colored belts, I enjoyed going to the studio to watch the action. We also went to Las Vegas for a few competitions as Ted was on his way to earning a black belt.*

*My favorite time was with the Black Porsche Club. Early in our marriage Ted wanted to buy a Porsche and we purchased a used burgundy 911. As I recall the monthly note on the car was more than the rent on our apartment, but we had a Porsche. He taught me to drive it on the parking lot of Reseda High School near our apartment. A few years later he traded it in for a brand new desert sand 911. It was quite the ride. After that purchase he wanted to join a local car club, Black Porsche Inc. It was a group of about 30 African American men and a couple of women who owned Porsches. The club gathered monthly to drive in and around LA to*

*showcase their cars. It was a social club that offered a wonderful outlet
for me. Every year the club held a dinner dance at the Bonaventure Hotel
in downtown LA. The event always sold out.*

*Monthly, after the club meeting, the members and their significant
others would get in their cars for a Sunday road trip. Sometimes we would
travel up to Santa Barbara for lunch, or down to San Diego for a quick
trip to the zoo, or out to Malibu for a picnic on the beach. We also went
to the Monterey Jazz Festival every year—something I had long wanted
to do but Ted never wanted to until we joined BPI. The club also took an
annual trip to Rosarito Beach in Mexico, and ski trips to Big Bear.*

*Seeing 30 African Americans driving Porsches was difficult for some
people. Once after a club meeting we pulled up to a café on the road and
the owner looked at one of our members and asked, "You boys delivering
these here cars?" Smitty answered, "No we boys own these here cars."*

*I even had the opportunity to attend The Bob Bondurant Driving
School. Complete with driving jump suit and gloves, I learned to drive the
track. I was actually pretty good and became very comfortable behind the
wheel on a racing track. I believe that the last five years of our ten-year
marriage were manageable because of the fun times with Black Porsche.*

*This married life wasn't what I wanted. Ted was a hard worker, a
good person, but the romance in our marriage left much to be desired. I
wanted to travel and to begin thinking about having children. Ted didn't
want either.*

Early July 1971. Through a friend I am offered the job of writing
and producing a radio documentary about the drug culture and the Jesus
freaks movement for KPFK Public Radio. I accept even though I'd never
written or produced a radio documentary before, but I'm a fast learner.
My first step was to start researching the Jesus freaks.

My research took me to a Christian halfway house in San Diego
where I met the head counselor, Laura. After talking to her about the
documentary she agreed to help with my research.

Laura was from San Diego, single, committed to her work, and a
devout Christian. She wasn't a warm and fuzzy person. She was reserved
but compassionate. She reminded me of a character in an Ingmar Berg-
man movie, cool and aloof. She told me she used to be a dental technician
but left that to work as a drug counselor for her church.

After a week I ask her out for coffee. At first she is skeptical about
going out. I tell her it's only to talk about the documentary. Over the next
month we work closely together on the project. When I finish the documentary we continue seeing one another. The relationship soon turns into

a romance.

Meanwhile, I haven't told my family I am seeing someone. When they finally meet her they aren't thrilled. To them she seems cool and distant.

With the documentary completed I am once again out of work and in need of a job. I go back on unemployment but I know that won't last forever.

In early August I am told my unemployment benefits are about to run out. A week later I'm at the unemployment office to pick up my last check when my counselor tells me there's a job opening for someone to teach English and Drama at LaSalle High School, an all-boys Catholic school in Pasadena, California. "Don't you have a minor in English?" my counselor asks me as she thumbs through my folder.

Ugh, I think. Teach. I don't want to be a teacher; I want to be a director. Well, I wasn't anything then so I thought, what the hell, I need a job; I have a degree in Theater Arts and, yes, a minor in English.

I contact the school and send them the paperwork they ask for and much to my surprise one week later I get a call to come in for an interview.

The interview goes well and I am hired! I'm going to be a teacher. Mom and Dad are thrilled. "At last!" Dad says. "You have a real job."

My initial feeling about getting the job is enormous relief. I am employed and with that I can finally afford to once again get a place of my own. I find a small apartment in Laurel Canyon.

It's not very big, but it's all mine. More importantly I'm out of my parents' house, and that's all I wanted. Just to be on my own.

Going in I am totally unprepared to be a teacher. I know nothing about course outlines, class objectives, learning skills, grades, daily course materials, homework assignments and most of all… I have zero classroom experience. I'd always said if I didn't know something I could pick it up pretty quick. But teaching…?

The day after I'm hired I drive out to the school and meet with the school Principal, Brother Gary, a 30-something serious man dressed in traditional monks' attire. He tells me he wants to build the drama program up so they can use it as one of the major selling points for the school's annual fundraising campaign. Next I go see Jerry, the Vice Principal. He's the guy who actually runs the instructional side of the school but he isn't a Brother. Jerry is very sharp. Early 30s, tall, lean with thinning red hair.

He gives me some really good advice. "Be sincere in wanting your students to do well. Because if they do well you're doing your job."

After that he gives me a stack of papers and folders that contains materials about the school, the textbooks for my English classes and the telephone number of my department chair whom I'm told to call for any advice and guidance.

As I walk out the door Jerry shouts after me, "And have fun!" Oh, yeah... fun. Having never taught before I find out very quickly... Teaching is hard work.

Classes begin and I quickly learn I am a natural-born teacher, especially when it comes to drama classes. Then when I start directing, everyone, students and staff alike, see the productions improve tremendously. The result, in just one year there, is a substantial increase in enrollment in the drama program. It doesn't take long for the program to become what Brother Gary wanted, a major asset for the school's fundraising campaign.

During my first year at LaSalle I re-take my graduate exam at CSUN and in June I'm awarded my Master's degree in Theater Arts.

At the end of my first year I get my evaluation and it is excellent. In spite of the fact that I don't like calling myself a teacher, especially when I am with my Hollywood friends, I'm becoming a good one.

Throughout my first year at LaSalle I keep seeing Laura. By now our relationship has become serious and we start talking about living together. Economically speaking, living together made sense. One rent is cheaper than two and driving back and forth to San Diego is getting tiring. So we start looking. Eventually we find an apartment in Santa Monica a few blocks from the ocean. We both love the location and the weather is the best in the world. We move in together at the beginning of August 1972. Soon after moving Laura finds a job in Santa Monica teaching at a local dental college.

I've always been ambitious. I become friends with a few public school teachers and learn what they are paid which makes me realize teaching at a Catholic school isn't the best paying job in education. So during my second year at LaSalle I begin to look around for a better paying position.

One day an ad in the *Educational Journal* catches my eye. Redmond High School in Redmond, Oregon is looking for someone to teach Drama and English. I reply to the ad and a week later I get a call from the Vice Principal. He conducts a phone interview with me. When it's over he asks me to come up in June for one more final interview with the Principal. I tell Brother Gary and to my surprise he wishes me luck.

The semester ends and I drive to Redmond thinking the job is mine for the taking. The Vice Principal had made it sound like, with my teaching experience and my background in production at the Greek, I was the right man for the job. I'm so sure I'm getting the job I clean out my desk and say goodbye to everyone at LaSalle.

In Redmond I meet with the Principal and it is evident from the moment we start talking that I am *not* getting the job. He's going to hire someone already in the district, the in-house candidate. So thanks for driving up and see you later.

Right after the interview I call Laura and tell her the news. She isn't devastated like I am. Then she says if I really want to leave LaSalle she'd be happy if I'd look for a position in the San Diego area. I tell her I'll think about it.

On my way back to LA, for no apparent reason, I decide to return via Ojai, a small community located in the Ojai Valley just north of Ventura, California. On a whim I drive to the office of public education and ask the secretary if there are any openings for a Drama/English teacher at the public high school. She gives me a funny look, then says, yes, it just so happens they are looking for a new Drama/English teacher at Nordhoff, the local public high school, and the interviews are being held as we speak. I hand her a manila envelope with all my professional papers. She takes it and goes into the office marked Vice Superintendent. A few minutes later she comes out and tells me to go in for my interview.

What, an interview right now? Is she kidding me? Nope, she's not kidding. The interview lasts about an hour. The time flies by. At the end the Vice Superintendent thanks me for coming in and tells me he'll call in a couple of days with his decision.

That night back in Santa Monica, I tell Laura about the Ojai interview. She asks a lot of questions then finally asks me the really important one. If I'm offered the position will I take it? I tell her yes.

The next morning Ojai calls and I'm offered the job. I accept and just like that I have a new teaching position at twice my current salary that is taking me out of Los Angeles. Wow! Things are moving very fast. I call Laura at work and tell her the news. She says we'll talk about it when she gets home. Talk about it? I've already accepted the job offer.

That night we talk and I tell her I want her to come with me to Ojai. She agrees but only if we get married. She thinks because Ojai is such a small community it wouldn't look right if the new drama teacher showed up with a woman he wasn't married to. I am hesitant when marriage is mentioned. Since my last marriage didn't work out I'm not keen on getting married again but she's pretty clear about her feelings. If I want her to go with me we'll have to be married. I finally agree but deep down I'm still not sure it's what I want. Not a good way to go into a marriage. Looking back getting married again wasn't a good decision on my part.

My parents are thrilled when I tell them about my new job. Then I tell them I'm getting married again. They aren't happy about that at all.

August 1973. Just prior to leaving for Ojai, Laura and I are married in a small ceremony in Los Angeles. It is very low-key unlike my previous wedding. My folks are there but don't show much enthusiasm for my new nuptials. No one from Laura's family attends. In fact, in all the time Laura and I are together, I never meet anyone from her side of the family.

Moving to Ojai is a big project. We have to move out of the apartment in Santa Monica, drive to Ojai, find a place to live, move in, find a new job for Laura, learn the geography of the area, and make new friends. All in three weeks. It's a whirlwind of activity.

In 1977 Nordhoff High School has a little over 1,300 students, more than double the size of the student population of LaSalle. The school is a huge part of life in the Ojai community. The community comes out to support all the athletic teams, along with the music and drama programs.

Soon after beginning work at Nordhoff I become involved with every aspect of school life. Besides directing theater productions I become the Public Address announcer at all football and basketball games, the advisor to the Drama Club, serve on the academic affairs committee, become a union member, build a TV studio at the high school, and at night, when I'm not rehearsing a play, teach television production classes for the local cable channel. In addition I find time to teach occasional night classes at Ventura College and the University of California, Santa Barbara. While I'm doing all of this Laura tells me she's not sure she likes living in Ojai. It's a bit too small-town for her. Give it time I tell her.

My first year at Nordhoff I direct three shows. The local newspaper praises the productions along with my work at the school. My colleagues and friends say I'm doing great things for the students, the school and the community. Everyone is happy for what I'm accomplishing except Laura.

At the start of my second year Laura tells me that living in Ojai is stifling for her. She again asks me to look for a new position in the San Diego area where she's from.

But I'm not interested in leaving Ojai. I am happy at the school and have no interest in moving to San Diego. She's not happy with that.

At the start of my third year Principal Duane, my boss, calls me into his office and asks me, "When are you planning on leaving?"

"Leave?" I reply "I'm not thinking about leaving. Is there something I don't know?"

"No," Duane says. "What I mean is, we've seen how good you are as a theater director and teacher and I know someday you'll be leaving for greener pastures. For a bigger school, maybe even a college."

"No, no," I say, "I'm not thinking about anything like that at all." And that was the end of our conversation.

I walk out surprised at his comments. Leave Ojai? It wasn't something I was consciously thinking about at the time. But the more I think about what he said, the more I begin thinking, "Maybe I should start looking for a job teaching at a college."

Then...

The day before the start of my 1977 summer vacation I go to the main office at Nordhoff to hand in my grades. As I finish handing in my grades, Lucille, the principal's secretary, calls me to her desk where she hands me a piece of paper. I look at it and see it's a job announcement from Moorpark College. They're looking for a full-time professor to teach theater and television. As I'm reading the notice Lucille says, "You should apply for this. It's right up your alley."

I laugh it off but she is adamant and tells me I should fill out the application right now then give her a copy of my resume and she'll mail it in for me. I tell her I'll come back tomorrow with it but she insists I do it that afternoon. She knows summer vacation is about to begin and once I leave campus I won't be back until September. So I go back to my classroom, get a resume from my files, fill out the application and write a one-page letter telling Moorpark College why I'm the person for the job. Thirty minutes later I'm back in the office with all the necessary paperwork. I hand it to Lucille who puts everything into an envelope and gets it in the mail. I wave goodbye and shout, "Happy summer. See you in September." My summer vacation begins. As I get into my car I'm thinking, "Where is Moorpark College?"

In early August I get a call from Moorpark College notifying me that they want me to come in to interview for the theater-television position. When is the interview? Tomorrow. What? 11:00 a.m. at the college.

I'm excited about the interview but when I tell Laura she just says, "What about San Diego?" I tell her let's see what transpires with the Moorpark College interview first. If that doesn't work out then we'll talk about San Diego.

The next day I drive to Moorpark College, which I've learned is located in the east end of Ventura County. A committee of 12 faculty and staff interview me. The interview lasts about two hours. I tell them about my experience at the Greek Theatre, working for CBS, Barney and cue cards, my time at La Salle and Nordhoff High Schools and my work as a theater director. The interview ends. I drive home feeling confident.

The next morning the phone rings. I pick up. It's Moorpark College on the line. I'm told the committee has selected two final candidates to

be interviewed by the college president. I am one of the two selected. My
interview is scheduled for the next day at 1:00 p.m.

The next day I drive to the college and go to the President's office
where I meet President Ray and Vice President Howard. The interview
begins and before I know it I am in a serious discussion about Shake-
speare with Howard who I learn has a PhD in Dramatic Literature. Of
all the luck, to be interviewed by someone who really knows something
about the Theater. Lucky me.

After an hour the interview ends and I'm ushered out the door. I walk
away thinking, I can do this job. I can be a college professor.

Once again the next day I get a call. It's the college President offering me the position. Will I accept? You bet I'll take the job. I hang up
the phone and start yelling, "I got it! I got it! I got it!" I am yelling to an
empty house. Laura is at work.

Wow, I think, Professor Les!

I call my folks and tell them the news. They are happy. I call my
friends. They are happy. I tell Principal Duane. He is happy. I tell his
secretary, Lucille. She is very happy. I tell Laura. She is less than happy.

In the fall of 1977, soon after I start at Moorpark College, Laura tells
me she's thinking about taking some time away to visit friends in San
Diego. She says she needs some time away to think. As soon as she says
that I know my marriage is over. Soon after that conversation she leaves
for San Diego and never returns. A year later we are divorced.

When I told my folks my marriage had broken up and I was getting
divorced, Dad didn't say much. He just shook his head and told me not
to make another mistake. As for Mom, well, she was pretty happy Laura
wouldn't be around anymore. Once Laura was gone Mom told me, "I
never really liked her. I didn't trust her. Did you realize when she smiled
she never showed any teeth! Just that tight smirky-smile of hers. You're
better off without her. She wasn't good for you." That was Mom. Always
sticking up for me even when I did dumb things.

Looking back I thought my marriage to Laura was working. We didn't
quarrel or have fights. But once we moved to Ojai our lives changed.
Most of my time and energy went into my directing and teaching and not
enough to her. After she left I thought, I may be a good director but I'm
not so good at being married.

While my marriage had ended, my career was looking up. Mom especially liked to tell people her son was a college professor. I guess for
a Jewish mother, if you can't be a doctor or lawyer, being a college professor is okay.

*The Employment Office was a good place to work, but I really want-
ed to work at a community college. With my MA in hand I was advised
to volunteer some time at a local mental health clinic to enhance my
resume. A few months later I secured a position at the Pacoima Mental
Health Clinic.*

*Working in mental health was a true learning experience. I had a
fabulous mentor, Dr. Alicia D., a Hispanic woman who was brilliant. She
loved working in a community where her bilingual skills were desperately
needed. Her sister Ruth also worked in the clinic assisting with the adult
daycare program. I learned so much from both of them and they were
absolutely the most fun to hang out with. They came from a big family
and I got to meet all the brothers and sisters, even the ones who lived
in northern California. I would have to write another book to fill in the
details of the craziness we enjoyed together. Suffice to say everyone in life
should have some time with the D. family.*

*I had been working at the Pacoima Mental Health Center for about a
year when I received a call from a friend telling me about a job opening
at Moorpark College. Moorpark College was looking to expand their
counseling department and was interested in hiring more women as 50%
of the students were women and only 2% of the counselors were. I had
just finished a Master's degree in Educational Psychology, had experience in employment service with the Department of Employment and cur-
rently was working as a mental health counselor. My resume exceeded the
job criteria.*

*I submitted the necessary paperwork and received an invitation for
an interview. I was told to drive out on the 118 Freeway until it ended,
and then take a small side road until I was sure I was lost and the college
would be right after that point. The directions were spot on. The campus
was located on a hill in the middle of nowhere. That is often the case with
donated property, but it was a great location with lots of potential for
expansion, which the college did several years later.*

*There were 15 people on the interview panel. Thankfully I'm pretty
good at interviews so the number did not intimidate me. I felt I was putting in a strong performance but toward the end of the interview I noticed
people passing around notes. I tried to concentrate on the questions and
focus on the person talking to me, but the note passing was very distract-
ing. Of course, I thought the notes were about me. Well, I found out much
later that the notes were actually about their upcoming retreat. Rather
rude during an interview, but in spite of the distraction the interview was
successful and I landed the position and started working at Moorpark
College in February 1972.*

*What was especially fortuitous was that the day after my first interview I returned to the clinic only to be handed a pink slip. Yes, I was officially laid off. The office was closing. It was clearly a good thing that I had been job hunting.*

*Moorpark's counseling department had a wonderful reputation with the faculty and most importantly the students. It was an innovative group of people who had received statewide recognition for the development of their Career Planning and Placement Center and accompanying textbook.*

*Early on I learned one of the department's responsibilities was to host the annual welcome back luncheon for faculty, to be held in September just before the start of the semester.*

*We were called to a meeting in the Dean's office to plan the event. I was immediately excited because the event was to be a barbecue, my kind of party. Assignments were made for setup, food prep, clean-up and shopping. I drew the card for set up and food prep. The meeting was going along fine until the Dean assigned one of the counselors to pick up the hot dogs and hamburgers. What? A barbecue in my part of town was ribs, chicken, hot links; a barbecue in the Simi Valley suburb was cooking outdoors. I was really stunned but smart enough not to say anything, my first lesson in working in a new cultural environment.*

*Cultural differences continued. The college sponsored a very successful program for women wanting to reenter college. Language was very important and certain terms were frowned upon. In my community, I would say things like, "Hey lady, how's it going?" I was told by one of my female colleagues not to say that. "Lady" was a term used for women who drank tea with their pinkies up. I told her, "No, lady in my part of town was a greeting for friends, your soul sister." After several discussions on the issue she finally understood the difference. I was not about to change my language because of the new feminist way of language sensitivity.*

*Shortly after I was hired, Rosa, a new counselor, arrived on campus. She was the department's first Hispanic hire and being the second woman of color on the staff we became fast friends. Not long after starting work at the college, she planned a trip to Mexico City and invited me to go with her. I had never traveled outside of the country, so I was very excited to tag along.*

*When we arrived at our hotel, we immediately took off for "La Zona Rosa" which was the main tourist area of the city.*

*Rosa was very friendly and soon met a very handsome young man whereupon I immediately lost my guide. From then on I was on my own.*

*With my Spanish dictionary in hand I took off to explore Mexico City.*

*My first stop was a tour of the museum. I found the next available English speaking tour and off I went. After my time at the museum, I walked along the streets, again with dictionary in hand, attempting to navigate my way around the city. Everyone I spoke to was very helpful even with my clearly minimal Spanish skills. Eventually I met two elderly sisters and they became my new guides.*

*One night we went to see the pyramids outside Mexico City. The pyramids would speak to each other by way of colorful lights including the recorded voice of the actor Ricardo Montalbán telling the history of the pyramids. What fun! We laughed and laughed and drank margaritas.*

*When I returned to my hotel, I went to my room and found the "Do not disturb" sign hanging from the doorknob. I gently knocked and my roommate requested I wait in the lobby for a while. I went to dinner with the sisters. In spite of being deserted two hours after our arrival I managed to have a great time in Mexico.*

*At Moorpark I became active in the faculty union, the California Federation of Teachers, and was encouraged to participate in the local chapter. I began to learn about the politics of education, how the unions operated, the importance of the faculty contract and how the work of the union impacted the college work place. I was asked to attend statewide meetings and began to discover what was happening at colleges around the state. I took regular trips to Sacramento. It was the beginning of what would be a long foray into state politics.*

*Occasionally I would bring my grandmother to campus for various activities. She toured the campus and I introduced her to my colleagues. I was very proud to have her visit my place of work. I don't believe she fully understood my job, but she knew I was a counselor and that I helped students. She was very impressed when I explained that my schedule was always full because many students requested to see me for counseling appointments. She met my boss, Dr. Bud, a very large, 6' 4" man who was Dean of Counseling. Of course the first thing she told him was that she did not like me driving home late at night (I worked till 9:00 p.m. on Tuesdays). It was fun watching my very large Italian boss assure my grandmother that he would make sure my drive home was safe.*

*Grandmother had once told me that going to college would "wear out my brains," but now saw that my work in college had paid off, because it was my college degree that put me in the position to have this wonderful career of counseling at a community college.*

*Professionally, I was growing as a counselor. I worked very hard and developed a reputation as someone to be counted on. I took pride in en-*

*suring that I gave the best advice to students and I did not shy away from the long hours. I seldom took time for lunch, preferring to eat at my desk to maximize my student contact.*

*I was asked to serve on the curriculum committee and to represent the counseling staff on several other college committees. I challenged the faculty to do a better job of building the schedule of classes so that students had a better chance to enroll in the classes they needed to graduate. My persistence paid off, the scheduled offerings were adjusted so that classes students needed to graduate did not overlap and students could more easily complete the necessary requirements.*

*My reputation grew as a tough negotiator in meetings and as a strong student advocate. I was told by one of the professors that I would soon become an administrator and probably a college president one day. I told him he was crazy, that was not what I planned on doing at all. Little did I know he was absolutely correct because within a year of his comment I had applied for and accepted an administrative position.*

# CHAPTER 7

## *Moving In*

*N*EAR *the end of 1978 my grandmother had been in and out of the hospital and we realized that now it was necessary to place her in a facility where she could get daily care. She could no longer live alone. The thing that was most surprising to me was my sister's reaction to her illness. Suddenly, the sisters changed personalities. Beverly, who up to now could not make a decision about which peanut butter to buy, was making all the decisions about my grandmother's care, while I was reduced to tears daily and could not think straight. When I went to visit her in the hospital the tears began as I parked the car and started walking toward the hospital building. I remember sitting on her bed, watching Beverly make all the decisions and wondering, "Who is this woman?" She was authoritative and in a take-charge mood I had never seen before; I was a blithering idiot.*

*After a few weeks Beverly found a board and care facility to move grandmother to. Every day she went by to check on my grandmother, usually at odd hours. My sister is always skeptical, but I agreed with her unannounced visits to check on how our grandmother was being treated. We moved some of her bedroom furniture, pictures and other belongings to the facility to make her feel more at home. I would sit with her and help her with dinner. It was so hard seeing her become more and more frail. I knew she would not be with us much longer and my heart ached at the thought of losing her.*

*One day I was talking to Sheila about how my grandmother was hanging on. She said maybe no one had told her that it was time to let go.*

*Shelia's comment made sense to me so the next day when I went to visit my grandmother I knew it was time for me to tell her it was okay to let go.*

*I sat next to her bed as she was sleeping. When she opened her eyes I asked how she was and she said she was tired. I told her it was okay to let go, to rest, to be at peace. She smiled and closed her eyes and drifted back to sleep. She was lethargic, sleepy, not totally coherent. I talked to her softly, and though it was the hardest thing I had ever done, I again told her that it was okay, she could let go and go see her husband, my grandfather. I don't know if that made a difference, but in the next day or so she passed away, February 4, 1979. I was devastated. Her death was harder on me than my grandfather's because now I had lost both of them. Clarence said to me, "Well, now we are orphans."*

*Les was wonderful and caring with me after her passing. Some days I felt like I could barely breathe. I was glad she was no longer in pain, having trouble breathing, feeling her joints ache and just being tired. But I missed her.*

*After she died I would wake up screaming. Les was so compassionate and would hold me until I stopped shaking. I would have dreams where I was talking to her and suddenly realize that she had died.*

*This amazing woman was my heart; she had had a tough life but always did her best to raise a happy, healthy family. She made me extremely proud to be her granddaughter. I just ached and ached now that she was gone. For years after her death I resented Mother's Day. I could not look at a red rose (her favorite) without tearing up. My emotions remained raw, fragile. Sitting in the movie theater, if a sad scene came on the screen I would tear up and begin to cry. Les knew what was happening and would hold me till the pain passed. She sits on my shoulder every day and is with me.*

*The cycle of life demands that we care for our departed. Culturally we now had to deal with the preparations for her services, something I was just not ready for. Again, Super Beverly stepped up and put everything together, making all of the arrangements. Services were to be held at Angeles Funeral Home with a repast at Beverly's home. As we were working on the services I said something to Les about what he planned to wear. He looked at me with a blank stare and then I realized, oh yes, this is the Ojai guy. At the time he was simply not into the suit and tie circuit. So I said I would take care of it. Buying what I was used to, I picked up a pair of gray slacks and a dark blue Pierre Cardin blazer, a fact that would prove ironic in a few days.*

*I called Ted to let him know of mother's passing. He asked if I wanted him to pick me up for the funeral. I thanked him and let him know that I* had met someone and he would be going to the funeral with me.

I was a total wreck. I assigned Cousin Erni to be with me because I knew I would fall apart and Cousin Sheila to be with Les. Our relationship was a bit new so it wouldn't be appropriate for him to be in the immediate family car. He rode with Sheila. As we drove up to the funeral home, I saw Ted standing with Bobby, my Cousin Erni's ex. It was interesting because when we were married to them, Ted and Bobby were not fond of each other, but now they had something in common. Erni and I had left them about the same time.

At the service I sat in the front row with Beverly, Aunt Rubey, Aunt Patricia, Clarence and Robert. Reverend Williams presided. He had known mother for many years and she had sung in choirs he directed. I held my brother's hands as he told us not to be sad. "Ethel was a fine woman, who lived a good life." His words were so passionate and sincere I found myself smiling for the first time in weeks. I felt a certain joy in his message to us, and yes, I felt like he was talking only to us, her children and grandchildren. His expression of respect and love for mother filled the room. I realized he was right. In spite of her troubled childhood, she had overcome so much to be the woman she had become: nurturing, caring and proud of her family. The service was just what my grandmother would have wanted.

When we arrived at the cemetery for the burial I found myself in a drama I hadn't anticipated. I found myself standing between Les and my ex. They stood on opposite sides of the burial plot and when I looked up I noticed they were staring at each other. Both were wearing dark blue Pierre Cardin sports jackets, and gray slacks. It was an extremely awkward moment. I thought of two cats stalking each other. I was relieved when we returned to the cars to attend the repast at Beverly's house.

The family gathered to celebrate Ethel Countee and to spend some time together at what was a difficult life event for all of us. Losing the family matriarch made us realize that a new era had begun, so being together that afternoon was a source of comfort. My Aunt Alice, Uncle Chuck's ex, had made a large pot of her famous gumbo. She was Creole and her cooking skills were a testament to her Louisiana upbringing.

I sat on the front porch with Les and my brothers eating a large bowl of Aunt Alice's masterpiece. We had just finished eating and I was standing to go into the house when I heard the engine of a Porsche coming down the street. My ex had decided to come by.

Les was walking in front of me and I stopped him to let him know my ex was about to join us. I asked Les if he wanted to meet him and he told me, "No, thank you. I know who he is and he knows who I am. I don't *think an introduction is necessary."*

Les continued upstairs to say goodbye to my niece who had come down with the chicken pox and had not been able to attend the service. Just as he came down, my ex walked into the living room, and they silently passed each other. I took a deep breath, said bye to one and hi to the other, another awkward moment.

After my grandmother died, I felt that it was time for me to focus on my future. I realized that for the past few months I had been consumed with my concern for her. My divorce was final and we had reached a settlement. I had received 50% of the market value of the house in Northridge and the funds were sitting in the bank. I had seen recently divorced women race through their financial settlements and didn't want that to happen to me so I decided it was time to invest the money; buying a house seemed like the best way to do that.

I decided that Les and I would buy the house together, even though we weren't married. I truly felt Les was my life partner and wanted him to know there was no turning back for me. A joint investment in the house seemed like a good way to solidify that premise. It was a totally stupid "in love" thing to do. If my daughter did it today I would have a fit. It seemed perfectly logical, but in the pit of my stomach I sort of knew that there was the ever-so-slight possibility that this whole thing could go south.

I had no real commitment from this man. We had an extremely passionate relationship, but that was not something you hang your financial future on. Thank goodness I was right.

I had a colleague, who was fairly new to the real estate world, act as my agent, a mistake. We found a house in Canoga Park with four bedrooms and a fairly good-sized backyard. The owner was a Holocaust survivor, a widower who lived alone. Les commented that he was glad we were supporting this man who had suffered so much. Shortly after we moved in disaster struck. The roof needed repair and our first water bill indicated that there was a leak somewhere under the house. Our agent should have caught both problems but she didn't. First real estate lesson: don't choose an agent because she's a friend and you're trying to help her out. We spent the spring dealing with the necessary repairs. But when we finally got everything fixed, we were able to host both families for holidays and birthdays.

A few months after my grandmother passed, my sister Beverly cleared up all of her finances and was able to divide the remaining funds among the four of us. I used my portion to purchase something that was very meaningful and that would remind me of my grandparents and their music. I bought an upright piano and it was a wonderful addition to our *home.*

*We noticed that our neighbor was failing to cut his front grass. We went next door to meet him, knocked on the door a few times, no answer. We found out from the neighbors that when our house went up for sale, the seller's real estate agent had the yard taken care of until the house was sold. We were told that a single man had lived there for years, a widower, and he was pretty much a hermit. I told our gardener I would pay him to at least cut the grass next door. He was reluctant, but I assured him (little white lie) that the neighbor said it was okay.*

*Not long after we moved into our new home we had a housewarming party. The barbecue was flaming. There was music, dancing, drinking, eating, and laughing. About an hour into the party, a strange man walked into our back yard. He had a slight build and looked frail. His face was long and he had the red nose of a drinker. Les and I went over to him and he said, "Hi, I'm your neighbor, Jack. I hope I'm not disturbing you but I heard the music and laughter and I just... I just felt like I didn't want to be alone anymore." He told us that he had never gotten over the death of his wife. He had taken to drinking and let his life and home go to seed. Before we could say anything, Aunt Rubey, in true Countee fashion, walked up, took his arm and told him, "Sweetheart, you just come along with me. Everyone, this is Jack. Don't worry, Jack, you're family now." I wasn't ready to adopt him, I was still upset about the bad condition of his yard, but after hearing his story my heart melted a little.*

*Soon after, Jack started attending AA meetings and met Libby. She moved in next door and turned Jack's life around. We found her to be a jewel of a person. Jack passed away a few years later but we still remain friends with Libby.*

In the summer of 1979 Tyree and I decided to take a trip to Great Britain. The previous summer Tyree had gone to Europe with a group from the college and was excited to go back with me.

Marge, my theater technician, and her husband Marty, an actor and one of the funniest people I knew, learned about our plans and said they too were thinking about going and mentioned we should go together. We agreed and the four of us started making plans for the trip.

Marty said he had an actor friend who lived in London but who was off doing a movie so his place was available to rent for our entire stay. Sounded like a great idea so we all agreed, let's do it. I thought, this is going to be fun.

In London we go to the theater and see some wonderful shows. *The Crucifer of Blood* with Charlton Heston playing Sherlock Holmes, the

Vietnam War drama *Streamers* and the musical *Evita*... and then Tyree took me to see *The Rocky Horror Show*.

That show was amazing. I'd never been to a rock musical that starred a transvestite from another planet. It was awesome! The audience loved it, I loved it and I knew that I'd found a show I hoped to direct one day at the college.

After a week in London the four of us fly to Paris for the weekend. We spend three days wandering around the City of Lights.

On our first night in Paris we walked down the Champs-Élysées and had dinner in a five-star restaurant. The food was excellent but the prices were staggering. Marty complained throughout the meal that the prices were too high. I have to say, I agreed with him.

Our short trip ends and our first taste of Paris is over. The city has gotten to me and I wasn't through exploring it. I hoped someday to return. I didn't realize it would be a lot sooner than expected.

We return to London, rent a car and take off for a 10-day driving tour through Wales, the Lake District and then up into Scotland. We had a great time and I even got reasonably comfortable driving on the "wrong" side of the road. I especially loved Scotland with its green meadows, old stone walls and ancient castles. We even looked for "Lizzie" the Loch Ness monster at Loch (Lake) Ness. Great fun.

After returning to London, Tyree and I decided to re-visit Paris one more time before flying home. Marge and Marty decided not to join us and instead they went to Ireland.

Without Marge and Marty, our second trip to Paris was even more romantic than the first. We stayed on the top floor of a small hotel in a room that had a balcony that looked out over the rooftops of Paris. At night the view was magical. Paris is a very romantic place.

Our trip ends and we fly home. After returning, a few friends asked if we ever got hassled while in England being a black and white couple. I told them we didn't have any problems. I didn't think we would but I was always aware that things could happen. But nothing did. The Brits were cool with us.

However, when we get back I realize Tyree and I have contracted a bug. It's called the travel bug and we have it bad. I know this bug will never go away. It's something that will stay with us for the rest of our lives. Something we both will come to share and enjoy. Travel, seeing the world, becomes an important part of our lives.

*One night in Scotland we turned a corner and saw a castle up on a hill. I said, "Wouldn't it be wonderful to stay there?" Well, as it turned*

﹅ *out, it was a hotel and we were able to get a room. That night Les went down to the bar and I sat in bed overlooking the countryside and wrote a letter to my sister. I could only imagine what my grandmother would have thought of this setting. It was like a fairytale.*

*On our second weekend in Paris, while walking along the Champs-Élysées, we found a lovely little restaurant and decided to stop for a bite. Just as we were finishing, the owner's 10-year-old daughter was placed at the front door in a Dallas Cowboys cheerleader outfit. With the Cowboys' fight song playing in the background, she proceeded to dance with a baton. Since she was blocking the front door we had to sit through her entire routine, pretending to enjoy it, and it was awful. The place was tiny so all reactions were noticeable. We smiled and clapped with everyone else—it seems they all knew her—and when it ended we were able to escape out the front door. Paris and a junior Dallas Cowboys cheerleader, definitely a lasting memory.*

*So what made our second weekend in Paris so memorable, besides the junior Dallas Cowboy cheerleader? We walked for hours along the boulevards of the city. Resting at a sidewalk cafe, I pinched myself, realizing that I was sitting in Paris with my love, sipping a glass of wine, watching the people walk by and enjoying the incredible evening lights.*

*Spring semester 1980 was very busy on campus and I was working at top speed to cover counseling appointments. My door was always open to students and I always went the extra mile to help them.*

*Near the end of the spring semester I was notified by the honor society Alpha Gamma Sigma that I had been nominated for the outstanding instructor of the year (1979–80 academic year). I was really touched that the students had taken notice of my efforts and nominated me for this award.*

*My friend Miriam, who I had known since my first marriage, had moved to Hong Kong. She was Israeli, married to an American, and had a seven-year-old daughter. She was the person who had let me move my belongings to her garage when I moved out of my house. Miriam was expecting their second child in the spring and was feeling very homesick. She wrote and asked that we come stay with her for the summer. She, Matthew and their daughter were living in the European colony. We were very excited and agreed to come as soon as classes were over in June.*

*We arrived in Hong Kong in the evening. Matthew was at the airport to meet us and immediately took us to meet Miriam at the Jumbo, a large floating restaurant in the harbor. We ate on the top floor and watched a group of Americans perform Vegas showgirl-style dancing. The center-piece on our table included a lobster with twinkling lights where the eyes should have been.*

*The next morning we were able to see their house in the daylight and it was wonderful, complete with a view of the harbor. Our hosts had a full-time live-in maid to help with Kylie and the new baby. They were wonderful hosts and took us out every night and insisted we see the sights during the day.*

*Miriam felt we should travel as much as we could around Southeast Asia. Our first trip was to Canton, now called Guangzhou, on Mainland China. Guangzhou, located northwest of Hong Kong on the Pearl River, is a city of over a million people and the birthplace of dim sum.*

*We found a five-day trip at the American Express office and joined 20 other English-speaking tourists for the trip. We were an eclectic group from New York, Los Angeles, Texas, and Belgium. We traveled on a hovercraft to the mainland escorted by rifle-carrying Chinese soldiers.*

*Once we landed we saw that armed guards were everywhere and our movements were strictly orchestrated. It was like stepping back in time, the streets were full of bicycles, no traffic lights, or at least none that anyone paid attention to. The buildings looked run-down, like all work had stopped 20 years before, with peeling paint and wood in need of repair. Our hotel was very Spartan with no locks on the doors. One night I accidentally left my purse at the bar, went upstairs to bed and realized an hour later that my purse was downstairs. Les and I raced back down and it was still sitting on the table where I left it. One did not take something that did not belong to them in Canton.*

*One day we had an interesting exchange with our tour guide and one of our fellow travelers from New York. Seeing hundreds of bicycles parked on the sidewalks with no locks on them, our New York traveler was flabbergasted. "Where are the locks?" he wanted to know. Our guide could not understand the question, why does one need locks? Why would someone take a bicycle that was not his or hers? That was a concept foreign to our guide.*

*One night we went to the People's Park for an outdoor concert. Thousands were watching the dancing on stage; we were standing at the back of the park. Our traveling companion took out her camera, took a picture and the flash went off. Heads turned and suddenly we became the show. I was traveling with my hair in braids with beads on the ends. Les had curly hair and a beard and our friend was a blond, blue-eyed woman from Texas. Personal space was not a concept the attendees understood so all eyes followed us wherever we went. When the concert ended, after a lot of gesturing and "air honking" like a car, we found a taxi to take us back to our hotel.*

*While in China we also visited a commune and were invited to lunch with the commune leader. Off course I lucked out and got the seat next to him. The first offering was Bird's Nest soup that actually looked like gray dirty dishwater. Insulting or not, there was no way that soup was passing my lips. Most of the women on the tour felt that way but almost everyone gave in to tasting it. I smiled at the leader, fanned my mouth and said, "Too hot, too hot."*

*One day we saw a man on the street wearing a Mickey Mouse shirt. He smiled at us and said, "Disneyland," apparently his only English word.*

*Next Miriam suggested we take a trip to Penang, Malaysia and Singapore, so we booked a flight south. The night we were to leave, a hurricane warning almost stopped our trip, but after helping the maid put masking tape on all the windows (in case the hurricane blew them out), we took off for Penang.*

*The flight was rough and we landed in the middle of the night. We were driven to our hotel on a pitch-black road and could see nothing of the island. The next morning when we awoke, the crystal blue ocean was just a few feet from our room. The palm trees swayed in what was a picture-perfect tropical setting.*

*We headed for breakfast and at the restaurant ran into a couple we had met on the plane, Steve and Anne from England. They were waiting for their 10-year-old daughter, Siobhan, to arrive. She was at a boarding school back in England and was scheduled to meet them on the island that afternoon for a holiday vacation. I was very impressed that a 10-year-old would be flying solo on such a long flight to meet her parents.*

*Our first day at the beach Les and I headed for the water to snorkel and Jet Ski, my first time for either activity. A few hours later, Les noticed how red his feet were and discovered he had third-degree burns on the tops of his feet. The sun was that intense.*

*That night at dinner we met Siobhan and the five of us spent the next five days together. She was a delightful child and we were so glad to have met them.*

*One day we all sailed over to a small island and spent the day on the beach and in the water. Our guides prepared a barbecue feast with shrimp, lobster, fruit and lots to drink. It was a wonderful outing and one I will always remember.*

*Another fascinating experience was eating chili crab. We found a taxi to take us out to a restaurant that turned out to be a few picnic tables set up on the side of the road. Rolls of toilet paper sat along the top of the table and waiters poured your order of crabs on the tablecloth then covered*

*them with chili sauce. The line was two deep around the table waiting for*
*us to finish eating and get up. It was a real local favorite.*

*After our week in Malaysia, Les and I took off for Singapore and the*
*Raffles Hotel where, when it opened, neither of us—a black and a Jew—*
*would have been able to reside in this old British mainstay.*

*The highlights were Boogie Street, drinking Singapore Slings in the*
*Long Bar every night, playing with the gibbon monkeys who ran wild in*
*the local parks and eating the most amazing food. Singapore was truly an*
*adventure, and it would become a life-changing one.*

The Raffles, an old colonial-style hotel located near the Chinese
section of Singapore, was built in 1887 by two Armenian brothers and
named after Stamford Raffles, the founder of modern Singapore.

On our first day we went to the famous Long Bar located on the first
floor. The place looked and felt like an Englishmen's club. A long bar
filled one side of the room and wooden booths lined the walls. Tables and
chairs filled the center.

One table with four chairs was very famous. That's where the writers Somerset Maugham and Noel Coward would sit and drink Singapore
Slings when they stayed at the Raffles. So, in honor of them, every evening Tyree and I would go down to the Long Bar, sit at the famous table
and drink Singapore Slings.

When we got our final hotel bill we noticed we spent *a lot* of money
drinking Singapore Slings. But it was worth it.

Then there was Boogie Street. Friends of ours who'd been to Singapore told us very little about Boogie Street, only, "If you go to Singapore
you have to go there."

"Just remember," they told us, "it opens at midnight."

Well, any street that *opens* at midnight I knew I wanted to see.

On our second night in Singapore we head out from the Raffles at
11:30 p.m. in search of Boogie Street. We have directions but no idea
what we'll find when we get there.

Boogie Street isn't a real street. Rather it's an intersection where people come to party. Once we arrive we find the intersection is filled with
wooden tables and chairs. Along the outskirts of the intersection are numerous stores that sell all sorts of bootleg items from music tapes to elec-
tronic equipment to knock-off clothing, handbags and cameras. Strands
of flashing colored lights and Chinese lanterns make the place look like
a Chinese Christmas tree. Then there is the music. Rock and roll blasts
from speakers located throughout the area.

Hundreds of people jam the space. We look for a place to sit. Nothing is available until we spot a table along the outer edge where two people are seated. We shoulder our way through the crowd to the table and ask the couple seated there if we can join them. They say yes. We sit down and the evening adventure begins. Introductions are made.

"Hello, I'm Jimmy and this is Lola."

Jimmy is a young-looking man wearing a white suit, with a white shirt and black tie. He has long black hair and a small thin mustache. Jimmy is half Chinese and half black. Lola is a blond Australian woman already slightly inebriated.

"You know about Boogie Street?" Jimmy asks.

"Not really," I reply.

Suddenly, the most beautiful Asian women I've ever seen appear from the surrounding buildings. They all wear high-necked Chinese dresses with slit skirts and high heels. Their hair is stacked high on their heads and their makeup is perfect. They are stunning.

They enter and begin to mingle with the crowd. As they pass through the tables men grab them and pull them onto their laps, as photographers magically appear carrying Polaroid cameras to take their picture... for only $5. The men manhandle the women trying to feel them up but no one seems to get angry and the women handle it well.

As I watch this take place I ask Jimmy, "Is this it? Booze, loud music and beautiful Asian women walking around being fondled?"

"They're not women," Jimmy tells me.

"Really?" I take a closer look.

He smiles, leans over and says, "They're transvestites. Want to meet them?"

"Oh, yeah," I reply.

Jimmy waves over two of the ladies. They come over and sit down at our table.

Once seated the ladies pay little attention to me but instead are more focused on Tyree. What fascinates them is her hair with braids and beads. In no time a crowd of ladies all interested in her hair surrounds her.

Jimmy tells me the girls are on a tour of Southeast Asia, and Singapore is their first stop. And guess what? He's their pimp. For the next hour all of his girls visit our table to check out Tyree and flirt with me.

After an hour Tyree has had enough and says to me, "We need to go." But I'm having too much fun with my new friend, Jimmy the pimp, so I say, "Let's wait a little."

"Leslie," Tyree replies, "we need to go."

Now, I learned early on in our relationship when Tyree calls me Leslie in that certain tone of voice she is serious. So I stand up, pay my respects to Jimmy and say goodbye to the "ladies."

On our way back to the hotel Tyree looks at me. "Did you have a good time?" she asks.

"Oh, yeah," I reply. She laughs and shakes her head, "You are so pathetic."

I loved Boogie Street.

*Our summer trip to Southeast Asia was just about to end. It had been an exciting and eye-opening seeing Hong Kong, Mainland China, Malaysia and now Singapore. But for me the trip carried an underlying sense of dread. I was concerned. While our relationship was passionate and exciting, the discussion of a full commitment to this relationship, that is getting married, was absent. I felt like I was on one path and he was on another. Les was having a ball in this exotic part of the world and I was coming to the realization that we would be going home in a few days and we were not moving in the same direction. I realized that he was comfortable with us continuing to live together and having a great time. I was not.*

*Sitting at breakfast in the Raffles Hotel on our last morning in Singapore my feelings were coming to the surface and I knew we had to have a serious discussion about our future before we returned to Hong Kong. I had left a marriage; we were living together with no understanding of where we were headed. Furthermore my biological clock was ticking.*

*Just before we left for this trip Les had said to me he did not understand why the state had to be involved in our relationship. I thought to myself, "Well, the state was involved in your relationships before, but with me it's time to make this new distinction?"*

*It was time so I broached the subject. "So, where are we headed?" He stumbled at first, not sure what to say, but the tone of my voice and the look in my eye must have spoken volumes, and maybe in spite of our having a wonderful time on this trip, he knew this was hanging in the air.*

*His next sentence was a surprise. He talked about making this relationship permanent. Later he told me that he realized I was slipping away emotionally and he had better step up or he would lose me.*

*We talked about next steps and decided why not now. When we returned to Hong Kong our friends sent us to their jeweler in the Hong Kong Hilton to pick up our wedding rings.*

On our last morning at breakfast in The Raffles, we start talking about us, and pretty soon the discussion becomes serious. Tyree tells me, for her, a major part of our being together means being married and having a family. Don't I feel the same way?

For a moment I don't say anything. I know marriage and children mean commitment. Serious, rest of your life commitment, and I'm still gun-shy about that word. I attempt to say something funny, but Tyree is very serious about this.

"If you want to be with me," she says, "then marriage and children are part of the deal."

Well, that's clear enough for me. If I say no then I will lose this amazing woman, and I know one thing for certain, I don't want to lose her.

So I nod my head and tell her I agree, realizing at that moment I had agreed to marriage and kids. Well, no turning back now, I thought.

We return to Hong Kong and get married in a civil ceremony. We are now Mr. and Mrs. Wieder.

We leave our friends and fly back to Los Angeles knowing our lives had changed. We were now married and actively attempting to start a family. This was a far cry from the person I used to be. I was nervous but happy about what challenges lay ahead.

# CHAPTER 8

## *Les, Tyree and Baby Makes Three*

RETURNING *from Hong Kong, we announced we had gotten married. Family and friends were elated for us. Our friend Nancy threw a party for us to celebrate. Family, friends, and colleagues from Moorpark came together to dance. The invitations said, "They finally did it." We had actually only known each other for two years, so it was not that long, but for some, including me, it was long enough. The cake was decorated with a large tree, signifying the start of a growing relationship.*

*We began the fall semester at Moorpark as husband and wife but I did not change my name. With both of us working on the same campus, I wanted to keep my personal and professional lives separate. Now, however, I realized it was time to learn more about my new husband's heritage. I knew little about Judaism, the Jewish faith, customs and traditions.*

*I had spent the previous months enveloped in the passion of our romance. I now looked to broaden that passion to include what would become a significant part of our relationship, a significant part of our future.*

*Maybe I should really have done that before committing to a new life together, but love and passion came first. The reality of one's heritage came next. Now it was time for me to learn exactly what I had moved myself into.*

*When I was growing up Jews were seen as people with lots of money and we knew there were lots of Jewish comedians because that's what we saw on TV. I also knew what Jews didn't do. They didn't eat pork and they didn't celebrate Easter or Christmas. Of course I knew about the Holocaust but my knowledge of the Jewish world was pretty limited.*

*I began to look for ways to learn more about Judaism. One day I saw an ad in the UCLA Extension catalog for a nine-week course called "Feminist Aspects of Judaism." It wasn't exactly what I wanted, but it was something.*

*The class had about 20 students. Most were Jewish women who had not been observant Jews since childhood and wanted to reacquaint themselves with their religion; a few were non-Jews involved with Jewish men who wanted to know more about the religion of their new significant other.*

*During introductions I shared with the class my recent marriage and my desire to learn more about the religion of my husband. In the class my situation of being in an interracial relationship was unique.*

*The instructor for the class, a wonderful woman named Paulette, was very active in the Jewish community and for years had been a fundraiser for a Jewish organization. She was a willing mentor for me in my quest for information. As a matter of fact, our relationship has lasted long past that class taken 30 years ago.*

*The class was a primer on Judaism. In addition, Paulette made sure we were invited to Shabbat services and Jewish events in the community to get a more complete look at Jewish life. What I learned about Judaism during this time was very positive.*

*I loved the tradition and rituals of the holidays and began to love the teachings of the Torah. I felt close to a religion and a people that believed so strongly in equality and social justice. I came to realize the Jewish understanding of the pain of slavery and centuries of discrimination.*

*At the end of our nine weeks several of us wanted to continue our studies. Paulette arranged a follow-up class for early 1981. In February she offered a six-week extension of the class.*

*Early into the spring semester I received a call from a friend who worked at Los Angeles Mission College telling me they were going to announce a position for an Associate Dean of Student Services and that I would be perfect for the job. Would I consider applying? I had never thought about an administrative position, but they didn't open up very often and this was in my area of expertise, so why not? I talked it over with Les and he encouraged me to go for it. I completed the application and was called in for the first interview. I was successful and told I would be called for a second interview with the president.*

*The next week, Les and I took a trip to Mammoth Mountain and stayed at Cousin Ron and Sheila's condo. We did a bit of cross-country skiing, mostly because I kept falling on the bunny slopes trying to learn to ski downhill. I was also very tired the entire weekend and spent a con-*

*siderable amount of time sleeping.*

The next week I went to the doctor and my suspicion about my sleepiness was confirmed. Les and I were to become parents. We were both ecstatic.

Needless to say my family was over the moon about the pregnancy. My only regret was that my grandmother would not be with me to share in this joy. Les' parents were very happy as well; I think they could see their wandering son was really settling down.

For spring break Les and I joined our friend Nancy (who had hosted our wedding reception) and her husband for a trip to New York; it was my first trip to the Big Apple.

We went to Lindy's for cheesecake, Greenwich Village for pizza, the Carnegie Deli for pastrami and ate lots of Nathan's hot dogs along with some wonderful Italian food; yes, food was an important part of the trip.

I really got the full tour of New York, which of course included theater. On our final night in the city we were able to get tickets to see Lena Horne: The Lady and Her Music. We were thrilled that we were actually able to get tickets!

Lena was amazing. There were several older black gentlemen sitting behind us making very affectionate calls to her and they kept Les and me in stitches for the whole concert. When I was not laughing or applauding I was crying.

This was Black History at its best. I thought of my grandparents singing and playing some of the songs she sang. It was a perfect ending to a perfect week.

The next weekend after returning home Les and I headed to San Diego for his Cousin Peter's wedding. I was going to meet more of Les' mom's family.

We drove down with Les' parents. When I got into the car I was very surprised to see Hilda wearing a gigantic Star of David necklace, not something she usually did. Turns out since this was to be a Christian ceremony she wanted to make a statement, and the necklace surely did that. Actually the event went pretty well and I was even included in a family photo.

Shortly after that weekend I was called in for my second job interview at LA Mission College. But now I had a dilemma. Should I mention to the President of the college that I was pregnant? After consulting with a couple of folks including my current President I was advised that I was not obligated to pass on this information, just to wait and see what happened with the interview. After all, I might not even be selected for the position. The interview went fine and I walked away feeling very good about my *prospects.*

*A few days later driving home from Paulette's class I began to have terrible cramps. I walked in the door and went immediately to bed, trying to fall asleep, hoping that would help. It did not. By 1:00 a.m. I could not ignore the pain any longer and called Dr. Forbes, my OB. He asked if I was bleeding. "No," I told him. He told me to come see him first thing in the morning. The pain subsided a bit and I was able to get a few moments' sleep. When I woke up, I got dressed and we headed off to see the doctor.*

*By the time we got there he was busy with a patient so we had to wait a bit and that's when the pains started again. Finally he called me in, gave me a quick exam and then called Les in to tell him he would have to drive me to the hospital as an emergency exploratory surgery was needed.*

*That's when I told him to hold on, I wanted a second opinion. He said, "Sure," and then preceded to tell his nurse to call the hospital for an anesthesiologist and an operating room, he would meet us there in 15 minutes.*

*When we arrived at the hospital I was taken immediately to surgery. Unfortunately, when I got there, there was a complicated surgery still going on in my scheduled operating room. Consequently I lay in the hallway for about 30 minutes waiting for the room to become available. Finally the room was cleared and I was rolled in.*

*The anesthesiologist came in to give me a spinal, but unfortunately he was unable to locate the proper spot, sticking me several times trying to locate it with the needle. I was curled on my side and I could see Dr. Forbes pacing, waiting for the anesthesiologist to finish his work. Finally he made the connection, and I went into a twilight resting state.*

*It seems over the past few weeks fibroid tumors had grown in my uterus and were competing for space with the baby. Because the tumors were fixed to the uterine walls, they could not be removed. The doctor repositioned everything as best he could, hopeful I would get past this difficult phase. The last thing I remember was the sound of staples being attached to my stomach*

*When I awoke from surgery Dr. Forbes explained that the exploratory surgery went well, but we would have to wait and see with a 50-50 chance of everything going well with the pregnancy. The next day as I sat in my hospital bed and contemplated what the doctor had said I began to cry for the first time during this ordeal. I looked out the window into the parking lot and saw my sister Beverly, my Aunt Pat and Cousins Sheila and Erni. They had come to cheer me up but alas found me in tears because of the news from the doctor.*

*In her attempt to cheer me up, my sister announced that she had just purchased some beautiful white yarn and would be knitting the baby a christening outfit. In dismay, I looked up at Sheila, asking with my eyes that she explain. So Sheila said, "Beverly, Jewish babies do not get christened."*

*Her reply, "Really?"*

*All of a sudden, my sister who had not seen the inside of a church since my grandmother had died was concerned about my baby being christened. We all had a good laugh and I stopped my tears.*

*Then she told me she was going to just take the baby one day when I was not home and have it baptized. I explained that it was really okay as millions of people in the world were not baptized and they do fine. But I thought I had better keep my eye on the baby for a few months just in case.*

*In my post-op visit Les and I had a serious conversation with Dr. Forbes about the upcoming delivery. The doctor explained that, with the position of the tumors, a natural childbirth would be impossible. He was going to schedule me for a C-section.*

*I told him I wanted to have a natural childbirth. This might be my one and only delivery. I told him women have been having babies for centuries without C-sections. He then said, yes, and many of them died. Point well taken. He won the argument and the procedure was scheduled.*

*I had to take it easy for a few weeks, but the surgery did not have any long-term impact. However a few weeks later I got the same cramps and had to call Dr. Forbes again. This time he could do nothing other than manually manipulate my cervix to see if he could "rearrange" the fetus. It was very painful. I never experienced morning sickness, but in exchange I had two painful episodes, including the emergency surgery.*

*It was during my recuperation that I received a call from the President at LA Mission College offering me the job of Associate Dean of Student Services. He had called Moorpark and they told him I was home on illness leave. He called me, concerned, and I told him what had happened. He listened and then said he would hold the position until I was ready to return to work. He was building a long-term team and pregnancy and childbirth were temporary conditions. I was to begin my new position as Associate Dean of Student Services at LA Mission College on July 1, 1981.*

*In mid-June, before leaving Moorpark College, the staff gave me a great send-off with a surprise baby shower. Our friend Nancy and my Cousin Sheila hosted my second shower in November. This was for family and friends. My third shower took place at LA Mission College a few days later. When you wait until you are 35 to have your first child, everyone is so excited and happy they can't wait to shower you with baby gifts. Seriously, the only items we purchased for the baby were nursery furniture and a diaper bag. Three baby showers and not one diaper bag. We found the perfect one. It was a very practical brown canvas model that Les used for years after baby duty as a camera bag.*

When Tyree got pregnant I was really happy. The idea of having someone I'd be responsible for the rest of my life actually felt exciting. I was raised like an only child in that my sister was 13 years older than me so when she graduated high school she immediately went to New York to train to be a nurse, leaving me the only child in our house. I was five. So for the most part I grew up alone. I had friends and didn't feel lonely but I didn't have a sibling around to share my life with.

As I became older I felt having children would stifle my ambition and take away my chances of becoming a successful director. Looking back it was stupid to think that way. Once I changed my mind and found out I was actually going to be a father, I wasn't scared about it. Well, maybe a little, but that had more to do with how to raise a child than with being a father.

When we saw *Lena Horne: The Lady and Her Music*, the audience exploded with applause, shouts, whistles and cheers as soon as she stepped on stage. Wow! She looked amazing. She was 64 years old but looked 20 years younger. She was beautiful and filled with energy. Then she started to sing. Her voice was smooth and sexy and strong. It was a stunning performance and afterwards I was so taken by her I started thinking if we had a girl we should call her Lena Horne Wieder. I told Tyree. Didn't happen. But for a moment....

*On July 1, 1981 I started my new position as Associate Dean of Student Services at LA Mission College. I would only be able to work for five months before I took off for maternity leave so I dove in full force to meet my new colleagues, get to know the campus and become familiar with the community. I would be supervising several departments in Student Services. Everyone was very welcoming and the Student Services staff was very supportive of their new Associate Dean.*

*In addition to adjusting to my new role as an administer at a new college and the fact that in a few months I would become a mother, I also began to more seriously consider how Judaism might become part of our life together. I had signed up for Paulette's class because I wanted to learn the basics of Judaism and her class had the additional benefit of adding information from a woman's perspective. Les and I had discussed religion briefly, but had not made a firm decision about the direction we would take on religion in our home. Now there was a child to think of. I began to think about the possibility of converting to the Jewish faith. Converting to Judaism was a monumental decision but not necessarily a difficult one to make.*

*The world would always see our child as African American. As a black child, you are constantly reminded that "one drop" of black blood puts you on the auction block. I remember stories of light-skinned blacks passing for white and later being discovered and lynched for having that single drop of black blood. However in the Jewish faith the Jewish identity was carried through maternal descent. In 1981 the Reform movement had not yet moved to Jewish identity through paternal descent, which occurred in 1983. So here I was about to have a baby who, if I did not convert to the Jewish faith, would not necessarily be seen as Jewish.*

*Another aspect of my decision was that while I grew up in a Christian home and my grandparents were devout Christians I never had strong feelings about the religion. I never understood the passion from members of my grandparents' church. I watched, was respectful, but was never as committed to the faith as those around me.*

*I knew very little about Judaism, but my sense of the religion, added to what I had learned in Paulette's classes, gave me the comfort level I needed to move forward. I felt connected to the pragmatism of Judaism.*

*Les and I discussed my feelings and the difficulties of an interracial marriage and the difficulties of practicing two different religions.*

*I contacted Rabbi Jacobs, a referral from my Israeli friend Miriam, and he suggested I contact the Union of American Hebrew Congregations. They referred me to the "Jews by Choice" program. To my surprise Les decided to attend the classes with me.*

*There was a lot to learn: religious training, cultural concerns, history, food, language and traditions. Since I was already a few months along, Rabbi Jacobs assured me that if I went into labor before I finished the class, he would be at the delivery room to perform my conversion prior to the baby's birth.*

*What was a bit disconcerting for me was the fact that one of our best friends attempted to discourage my decision. She told me "real Jews" would never accept you. By real Jews, I think she meant Orthodox Jews. One of her friends said, "Don't you have enough issues being black?" Not exactly what I expected to hear from Jews, but it opened my eyes to their feelings about Judaism. I was a bit taken aback by their lack of support. However, I did know that my family would be accepting of whatever decision I made.*

*The Jews by Choice program was 18 weeks with classes at a local synagogue. There were about 40 in the class, mostly couples.*

*At our first session introductions were made around the room and we were given a three-inch binder with reading material for the program. We were to cover a detailed look at Judaism, the history of the religion, holidays and their significance, culture and Jewish living. There was a lot to learn and I found the discussions interesting and very helpful to my learning about this new world I was entering.*

*A main goal of the program was for those of us in the class to become familiar with Jewish concepts and values. We did this through our discussions and lots of reading material. Les was very engaged with helping me weave my way through all I had to learn, including a rudimentary review of the Hebrew language.*

*We began the classes in mid-July and they continued up until I went into the hospital to deliver the baby. As timing worked out, I missed the final session, but the Rabbi passed me with his blessing.*

*We held the conversion ceremony at Temple Judea four days before my scheduled C-section. Rabbi Jacobs had asked us if we were married in the Temple, and when we said no, he suggested we remarry right after my conversion, and that is what we did.*

*So there I stood, nine months pregnant and getting married. Rabbi Jacobs talked about the blending of our two cultures and how we would find joy in that blending.*

*Afterwards we went back to the house for a small celebration. A little while after we got back to the house Les' dad called me into the bedroom and with tears in his eyes thanked me for making the decision to accept his faith as my own. It was a truly touching moment for both of us. He was very happy. Somehow I knew my grandparents would have approved as well.*

I am a Jew. I was born and raised as one. Both my parents come from Jewish parents. There was never a doubt in my mind what faith I was. However, I was not raised in a strict Jewish home. We didn't go to the synagogue every week and didn't celebrate Shabbat every Friday evening. We did, however, attend High Holy Day services for Rosh Hashanah and Yom Kippur, celebrated Passover and I had a Bar Mitzvah. Otherwise my life was not very religious.

With my earlier marriages religion wasn't an issue. Peggy, who was raised as a Catholic, was a lapsed Catholic. Laura, who was a Christian and who went to church, never openly attempted to convert me but often did speak about her faith. A few times in our relationship I attended church services with her but mostly for the social aspects. I never once thought about converting to another religion. I was a Jew and that was that.

When Tyree and I made the decision to start a family we spoke about the issue. How would we raise our child? Even though I wasn't religious I always felt if I ever had a child he or she would be raised Jewish.

As Tyree's delivery date drew closer we began to talk more about how we'd raise our child. We didn't want to raise it without any religious background. My parents didn't say much about it but I knew Dad had strong feelings regarding the issue. He had lost family in the Holocaust and although not a religious man he was hoping we'd raise our baby as a Jew.

The other aspect had to do with heritage. Our child would be the product of two very strong heritages, black and Jewish. It didn't matter if I was white, society would always see our child as black, and that was all right with me. But Tyree and I wanted to celebrate both of our heritages so when she made the decision to convert to the Jewish faith it made me very happy.

Afterwards, when folks would ask me about Tyree converting, I'd tell them, "Well, it was easier for Tyree to become a Jew than for me to become black."

*After arriving at the hospital the night before the scheduled delivery, two nurses came in to perform various pre-op tasks. They began by strapping a monitor across my stomach. At one point they began to show concern that they were not getting a reading from the fetus and continued to discuss the issue, oblivious to me lying beneath them. I could feel tears forming when suddenly they realized what they were doing and attempted to camouflage their comments. They quickly assured me that everything was okay; they were just having some trouble reading the instruments. For a moment I had panicked due to their insensitivity.*

*The next morning I dressed and put on my makeup—we had planned to film the delivery—and sat up in bed waiting for the trip to surgery. The nurse came in, took one look at my smiling face and told me to remove the makeup. Apparently you cannot go into surgery wearing makeup.*

*The surgery went well and Les and I had a wonderful baby girl, 6 lbs. 8 oz. She came with a head full of dark brown curly hair and a wonderful smile. The doctor informed us that she was bit jaundiced, but they also weren't sure because Shavonne was sort of an in between color. At any rate the baby was put under the bright light for a few hours until the jaundice cleared.*

*The next day the baby's birth certificate came up for me to check. I looked it over and noticed that father was marked as white and mother was marked as white. Oops, that had to be sent back to records to be corrected. That afternoon my lunch came with a new corrected birth certificate and a small glass of red wine ordered by Dr. Forbes. The night before we brought our baby home Les and I had a lovely candlelight supper sponsored by the hospital.*

*When we arrived home, Beverly came to take care of us that first week. She cooked every one of Les' favorite dishes; I had no appetite but happily watched Les enjoy the feast.*

In 1981 I started a production company. I formed it so I could produce and direct theater, commercials and music videos outside of the college. It was a way of keeping one foot in the commercial world. However, my first production had nothing to do with theater or television. It was much more personal.

New parents were being allowed to film in the delivery room, so early in Tyree's pregnancy we had talked about filming the birth. I figured with the equipment I had at my disposal, I could do a first-class production. Dr. Forbes agreed to it as long it didn't get in the way. This will be fun, I thought. Tyree, however, wasn't so thrilled, but after discussing it with her and making a promise the camera would be discreetly placed she decided it would be okay.

Now, I knew I wasn't going to be able to operate the camera that day, so I needed to get a camera operator, someone I could trust inside the operating room. I selected Mickey, my former student, who had worked as a television cameraman before coming back to be my theater tech at the college.

December 1, 1981, 11 in the morning. It's time to set up the camera. The nurses are very helpful, all the while chuckling at what I'm attempting to do.

Mickey and I set up the camera in a corner of the delivery room. The nurses come over and drape the camera with a couple of surgical sheets and hand us surgical gowns, masks and caps, along with paper booties to place over our shoes. 15 minutes later we have everything set, just as Tyree is rolled into the delivery room. They start to prep her. I'm standing over Tyree's right shoulder looking down at her exposed pregnant belly.

Dr. Forbes enters, looks over at the camera, then back at me and asks, "Rolling?"

I nod and say, "Yeah, we're rolling."

"Okay," he says, "then let's get started. Scalpel."

He holds out his hand and the OR nurse places a scalpel in it. Then, just before he starts to cut, he explains what he's about to do. He is very precise in his explanation of how he is going to cut Tyree's abdomen, open her up and take out the baby.

Without any warning he quickly slices Tyree's abdomen and a small amount of blood flows. As a nurse moves to swab the blood we all hear a thud sound. Dr. Forbes looks up at the camera and starts to laugh.

"I think your cameraman's got a problem," he says. I look up and see a nurse dragging the unconscious body of Mickey out of the OR. He's fainted. The good doc looks at me and asks, "Everything going to be okay?" meaning is the camera still working.

I look over and see the camera is locked off, meaning it is still pointed in the right direction and recording. "We're still rolling, Doc. No problem."

After a few minutes Mickey reappears, taking up his position next to the camera. Doc notices him and asks how he's doing. He says he's okay. "Did I miss anything?" he asks. Everyone in the room laughs. Doc Forbes says, "Not yet. We're just getting to the good part." And with that he reaches in, spreads my wife's abdomen wide open and gently removes a little baby girl.

Then the following happened in what seemed like slow motion:

1.  Dr. Forbes holds up a baby girl with umbilical cord attached. He looks the baby over and says, "Baby girl, with all her fingers and toes."

2.  A nurse reaches over holding a towel and Dr. Forbes places the baby in it.

3.  Dr. Forbes hands me the scissors. I cut the umbilical cord and the nurse places the baby on a small scale and calls out her weight.

4.  I turn and face the scale as the nurse hands me the baby.

5.  Another nurse rolls in a small bathtub. I take the baby, place her in the warm water, look down at her little face and notice her eyes are still closed. I gently begin to wash her.

6.  I smile and suddenly she opens her eyes and looks directly into mine. It is the greatest feeling I have ever had in my life. I instantly bond with my daughter. Tears fill my eyes.

7.  The nurse takes the baby and places her on Tyree's breast. Tyree

smiles and we look at each other. It's the most moving experience we have ever shared.

Cut. Print. It's a wrap!

The video turns out great. Mickey is able to zoom into me holding the baby and seeing her open her eyes for the first time. That moment is priceless. Afterwards the doc asks for a copy of the tape.

After the birth I go out and greet the family mob that has appeared at the hospital. My parents are there as is Tyree's family. When they see the baby they all say she is beautiful, but then all newborn babies look beautiful to grandparents and family.

When we get home we place the baby into her crib and stand looking down at our sleeping daughter. I'm mesmerized by everything about her. Now, for the first time in my life, I feel I have real purpose.

*We named her Shavonne Rebecca Wieder (better than Les' first suggestion of Lena Horne Wieder). It was the only girl's name that we truly liked. It came from our traveling companions in Penang, but we changed the spelling to fit a US pronunciation. Les' mom was a bit concerned about the name Shavonne. What kind of a Jewish name is that? Fortunately we were set with Rebecca, which honored my maternal great-grandmother and afforded us a good Jewish name to satisfy Les' mom.*

*From the very beginning Shavonne proved to be an easy baby. She was able to sleep through the night by the time I returned to work eight weeks later. She rarely cried and had an excellent temperament.*

*Since we both had demanding full-time jobs we knew we'd have to have some type of daily childcare once I went back to work so we headed to a local employment agency to find a suitable nanny. Before leaving the house we agreed on five basic principles. First, the person must speak English; second, as she was working for us Monday through Friday, her weekend home had to be close by; third, she must have references; fourth, she had to have been in the US for a while; and fifth, we would not make an immediate decision but go home and discuss who we interviewed and then decide how to proceed.*

*After an hour or so at the agency, meeting many prospective nannies, we settled on Sandra from Guatemala. Why? Because of all the candidates we saw she was the first to walk over and pick up the baby to hold while we talked to her. It honestly seemed that Shavonne took an instant liking to her.*

*That evening as Sandra settled into her room we sat on the sofa with a glass of wine in hand laughing at ourselves. Sandra spoke not a word*

*of English, her relatives lived in a city 30 miles away, she had no refer-
ences, had just arrived in the country a few days before and we had hired
her on the spot. We went with our gut feeling and she turned out to be a
wonderful choice.*

*With her at the house Sunday night through Friday afternoon, it took
a tremendous amount of responsibility off my shoulders in worry and
concern about our new arrival. Shavonne did not have to be awoken at
6:00 a.m. to be dressed and carted off to childcare; and when I came
home I was able to drop my briefcase and just play with our baby, give
her a bath and spend some quality time before bed. The arrangement was
truly a blessing.*

*I was settling into my new life—mother, wife, and administrator—a
lot of changes in a short time. Most important to me was my role as a
mom. I was not a timid mother, nervous about her new baby. We grew up
babysitting at an early age so I was very comfortable with a newborn.
Being a mom was something I had looked forward to for a long time, so
I was ready.*

I never thought I'd have a child. I had always said during my previous marriages that I didn't want a family. It was a selfish thing on my part.
I didn't want the responsibility and none of the women I had previously
been with had given me the confidence I needed to become a father.

I loved being a dad. I learned quickly how to take care of my daughter. I learned how to change her diapers, how to feed her and how to rock
her to sleep. I loved holding her. Very early on I felt we had a special bond
that would stay with us forever.

For the first year I was lucky to be around a lot more than most fa-
thers. That was because I took a leave of absence to work on a screenplay.
I wrote at home, so I was there watching my daughter grow, seeing her
take her first steps and hearing her first words.

In the spring of 1982 I decided to direct the musical *The Wiz* at the
college. This production was one of the most enjoyable productions I
ever directed and an especially noteworthy one for me.

Although the original Broadway cast was entirely African American
my production was multi-racial. Lots of people told me they enjoyed seeing that on our stage. The best part of the production was my daughter
attending rehearsals and being made an honorary member of the production with her own production t-shirt.

The staff had made t-shirts with "The Wiz" on the front and the
person's job title on the back. Tyree had a special baby shirt made for
Shavonne that read on the back, "Directed by Daddy."

The show was produced in March and sold out the entire run. Excellent reviews. Everyone was happy. But the run wasn't over when it closed at the college.

Right after our first week of performances, I got a call from the Santa Monica NAACP. It seems a member of their board had seen the show and raved about it to her fellow board members. They wanted to know if I would take the production to Santa Monica for three special performances to help raise money for a young African American student that needed a heart transplant. He was a star athlete and an honor student at Santa Monica High School. They offered to fund the production's move.

In the end we did three shows at Santa Monica High School and raised $50,000 for the boy. Afterwards I received hundreds of thank you cards. It was a wonderful experience for everyone involved.

# CHAPTER 9

## *A New Family*

W<small>E</small> *were enjoying our baby, our home and learning to balance work and parental responsibilities. To our surprise, six months after Sandra, our nanny, had been working with us, she came home one Sunday night with a young woman. She announced that she had to return to Guatemala and brought her niece, Lillian, to take over her position.*

*Les, who has the patience of a gnat, immediately said it was a bad idea, and it wasn't going to work. I looked at him and was about to say, as the saying goes, "Negro, please...." Then I remembered he was not a Negro (that happened sometimes). So instead I said, "Well at least if she has to leave it was good of her to give us notice and bring her own replacement. Let's give it a try."*

*Lillian was 19, spoke a little English and had been in the US for a while. Sandra agreed to stay for a week with her niece to get her acquainted with the baby and the house. Lillian turned out to be as wonderful as her aunt.*

*As I had done with Sandra, I took Lillian to the local high school to attend English classes; but unlike Sandra, Lillian's English skills improved rapidly. By the time she left us, her English was pretty good and my Spanish had diminished.*

*December 1, 1982 was Shavonne's first birthday. For her party we decided on a* Sesame Street *motif: pink and yellow flowers, a cake with Big Bird and lots of balloons. Since at 12 months Shavonne did not have a lot of friends, her cousins, aunts and uncles made up the guest list. I was so busy decorating and selecting a menu for adults and children, I totally didn't think about activities for the kids. My cousins came to the rescue. Erni and Cynthia organized games on the spot using kitchen utensils and lots of imagination. The party was reminiscent of family parties when I was young, all the cousins, aunts and uncles in one place, laughing, playing games and dancing. The party went well into the evening; Shavonne was asleep before the guests left.*

Near the end of 1982 my best friend Gene Lay moved from Simi Valley to Chatsworth, a small community in the northwest corner of the San Fernando Valley. When I went to his new home I realized I liked the neighborhood and told Tyree I wanted to move into a bigger house, one with a pool. So I started looking for a place in rural Chatsworth near my buddy.

In December 1983 we are shown a house in the right neighborhood but it doesn't have a pool. After we turn down that house our agent tells us there's another house just around the corner that's going on the market the next day. It's vacant and if we're interested she can show it to us. So we drive around the corner to take a look.

The moment I walk through the front door and step inside I know this is the house for me. The entire back of the house is all large windows and sliding glass doors that look out onto a large yard with a huge swimming pool, surrounded by tall hedges, flowerbeds and palm trees. The yard and gardens are beautiful but I can't take my eyes off the pool. It's long, wide and even has a diving board.

"I'll take it!" I shout. Our real estate agent groans and says, "Les, you're not supposed to say that. Takes away my bargaining position." Everyone laughs but I'm not kidding.

It's the right size: four bedrooms, three baths, a den with a wet bar, a large living room / dining room and a good-size kitchen. It's also one story and, did I already mention, the pool is amazing. A week later we buy it and in February we move in. We've been there ever since.

Right after we moved in Gene started coming over on Sunday mornings to watch NFL football. I had recently bought a six-foot Sony projection TV and Gene loved the large screen. He always brought two six-packs of Budweiser beer with him. We'd sit and watch the games and drink beer and talk football. Tyree and Shavonne would join us to watch the games and Gene always played with Shavonne. He was great with kids and she loved him and called him Uncle Gene and would watch him like a hawk.

One day, we were driving by the Budweiser Brewery just off the 405 Freeway, and from the back seat Shavonne started calling out, "Uncle

Gene! Uncle Gene!" We thought she'd seen him in a car driving past us but no, she had seen the Budweiser sign and recognized it as the beer Uncle Gene drank every Sunday at our house. Just goes to show you, kids see *everything!*

Gene and his wife Sharon were our closest friends. We socialized together, took vacations together and hung out with them a lot. Every year for 20 years Gene and I would go down to Baja for a week to fish for marlin. For me Gene became the brother I never had and since he passed away I think of him often.

*A few weeks after the move Lillian gave us notice that she would be leaving. Like her aunt, she had been a wonderful addition to the household. Shavonne had just turned two.*

*Right after we moved in I noticed a woman down the block with three toddlers in her front yard and a teenage boy. One day I saw him in the grocery store and asked if he had younger brothers and sisters. He said, "No, my mom does daycare."*

*Well the next day I went to see her and found out that not only did the woman provide daycare in her home, she and her family were the only other African Americans living on the block.*

*Nana, that is what everyone called her, was wonderful and Shavonne spent the next six months with her. By June, Nana told me that Shavonne was ready for preschool and I should begin to look for the right placement. After checking out pretty much every preschool in the area, I settled on Pinecrest, a progressive preschool where she stayed for preschool and kindergarten before she moved to Germain Street Elementary School for first grade.*

*All in all the school was exactly what we wanted: wonderful teachers and a great learning environment. However, every time we were treated with a new vocabulary word or burst of demonstrated knowledge about something I would ask, "Where did you learn that?" She quickly replied, "On Sesame Street." So why were we spending all this money for a private school? But some things she did learn at school, like the day she came home to inform us that little boys had pee-pee things. Apparently preschool restrooms were coed.*

*We also began to understand what a brilliant child we had. One day when I went to pick her up she told Ms. Jenny, her teacher, "Remember to pick up your shoes!" I shot a quizzical look at the teacher and she told me, "Oh, Shavonne is our class helper. She remembers everything, so in the morning we let her know what we need throughout the day and she reminds us. We also have her serve as the 'new friend' to take new children*

*around to meet the other kids. She's quite the class leader."*
*So early on we were proud parents.*

We now have a house with a pool and a toddler. We discuss fencing the pool but realize even if we do that, our baby still needs to know how to swim, for her own safety. I think, no problem. I'm a champion swimmer. I can teach her myself.

"How did you learn?" Tyree asked.

"Well, one day at the beach when I was about two Dad suddenly picked me up and threw me into the water and yelled, 'Leslie, swim!' And that's how I learned."

Tyree isn't keen on that idea. She thinks I should take Shavonne to a certified swim instructor who specializes in teaching toddlers to swim.

In early summer Tyree finds a "Mommy and Me" swim class and signs us up. We're ready to go; rather I'm ready to go since Tyree won't be able to take Shavonne because the class is held during the day while she's at work. I'm excited about going. I figured, what's the problem? I'll be in the water with my kid. Should be fun.

First class... I show up and it's me, Shavonne and seven other mothers and their toddlers who are all girls. Our instructor is also a woman. I look around and realize it's just the girls and me. Nice.

First thing our instructor has me do is stand on the side of the pool in the deep end and drop Shavonne into the water. "Just drop her in," she tells me, "and don't worry. They'll know what to do. They've lived in water for nine months. They'll go down then pop right back up and swim back to you."

So I drop Shavonne into the water and sure enough that's exactly what happens. Down she goes then pops back up and dog paddles back to where I'm standing. The kid's a natural!

The class was fun. In no time the ladies and I are all on a first-name basis. They love Shavonne who has turned into quite the little water rat. Later, as a teenager, she became a certified scuba diver. She was our little fish.

Okay, Graduation day... Swim school graduation takes place on a Saturday. Tyree is there. We walk in and all the mothers come over and say, "Hi, Les," "Hi, Les," "Hi, Les." "We love your husband." "Your husband is so nice." "You have a great family and your husband is so cool." Tyree smiles, looks at me and rolls her eyes.

"Mommy and Me" swim class. I loved it.

*Shavonne was a great imitator and, as children will often do, allowed us to see ourselves through her eyes. One afternoon I was in the garage cleaning up some boxes and, in her two-year-old way, she was helping. I turned over a carton and there was a long trail of ants. Shavonne exclaimed, "Look, mommy, goddamitshitants." I was truly stunned at the long word, but immediately knew where she had heard that phrase.*

*Les hates ants and I could so hear those words coming out of his mouth. I called him outside and asked Shavonne to tell him what she saw. After she described the insects a second time, he was truly embarrassed at being caught. I asked him to offer a different title for the insects. He quickly explained to our innocent daughter that they were in fact just ants.*

*And then there was the issue of correcting false impressions. She and I were watching a wonderful nature show on television that highlighted the migration of the African wildebeest. At one point a mother was giving birth to a calf. She stood so the baby could drop, as is the manner in which they give birth. Shavonne looked at me with excitement and said, "Oh, I see, mommy. They poop the babies out." I had to think for a moment, realizing that I had to correct the visual impression she had gotten. I explained that it may have looked like that, but really there was another opening where the baby came out. I could just hear her telling everyone she knew how babies were born. "We poop them out."*

*It's wonderful to see your children capture the essence of who they are. One afternoon at Cousin Sheila's house we were all gathered for a family event. Shavonne, age three, was in the living room with her Cousin Bridgett, who was about eight. Bridgette was explaining to Shavonne that she, Shavonne, was only half Jewish. Her mom explained that no, Shavonne was not half Jewish, both her mom and dad were Jewish. Shavonne quickly advised her cousin that, "Yes, my daddy's Jewish, my mommy's Jewish, I'm Jewish and my cats are Jewish too." Clearly, we were a Jewish household.*

When Shavonne was born Dad and Mom were in their early 70s so they weren't able to run around a lot with their new grandchild. But when they visited our place Dad showed a loving side toward Shavonne that he'd never shown to any of his other grandchildren. I think it was because I was his son and that made the difference, but who knows why? One thing, however, was clear; since Shavonne was born my relationship with them had become warmer.

One day Dad phoned and said he wanted to talk to me about something. I asked what about but he wouldn't tell me over the phone. So I waited until they came over. After they arrived he and I went outside and sat beside the pool to talk.

He talked about growing old and getting his affairs in order. Of course no child wants to hear their parent talk about their future demise but I was touched that he actually was talking to me about important matters and not just sports. He told me he had everything in order so that when he was gone Mom would be taken care of and he asked me to help her out with her needs. Then he asked me if I could loan him some money so he could pay off the remaining few things he still owed.

He promised me he'd pay me back but I stopped him and said, "You've given me so many gifts in my life, let me give this to you. It's the least I can do."

He looked at me and tears came into his eyes. I leaned over and gave him a hug and he returned it. Then, with his cheek up against mine, he whispered into my ear, "I'm very proud of you Leslie. You have a wonderful wife and beautiful daughter. Very proud."

I kissed him on his cheek and we got up and he gave my arm a squeeze and said, "Thank you." Then he walked inside and I knew something had changed in our relationship. For the first time in my life I felt we were equals.

It took a lot for him to ask me for that money. He was a very proud man when it came to money and his asking me meant he felt okay in allowing me to help him. It was a turning point in our lives. From that day on we became even closer. Now, when he came over, we'd always find time to sit and talk about life.

Over the next few years I watched as my parents grew older. Some carry it better than others. Dad didn't handle it well. Mom said he was having trouble sleeping. He was having anxiety attacks and getting up at three or four in the morning to go for drives. Driving, he told her, relieved his anxiety. She said he was afraid of dying.

*In the fall of 1985 we hosted my Cousin Cynthia's wedding in our backyard. Prior to the ceremony her groom, Les, and the family gathered to help us decorate the yard and get ready for the event. We set up chairs to seat 120 guests on the lawn and the caterers set the banquet around the pool. The party, it turned out, lasted until the next day. Shavonne was a flower girl, for the second time. Earlier she had served as flower girl in her cousin's wedding. Fortunately I was able to use the same dress. I shortened it and dyed it from pink to lavender, perfect for the new wedding.*

*The ceremony was lovely, except for the fact that Shavonne had to drag the ring bearer, her Cousin Conrado, down the aisle. Right after the*

*ceremony the chairs were rearranged, tables were added and the recep-
tion began.*

*At one point I noticed that the backyard was getting pretty empty. To
my surprise when I went into the house, I found everyone had gathered
around the television to watch a championship prize fight on pay-per-
view. It was wall-to-wall people. There were the groom, his five brothers,
the bridesmaids and most of the guests laughing and making bets on the
fight. I suggested to my cousin, the bride, she might want to break this
up, but she laughed and said no way, they were all having a good time.
When the fight ended everyone returned to the party outside and continued dancing. Several people stayed overnight, including the bride and
groom, so the afternoon wedding turned into a weekend wedding.*

*We were glad it was such a joyous occasion because it turned out to
be the last outing for Les' father. I remember him sitting in the living room
smiling and laughing with everyone else watching the fight.*

*A few days later, he passed away on Yom Kippur. I was so happy that
he had had that wonderful afternoon. Shavonne was in preschool and
when we went to pick her up we had to tell her that grandpa had died.
She had made a picture for him, and when we told her he was not with us
anymore, she simply asked if she could give it grandma instead.*

*Les was very close to his dad and losing him was difficult. In ad-
dition, we now had responsibility for Les' mom. For the first time in 55
years she would be living alone.*

September 26, 1985. The phone rings. I wake up and look over at the
clock beside our bed. It's 2:00 a.m. I think, no one calls with good news
at two in the morning.

I pick up the phone. "Hello," I croak. Tyree wakes up. It's Mom. She
tells me Dad's been taken to the emergency room at Encino Hospital.
"He's not feeling right."

"I'll be right there," I say.

I hang up and turn to Tyree. "Dad's in the hospital." We both get
up. She calls my niece and tells her what's going on and asks if we can
leave Shavonne with her while we go to the hospital. She only lives a few
blocks away. "Of course," she says, "bring her over."

We dress quickly, bundle Shavonne up, drop her off and head for the
hospital. We park and hurry into the emergency room and ask for Mr.
Wieder. I tell the nurse at the desk I'm his son. They tell us where Mom
is waiting. We go to her.

Mom tells us they don't know what's wrong with him. "He just got
up and said he didn't feel well and I should call an ambulance and I did,"

she says. "He's inside waiting for the test results. Go see him," she tells me.

I walk into a small room and see my dad sitting in a chair, leaning over with his elbows on his knees, head in his hands. He looks up when I enter and shakes his head. "I don't know what's happening. I just don't feel good." Then he smiles at me. "Why are you here?"

"Mom called," I reply, "so we came down." He asks about Shavonne and I tell him she's fine. We sit silently waiting. He doesn't look sick. The doctor appears. He tells us he's still waiting for the tests results to come back and to be safe he wants Dad to stay a few hours to keep an eye on him. Doesn't sound bad so Mom tells us to go home and get some sleep.

We drive home. On the way we decide we'll pick up Shavonne later that morning. It's now almost 4:00 a.m. As we step into the house, the phone is ringing. I grab the phone. It's Mom.

"Hurry, come back," she says. "His kidneys have failed. You need to come right away."

We rush back to the hospital. I go inside and find Mom in his room standing next to Dad who is now lying in bed. A blanket covers him. His eyes are closed. I walk up and stand next to Mom. She doesn't look good. She isn't crying but rather looks very sad and almost resigned. I look at Dad. His skin looks gray. I ask Mom what happened. She says, "The tests show his kidneys have shut down. It's very bad."

I look at Dad and take his hand. It's cold to the touch. Mom and Tyree leave the room and I'm left standing beside the bed holding Dad's cold hand.

I lean over and whisper in his ear, "I love you, Dad." He squeezes my hand. A tear rolls down his cheek. His eyes remain closed. He starts to speak and I put my ear near his lips. "I love you too, Leslie," he whispers. I stand there holding his hand. My dad is dying. I'm numb.

Mom returns and I walk out and find Tyree in the hallway. We stand there silently waiting. I can't believe this is happening. I mean, just a couple hours ago he was sitting up and looked okay, and now, suddenly.... Didn't anyone know his kidneys were failing? Didn't his doctor ever say anything about that? A million questions race through my mind.

Then we hear soft crying coming from inside the room. I hurry in and find Mom holding Dad's hand. I come up behind her and she says, "He's gone." Dad is dead.

Tyree says, "You need to call your sister. I'll take care of your mother."

I look and see Mom gently stroking Dad's forehead. I leave the room, call my sister and tell her the news. Dad is gone. I ask her to make the calls to the rest of the family.

I find it very hard to accept I've lost my father so suddenly. I'm angry and pissed, wanting to lash out, but I also know I have to be strong and take care of business and look after Mom. My father is dead, and as a Jewish man he needs to be buried within 24 hours.

We take care of all the arrangements and 24 hours later we have the funeral. Lots of people show up to pay their respects. Many of them I'd not seen for years. Nice things are said about Dad and then I get up and speak.

It's harder than I thought. I figured I'd gotten over the initial shock of him passing and I'd be able to say what I wanted to say without any problems. Not so fast.

As I speak I choke up. I loved my dad, and despite some problems we'd gone through during my rebellious years (the usual adolescent issues) we'd become very close since Shavonne was born. I reminisce about the fun times we had when I was growing up, and tell funny stories about him: our driving trips, the many sporting events he took me to, all the good times spent at the beach and in New York.

Everyone thinks they have the best dad in the world and for me he was just that. He had faults but in the end it didn't matter. He was my dad and I loved him and I knew he loved me unconditionally throughout my life, even when I screwed up.

I sit down, put my head in my hands and weep.

As I write these lines 30 years later I still miss him and think about him every day.

Mom never got over Dad's death. Eventually, she said she learned to cope with his loss, but it was at night when she went to bed alone that she felt his loss the most.

When my mom was in her late 80s she told me the only thing she wanted from me after she died was for me to remember her. I was surprised to hear her say that. "Of course I'll remember you," I replied. "You're my mother! How could I forget you?" She just shook her head and said, "You know what I mean."

# CHAPTER 10

## *Jewish Life*

*I* WAS *never a person who took the Bible literally, but I have always been a spiritual person. Les shares this with me. One of the first gifts he gave me was the book* Touch the Earth: A Self-Portrait of Indian Existence. *The book speaks to the spiritual nature of man's relationship with the earth and it began our first conversations about spirituality and its relationship to the Jewish faith. That conversation led to my reading more about Judaism and its history. It was so much easier for me to delve into a religion that valued Tzedakah, a word that some mistake to mean charity, but which actually means righteousness, justice or fairness. Giving to the poor is an obligation in Judaism. These are the values that brought me to treasure Judaism, and now we had the opportunity to build a family shaped on that history and its traditions.*

*We started with the basics. On Friday evenings we ushered in Shabbat, a time of rest and reflection from sunset Friday to sunset Saturday. We start the observance before the evening meal by lighting candles, enjoying "the fruit of the vine," sharing a loaf of sweet challah and reciting a short prayer for each. The cessation of work for that 24-hour period is a beautiful tradition that I have never been able to fully incorporate into my life. I'm told my A-type personality does not allow for rest. Still it's a weekly observance I understand and appreciate.*

*In the spring we celebrate one of our favorite Jewish holidays, the Festival of Passover. I was introduced to Passover in my UCLA class with Paulette. Les and I attended our first Seder together at her home. I learned even more in my Introduction to Judaism classes.*

*After Shavonne was born we attended Seders at a local synagogue, and at the homes of Paulette, her friends the Neimans and Les' parents. I believe this recognition of the exodus from Egypt spoke to me as a common experience for blacks and Jews, the ending of slavery. Jews all over the world come together with family and friends to celebrate the angel of death passing over the Jewish homes and sparing the life of the first-born child. It is a major holiday in the Jewish religion and of course is celebrated with study and a feast. Shavonne was now a toddler and we felt it was time for us to make our first Passover.*

*Our first Seder was held at our kitchen table and we invited Les' parents to join us. For the menu I followed each recipe to the letter. These were new dishes for me and I of course wanted the meal to be perfect. I prepared a chopped liver appetizer chopping everything by hand. Later I learned that was totally unnecessary and my Jewish friends all used a Cuisinart.*

*I learned that to prepare a Passover meal properly takes time. Also, there are certain dishes that are mandatory... for instance matzo ball soup.*

*My first attempt at matzo ball soup was quite naturally a disaster. They were hard and stayed at the bottom of the chicken broth. I called my friend Paulette, my Jewish mentor, and asked what to do? She told me the secret was to add seltzer to the mixture instead of water, and presto, I had fluffy matzo balls that were delicious. I was totally not ready to make chicken soup from scratch so I discovered Swanson's chicken broth. It was pretty good. It would be several years before I actually started to put a chicken in the pot to make broth. I couldn't work my way up to gefilte fish. While it is a true Passover traditional dish, I discovered many of our Jewish friends didn't find it the most appealing of dishes either.*

*I set the table with my grandmother's formal dinnerware (now bequeathed to me), our new Seder plate and candlesticks recently purchased from the Shalom House. I added spring flowers, a bottle of Manischewitz wine, and voila, I had set my first Passover table! As the celebration began Shavonne sat up in her high chair beaming with anticipation; she could sense that this was going to be a new experience. Dad was beaming with pride to see his son lead his first Seder.*

*Our subsequent Seders grew and we began to invite more family and friends. We have hosted up to 20 guests. We always invite people who have never attended a Seder before and they have all enjoyed the experience.*

*There is quite a lot to hosting a proper Passover Seder. This is a formal sit-down affair that begins with the telling of the Exodus. The guide* to be used is a booklet called a Haggadah (the telling); there are eight parts to the telling that are to be read in a specific order. In addition one must have a lot of traditional accouterments to set a proper Passover table. I felt a slight amount of pressure. All of my grandmother's training spoke to me to prepare my Seder in a manner that would make her proud. I learned that my Jewish friends all seemed to have items that had been passed down to them from their families. I had to start from scratch.

I purchased festive candlesticks, a holiday table cloth, a Seder plate, a plate to hold the matzos (the unleavened bread used to symbolize the bread baked by the Hebrews when they fled into the desert and didn't have time for the bread to rise) and of course a Haggadah for each participant.

Several years later we authored our own Wieder Family Haggadah, keeping all of the essential elements, but adding our own personal touches. Over the years we have revised it several times as technology has allowed us to be more creative and publish beautiful booklets with illustrations.

We have also collected Haggadahs including one from our trip to Israel. It's wonderful to see the differences, each one maintaining the order and structure, but changing the illustrations and content that deals with family, freedom, peace or other themes. For our Haggadah we borrowed from several different styles.

Our Haggadah has become very popular with our Seder guests. Every year at the conclusion of the dinner several guests always ask if they can take home their copy.

I have been asked many times about Christmas. Don't you miss celebrating Christmas? How do you handle the Christmas holidays? Do you put up a Christmas tree or not? I must admit that at first I did miss my holiday decorations. I weaned myself off Christmas decorations by substituting blue, silver and white decorations for the red and green. I searched the stores for Chanukah decorations, but they were few and far between. I soon realized that it was not necessary to compete with Christmas, so we did not. Shavonne visited Les' niece and her husband, who celebrated both Christmas and Chanukah, to help them decorate their Christmas tree, and they always had a lovely Christmas stocking for her.

Santa did not visit our house. That didn't bother Les or me but it did prove an issue for our toddler, Shavonne. One Christmas morning, most likely having heard her schoolmates talk of it, Shavonne wanted to know why Santa did not come to her house. It struck a pain in my heart for her because she was so disappointed. I was not prepared to respond, so quickly I told Les to move one of her Chanukah presents to the front porch. I then opened the front door to show her that Santa had left it on the porch because our chimney was too small for him to come down. How silly of me. I simply did not have the background to give her a better explanation. Later as my Jewish education grew, I better understood how to respond to the "December dilemma."

But we made every effort for the celebration of the miracle of Chanukah to be a strong tradition for our family. Every year when Shavonne was in elementary school, during our winter break, we would take a trip. It was usually during those two weeks that Chanukah was also celebrated. For several years we went to Arizona during that time and would take a menorah along with our Chanukah presents.

During the day we'd explore wherever we were staying, sometimes at a dude ranch, sometimes in the town of Sedona, a place we visited on several occasions. In the evenings we'd light our candles and exchange presents.

For our Chanukah celebration we always said the prayers over the lighting of the candles. The delicious part of the holiday is cooking in oil to commemorate the miracle of the lights. So scrumptious potato latkes, a Chanukah tradition, are fried and devoured.

As a child I usually received one present for Christmas, so the idea of getting eight presents was not something I was used to. I asked around and discovered that many people gave small gifts for seven nights and saved that special present for the final night so I followed that pattern. One year we hid an American Girl doll under the luggage for our annual trip to Arizona. That wasn't easy.

In her first year when Shavonne went away to college we sent her several small gifts for each night. But when she discovered that her friends from our synagogue who lived in her dorm received major presents each night from their parents, she immediately called home to let us know we had been slackers in the gift department.

Shavonne was proud of her mixed heritage. In high school she along with other members of the Jewish Club hosted a Seder at the school and invited students from other clubs, including the Black Student Union (where she also held membership) and Chicano Studies.

They served matzo ball soup, matzo crackers, and a salad—a limited menu, but it offered a taste of the traditional feast. She also provided a few pages from the Wieder Family Haggadah for the group to read. Most of the students were not familiar with Passover and shared with her what a great learning experience it was for them.

At our family Seders we always invite friends who have never attended a Seder to share the joy of that holiday with us.

Over the years we have been delighted that many of our guests have told us they wanted to return to our Seder. It is a wonderful feeling to have our family and friends enjoy the celebration.

*In the fall of 1986 we decided it was time to make a commitment to a synagogue. We had visited Temple Ahavat Shalom and several others in the area. Each synagogue is a bit different from the others. We attended an open house and met very friendly people who encouraged us to return. After attending a few services including High Holy Days we settled on Temple Ahavat Shalom*

*Those first few months and probably years at the Temple, I was on guard... oh, never so that anyone would be able to see it, but always waiting for a look or a comment that would question, in a negative way, why I was there. You don't grow up black in America without that training. No matter what people said, or how friendly they were, that slight edge of waiting to be asked why I was intruding was present. However, that was early on. As my time at the Temple lengthened, I learned that my decision to become a Jew, to actually convert, seemed to erase any question of my belonging.*

*Shavonne started Hebrew School and continued through her Bat Mitzvah and confirmation. Les and I became active members. Les directed several of the Cantor's concerts, wrote and directed a Purim Play and I even spent some time on the Board of Trustees.*

*Shortly after she started Hebrew School, one of Shavonne's teachers discovered that many of the children in her class had not had the benefit of a Hebrew naming ceremony, something that is traditionally done when children are babies. Shavonne was one of those children. The teacher contacted the class' parents and expressed her desire to hold a joint naming ceremony for all of the children. We thought it was a wonderful idea and I agreed to help with the reception following the Sunday morning service. The teacher graciously sent home some possible suggestions for the parents using the first letter of the child's name. We did not have a particular name in mind so the teacher suggested a Hebrew name that started with the letter S. We agreed with her suggestion and got ready for the ceremony.*

*Around 9:00 p.m. the Saturday night before the service I got a knot in the pit of my stomach and realized I could not go through with it. Just choosing something that started with the letter S was not right. This was a significant event in our daughter's life. The naming had to have meaning. In a panic, I called her teacher, apologizing for the lateness of the hour. I told her I was just not comfortable with what we had agreed to. She told me to take a deep breath and we talked it over.*

*We ended up with two names that would honor both sides of our family. Both Les' grandmothers were named Eleanor. My grandmother's name was Ethel. In Old English, German and Hebrew, Ethel means noble, and in Biblical Hebrew it is Adina. Perfect. Her Hebrew name would be Adina Elinoar. I was totally relieved.*

*The next morning in the sanctuary the Rabbi presided over the service and Shavonne announced her new Hebrew name to the congregation.*

Up until the time I became a father the thought of joining a synagogue wasn't on my radar. However, with Tyree converting to Judaism and Shavonne being born, along with our agreement that she would be raised as a Jew, it became something we both decided was needed in our family.

Since we weren't Orthodox it was clear we wouldn't be joining an Orthodox synagogue. We thought about perhaps looking into a Conservative one but finally we felt that a Reform synagogue would be our best fit.

Temple Ahavat Shalom felt right to us. The congregation was made up of several older families and many younger ones like ourselves. The services were held in both Hebrew and English and that appealed to us. Mostly it was because we felt the most comfortable with the people there.

We wanted Shavonne to have a Jewish education regarding the history and heritage of her faith and we both felt it would be important for her to become a Bat Mitzvah. She attended Hebrew School on Sunday mornings until fourth grade, and then attended Sunday mornings and Tuesday evenings after public school to increase her knowledge of Hebrew in preparation for her Bat Mitzvah.

# CHAPTER 11

## *Wieder World*

W<small>E</small> *were both working professionals, but I was still carrying the female role of cooking and cleaning. One day it occurred to me that we needed to change the system. So we tried you cook and I clean for a few weeks, but I soon realized that I was a much neater cook. Cleaning up after me was pretty easy; cleaning up after Les cooked was a chore.*

*So my new idea was this: each of us would run the kitchen from Sunday morning till Saturday evening. That is, on your week, you would be responsible for grocery shopping, cooking and cleaning the kitchen. That would give me one full week that I would not have to enter the kitchen. Hallelujah! Being the reasonable person he is, Les agreed to the plan. However, at first he complained that he didn't know what to cook. There were weeks of omelets, pizza, Chinese food and other assorted take-out options. I explained to Les that I had read an article in* Time *magazine in which astronaut Sally Ride said that growing up she often had nuts and fruit, or cheese and crackers for dinner. I told him if it was good enough for Sally Ride, it was good enough for our daughter. She could have Cheerios and she would survive. I figured that if in the weeks that Les cooked the menu left a bit to be desired, I would make up for it in my weeks. Gradually he began to open the cookbook and cook actual meals.*

*Your week / my week is a tip I have shared with numerous women over the years who have thought it was an outstanding idea; some even instituted the practice. It is a tradition Les and I continue to this day.*

*When she was seven Shavonne was hired for her first job, modeling as a flower girl in bridal shows. She worked for two seasons on the show* circuit. On her first few shows she had a dresser and hairstylist assigned to her, so my job was just to transport. On later shows, I served as her dresser. She usually did two shows on Sunday afternoons during the bridal show season. In between shows we hit the show room floor to sample cake and food from the various caterers. We spent time looking at floral arrangements, silver patterns and photography. Then it was back to the dressing rooms for the second show. Her paychecks went into her bank account for that future college fund and her treat was to stop at McDonald's on the way home.

That summer we took a trip to Club Med in Ixtapa, Mexico. Shavonne was with us, but the Club had activities set up for the children during the day, so we could lie on the beach and watch her playing with the other children. At dinnertime the counselors walked through the dining room to deliver the children to their parents. We cherished our time together and the alone time during the day gave us that honeymoon feeling.

In the fall, the acting president at LA Mission called me in to let me know that he thought one day I would be a college president, but he felt I needed more experience in Academic Affairs. I was stunned. I had never thought of myself as a college president. The following Monday, I became a Dean in the Office of Academic Affairs.

Shavonne became a Brownie in the first grade. We were very fortunate that she joined a troop with wonderful leaders. Les and I participated as much as possible with the troop, selling calendars and cookies, and participating in camping experiences. We even used our pool for water safety lessons.

In spite of her parents' lack of outdoor skills, she became an excellent camper. I attended several camping trips with her and the troop. While sleeping on the ground when I knew I had a bed at home I had to remind myself that this was a mother/daughter bonding moment and well worth it. On my first outing with the girls when they were in fourth grade, we arrived at the campsite and I was astonished to see them whip into action. The troop leader pulled out two camp chairs for us and invited me to have a seat. The girls put up the tents, took collapsed bottles and fetched water, started a fire and began preparing dinner, all without a word from their leader. Impressive.

As troop parents, we took turns planning activities for the girls. When it was my turn, I took them to the theater to see one of Les' shows, Little Shop of Horrors, and then out to lunch. Pretty much a Troop Beverly Hills moment, but that was all I had. Shavonne loved Scouting and was one of four girls in the troop who stayed through high school, eventually earning a Girl Scout Gold Award.

In the fall of 1987 a colleague of mine at the college told me he and some of the faculty were putting together a group to march in the Doo Dah Parade that was being held in Pasadena. Would we, Tyree, Shavonne and I, be interested in joining them? They were going to call the group, the New Gods of Los Angeles. We were supposed to dress in outrageously colorful clothing. It was all very much in keeping with what the Doo Dah Parade was about. Of course we said yes.

The Doo Dah Parade was started in 1978 when four buddies who had been drinking in a local Pasadena bar decided it would be fun to have an irreverent alternate to the very traditional Rose Parade. In 1978, January 1$^{st}$ fell on a Sunday, and the Rose Parade, which typically takes place on January 1$^{st}$, doesn't march on Sundays. So the guys decided it would be perfect to have it that year. Some of the early participants were Snotty Scotty and the Hankies, the Lawn Mower Drill Team, the Briefcase Drill Team and General Hershey Bar, among others. It was my kind of parade.

Parade Day. We drive to Pasadena, find a place to park and start walking to our group's staging area. Shavonne is six years old and the entire affair is like a giant crazy circus for her. Everyone is dressed in outlandish costumes and the happy, goofy mood of the morning is infectious.

As we get closer we see our fellow marchers assembling in front of a group of men dressed all in white, wearing clear cellophane bags on their heads. Shavonne sees the men and walks over to them. "Who are you?" my daughter asks one of them. "We're the Marching Prophylactics," the man replies.

Shavonne rushes back to us, looks up at me and says, "Daddy, what's a marching pro-phy-lac-tic?" I look over at Tyree for help. She smiles at me and says, "Well, daddy, what are they?" No help there. I'm stumped. How do I answer my six-year-old daughter's question?

I look around and realize our group has grown very quiet waiting for my response. "Well," I stutter, "ahhh...."

Just then, Mac Tonight, the McDonald's character, walks by. Shavonne sees him, gets excited and yells, "Daddy, Daddy! Mac Tonight! Can I go see Mac Tonight? Pleeeease?"

"Sure. Let's go!" And off we go looking for Mac Tonight. Saved by McDonald's.

It was an amazing day. In fact, to this day, whenever I mention that the Wieder family once marched in the Doo Dah Parade, my daughter always reminds me, "Yes, and we marched behind the Marching Prophylactics." See, kids never forget.

In the summer of 1989 the Wieder family took a road trip to the Canadian Rocky Mountains and the town of Banff, home of beautiful Lake Louise. For this trip we had family t-shirts made up with "Wieder Summer Tour" on the front. Pretty dorky but we loved them.

Our travel plans called for Shavonne and I to drive to Spokane, Washington the first week. At the end of that week Tyree would fly in from Chicago, where she was attending her Cousin Sheila's annual traveling slumber party. From Spokane we'd then drive into Canada. On the way back, we'd drive to Seattle, then turn south and drive home along the Pacific Coast Highway. The entire trip would take three weeks.

Before we left, Shavonne and I had several lectures from Tyree about going "potty." "Don't let her sit on the seats. Be sure they are covered. If they don't have paper covers, be sure to cover the seats with toilet paper." I must have heard that lecture 100 times before we left. We both assured her we'd follow her bathroom regulations.

On this trip I was driving our Ford Econoline van that had been outfitted inside for camping. Our first day Shavonne and I drive north along Highway 395, stopping for the night in a campground near Lone Pine. We pull into our space and get out to survey the area. As soon as we step out of the van we see we are surrounded by enormous motor homes. They look like whales surrounding a guppy.

We set up for our first dinner and build a campfire to heat our food. Shavonne takes out two cans of baked beans and a package of hot dogs. She opens the beans and pours them into a little pot that sits over the fire. Franks and beans for dinner. Yummy.

As we get ready to eat I notice all the folks from the huge motor homes are also sitting down to eat, but they're not having franks and beans. Instead I see them grilling steaks and chicken and corn on the cob.

While we are eating I go to open a beer and realize I've forgotten my opener so I tell Shavonne to go over to the motor home across the way and see if she can borrow one. A few minutes later she returns with the opener and with an invitation to join a family for dinner. She has already accepted so we go.

We have a really nice time and meet most of the families in the campground. Everyone seems concerned about what we're planning to eat while traveling. By now they've all heard about our baked beans and franks for dinner and several mothers want to make sure I don't feed Shavonne beans and franks every night. I assure them that won't happen.

Later that night I asked Shavonne what happened when she went to get the opener. She said when she got there the lady asked her if we were okay because we were eating franks and beans from a can and were driving a small van. She thought maybe we were down on our luck, etc.

So she invited us to dinner. We had a good laugh about it but after one more night on the road camping out we took to staying in motels the rest of the way.

The drive to Spokane was filled with fun and adventures. We traveled through mountains, farm country, forests and many small towns. Traffic was light and the countryside was beautiful. We got lost only a couple of times and ate at great local restaurants along the way. You meet lots of locals in places like that and it seemed everyone enjoyed talking to Shavonne, who was always ready with questions about where we were and what was good to eat.

Right after we got to Spokane I said to Shavonne, "Since you've been so good on this part of the trip maybe we'll get a puppy." Up to then Tyree and I had been talking about getting a dog but hadn't done anything about it.

When Tyree flew into Spokane to join us the first thing out of Shavonne's mouth was, "Daddy said because I've been so good on the trip I can have a puppy!"

"Oh?" Tyree says. Then she looks at me and says sarcastically, "A puppy? Really, Daddy? You said she could have a puppy?"

I try to explain, "Well, I didn't actually say she could have one..."

Shavonne immediately jumps in and says, "You said. You said. Please, Daddy. You said. Pleeeeeasse."

Tyree shakes her head, looks at me, rolls her eyes and says, "Please, Daddy. Please... Please... Pleeeeassse. Pathetic."

*During the trip to Canada, I checked in with my secretary and she told me the Vice Chancellor wanted to speak with me. We connected the next evening and he let me know there was a position open at the District Office as Director of Instructional Programs. I was a bit doubtful but my husband in his fashion said, "Let's see, you are on vacation, the Vice Chancellor tracks you down, tells you about the position, says if you are interested he will hold a spot for you in the application file, and you can call in and file a dummy application until you get back to LA. Yes, I think you should strongly consider the move."*

*I applied for the position, which was a one-year assignment, and, after returning from our trip, was selected to start in the fall. I assured everyone at LA Mission that I would be returning after the position ended. No one believed me. They all said once you leave you never return. I, however, honestly intended to.*

*My year at the District Office was a great learning experience. I was able to interact with the Vice Presidents of Instruction from all nine of the Los Angeles Community Colleges. I also traveled to Sacramento to meet with the statewide Chancellor's staff to discuss instructional policy issues.*

*Right after I started the position another exciting change occurred for the family through a series of unexpected coincidences. I was returning from an early brunch with friends and decided to run by Target for a quick errand. On my way into the store I noticed a box of puppies, all short hair and in a variety of colors from hound dog reddish brown to black. My eye caught a black female. I picked her up and was holding her when a woman who was the mother of one of Les' students came up and greeted me by name. She took the puppy out of my arms, looked at its tail, checked the ears and gave her a good inspection. She then explained that she used to raise dogs and this was a very healthy puppy. "It's a Viszla," she says. "What's a Viszla?" I ask. Her response, "It's a Hungarian hunting dog." Well, that did it; it was "beshert" (Hebrew for it is meant to be).*

*I took her home to fulfill Les' earlier promise that Shavonne could have a puppy for her birthday. He said it was the most spontaneous thing I had ever done. We named her Nicky and she was with us for 17 years, the best dog in the world.*

*Toward the end of my time at the District Office I was preparing to return to LA Mission when the Vice President's position at Los Angeles Valley College opened. I decided that as much as I loved working at Mission, the change might be interesting. It was a promotion to a large campus and a great career move. I was successful in my application and in the fall of 1990 became the Vice President of Instruction for LA Valley College, one of the largest colleges in the state.*

*The assignment began with some interesting challenges. To begin with, when I first arrived at my new office several affirmative action brochures were spread out on my desk, a not-so-subtle message. Next I was scheduled to meet with the Faculty Senate and Union leadership. They informed me that, though it was nothing personal, they wanted me to know that I was not the person they wanted as the new vice president. Then, on the opening day meeting with the entire faculty, there was a printed list of grievances against the president. The selection of the new vice president was number four on the list. Apparently there was a group of faculty who had hoped one of their colleagues would be selected for the position. Clearly this was not getting off to a great start; however other faculty were supportive of my selection so I decided the best thing for me to do was move into my new position and do the work. In a short time the tensions subsided as the naysayers learned I was indeed the right person for the job.*

*In the spring of 1993 President Bill Clinton visited the campus. What an exciting day! He was very gracious as he talked to students and staff. I only met him briefly and shook hands.*

*I would have a second opportunity to meet President Clinton 16 years later when I was serving as the Interim Chancellor of the Los Angeles Community College District. He visited LA City College on a political stop and I had the opportunity to spend some time with him before the event started. He was very focused on discussing his support of community colleges but was also interested in me: where I came from, my background and how I had come to be the Chancellor. It's said that when he's with you he's very focused on the conversation and I must agree that that was my experience.*

*I can only imagine how proud my grandparents would have been to know their granddaughter had the opportunity to meet and shake hands with the President of the United States.*

# CHAPTER 12

## *Theater, Challenges and a Bat Mitzvah*

$M_Y$ *first experience with live theater was appearing in a Christmas pageant in the third grade. I was a stable boy and when Joseph asked me if the stable owner would let them stay for the night, my line was, "I'll ask him, but I don't think he will." Next was in high school watching a production of* Paint Your Wagon, *and appearing in a few continuity skits for the annual High Jinks shows.*

*In college and when I was first married we did attend theater but usually for shows that featured black actors or stories about the black experience. When I went to work at Moorpark and was assigned as the counselor for the Fine and Performing Arts majors I attended the theater, dance and music productions at the college. After all, I had to up my game in order to better provide students with the information they needed.*

*Then I met Les and he was excited to, as he put it, introduce me to theater. I assured him that while my theater experience had been limited, I did have a working knowledge of the art form. Still, he was delighted to take me by the hand and lead me into the theater.*

*One of the first productions he took me to was a romantic outing to see* Side by Side by Sondheim. *Richly populated with wonderful Broadway show tunes, it was the perfect setting for a perfect date. We began attending plays at the Taper and the Ahmanson, as well as numerous small theaters around Los Angeles and Hollywood. Sitting with Les in the theater became one of my favorite things to do because I was sharing something with him for which he held a deep passion; and our discussions after the final curtain added more to the experience. Yes, enjoying theater together is a special bonding time for us.*

*At Moorpark College I was very impressed with how Les put a production together from start to finish: from selecting a play, to casting, set design, lighting, costumes, rehearsals including blocking, tech rehearsals, dress rehearsals, previews, opening night, the run of the play and finally closing night. It was a whirlwind of intense activity, long hours, and attention to detail. I took great pleasure in being a voyeur in his world. I loved seeing the production unfold. What was most amazing was watching him transform young and not so young actors into confident thespians. This man was so talented at what he did, and well respected by his students. He would not give them any slack; they were there to perform. He treated them like professionals and expected them to act as such.*

*I watched him dismiss a student who failed to come to rehearsal and did not call a few days before opening. Interesting thing was, this young man was the lead in the play. I, as a faithful member of the rehearsal audience, and the rest of the cast were aghast when he told the young man to leave the stage. He then proceeded to recast the parts, telling them all they had one day to learn their new lines. I was horrified. How could you do that so close to opening? He told me, "I will not allow anyone to disrespect me and the rest of the cast because they have the lead. You can always find another lead." His reputation as a no-nonsense director was sealed after that.*

*I was proud that time after time Les' productions played to sold-out houses; and what I enjoyed most were the plays that Les wrote and directed at the college and in Los Angeles and Hollywood.*

February 1990, Black History Month. I'm in my car driving to work. I'm listening to Public Radio when suddenly I hear these amazing recorded voices of African American men and women, all in their 80s, talking about what life was like as a slave during the Civil War. The voices are haunting. As I listen to them an idea for a play jumps into my head. I want to dramatize these voices.

The program ends and I hear the announcer say the recordings are part of a collection called the *Slave Narratives* recorded in the early 1930s and housed in the Library of Congress. I get very excited. I research the *Narratives* and the more I find out about them the bigger the project becomes.

I find there are hundreds of hours of slave narratives housed in the Library of Congress. The public can listen to them free of charge and for a small duplication fee get copies.

Right off, two things become clear to me: One, I'm going to have to go to Washington to listen to the tapes (this was before you could access them on the Internet); and two, I'm going to need more than a summer vacation to do the research and write the play.

I tell a colleague my idea about the *Narratives* and he says I should apply for a sabbatical. If I get it then I'd have time to do the research and write the play. That sounded good to me so I go off and write a proposal.

In a few weeks I get a call that my proposal has been accepted. The two semester sabbatical will begin in the fall 1990 semester. I now have a year to do the research and write a play. Tick tock... Tick tock.

The first thing I do is apply for research and travel grants. I receive three and I'm good to go.

While I'm doing research on the *Narratives* I come upon a woman named Sojourner Truth. Her name intrigued me so I looked her up and found she was one amazing woman who led an extraordinary life.

Sojourner Truth, I learn, was an illiterate black woman, born a slave in 1797 on a Dutch farm in upstate New York. She walked away from her slave master and came to a farm owned by Quakers. When her slave master caught up with her, the Quakers bought her and immediately freed her. After she got her freedom she became a famous traveling preacher who preached the evils of slavery and championed equal rights for women all over the North prior to and after the Civil War.

I become intrigued by her story and started to think of ways I could incorporate her into my project. However, after reading more about her I realize a couple of things. One, her story is a whole script unto itself; and two, I wanted to write it. All of sudden I'm conflicted. Can I work on two scripts at the same time? I decide to try.

In September, I fly to Washington and go to the Library of Congress and begin listening to the *Narratives*. There are tales of love, compassion, brutality and heartbreak. They are so moving that every day when I finish listening I come away emotionally spent. I soon realize because I only have a short time in Washington I'll never hear all the tapes. Instead, I select 30 hours of recordings to take back to Los Angeles.

My next stop is New York City and a visit to the Schomburg Center in Harlem to begin looking into the life of Sojourner Truth. The Schomburg is the preeminent research facility for African American History in the country.

I spend three days at the Schomburg reading everything I can about Sojourner Truth. Where she was born, where she lived, where she preached. The more I read about her the more her story fascinates me. Frederick Douglass, Abraham Lincoln and Ulysses S. Grant all befriended her. Not bad for an illiterate self-taught preacher.

After a week at the Center I travel to upstate New York and visit the region where Sojourner was born and raised. I spend a week following the Sojourner Truth trail along the Hudson River. I walk along taking in the sights, sounds and smells of the countryside just the way she did. Supposedly on these walks God spoke to her. No, I don't hear God speak to me, but I can appreciate what might have transpired with her. The landscape is breathtakingly beautiful and maybe she believed she heard something as she walked along. I end up in Northampton, Massachusetts where she lived for a time on a commune dedicated to the Abolitionist Movement. Then it's time for me to return to LA and start writing.

I have a contact in Los Angeles at the Public Broadcasting System, who has shown an interest in my Sojourner Truth project as a potential TV mini-series. So I decide to start writing the Sojourner script first. In less than two months I finish the script and submit it to PBS.

The executives at PBS pass on it. They don't say why. But I don't have time to worry because I have a bigger problem. It's now late spring and I'm way behind in writing my *Narratives* script which I've titled *Voices*, the script I'd actually been given a sabbatical to write. I only have a few months left before fall classes begin. Where the hell has all the time gone?

In two weeks I write a first draft. When I finish I immediately realize there's no plot. No conflict. Important stuff if you're writing a play. All I have are a series of black characters talking about their lives as slaves in America. I'm stuck and don't have a clue how to fix it. What do I do? I go for a drive.

Whenever I have a problem with something I'm writing I get in my car and drive north on Highway 1. For me the act of driving along the Pacific Ocean is both relaxing and stimulating and usually after an hour I come up with a solution to my writing problem. Only this time I drive five hours before coming up with an answer.

So what was the story I came up with as a result of my drive? *Voices* is a contemporary interracial love story about a black female playwright, attempting to write a play about the *Slave Narratives*, and her white college professor fiancé. It's about how the voices on the tapes she's listening to come to life and have a profound effect on their relationship. And, no... the play is not autobiographical.

By the end of July I finish the script and start putting together a workshop production in Hollywood. In early August the show is ready and the workshop production opens. People love it. Columnist Al Martinez attends the opening and writes a glowing review for the *LA Times*. We have a winner.

Fall 1991. I begin pre-production on the full-scale version of *Voices* for the college for Black History month in February 1992. I hold auditions throughout September and October, and by the end of November I have assembled my cast.

The ensemble cast is a group of students and staff members. I also cast Shavonne in the play. She portrays a child who is auctioned off at the slave market. It's a very moving scene that closes the first act and one of the strongest images in the entire production.

Soon after Shavonne portrayed a slave girl in *Voices* I cast her in a Purim play I'd written for our Temple. And what was her part in the Purim play? Why, that of a Jewish slave girl.

Later, Tyree said to me, "Do you realize you made our daughter a slave in both of your plays?"

"Oh, yeah... I guess I did," I answered. We both laughed about it but it was something Tyree never let me forget.

February 1992. *Voices* opens at Moorpark College. The play is a huge success, playing before packed houses the entire run. Reviews are excellent. All the time, work, travel and energy I have put into my sabbatical project have been a success.

During the run several professors brought their classes to see the show and vigorous discussions about race relations followed every performance.

I was very proud of this production. For one thing it solidified for me the fact that I could write a successful play that moved an audience. I remember people left the theater every night talking about the production. And if there's one thing a playwright wants it's for the audience to talk about his or her play after seeing it.

Soon after *Voices* closed I decided to go back to my Sojourner script and turn it into a two-hour play. I figured it would take me a couple of months to do the revisions. Wrong. I worked on it off and on for several years while teaching, directing and working on other projects. Finally in 2003 I figured out how to make it work.

*In the early '90s the family suffered several losses beginning with Aunt Rubey. She was stricken with cervical cancer and the family came together to support her. We found a woman to stay with her during the day while we were all at work; and every evening and on the weekends, family members took turns staying with her. She had divorced Uncle Herbert several years before so having full family support was comforting to her. She was very ill for several months and suffered till the end. She was a generous spirit, always caring for others, often before herself.*

*In the spring of 1992 the community was hit with the Rodney King*

*Riots. It was a very divisive time in the city of Los Angeles. After the not guilty verdict came down in the trial of the officers who had beat Rodney King, the city erupted in violence. Not knowing what was going to occur, I had left our home in the Valley to attend the Annual Community College Vice Presidents Conference, just north of San Diego. It was an event I really looked forward to, with great networking and excellent opportunities to catch up on the latest issues regarding community college administration. I drove down with a colleague on Wednesday before the verdicts were announced. Les was scheduled to drive down to get in some golf and, when the conference ended on Saturday afternoon, spend time with me so we could have a nice little romantic getaway. He was left with the task of taking Shavonne to spend the weekend with my sister Beverly, who lived in Los Angeles.*

*Late Wednesday afternoon after the verdicts came in, I sat at the conference room watching with horror the looting and burning on TV. Les had already left to drop off Shavonne when the verdicts were read, and I was afraid he would be in the middle of the unrest. He called me when he got to Beverly's house and told me not to worry. Beverly lived right off the freeway and the action at this point was on surface streets. He said he would hop on the freeway and be on his way to me. I told him maybe he should go back home. He might drive through the middle of an angry black mob that wouldn't care that he had a black wife and that his daughter was biracial; they would only see this white guy driving through the streets. He assured me he would be fine. He arrived a few hours later and we tried to enjoy our romantic getaway but ended up watching the unfolding violence on the news.*

*But there were positive events for us that spring as well. Earlier in the spring, my college president strongly suggested I return to school to study for a doctoral degree. She was quite a forceful woman and wouldn't take no for an answer, so at the start of the spring quarter I trotted off to UCLA to enroll.*

*She was very supportive of me taking on this new challenge and adjusted my schedule to accommodate my classes at UCLA. Unfortunately there are always naysayers to contend with. One of the more cantankerous faculty members wandered into my office after hearing that I'd started a doctoral program. He commented, "I heard you started at UCLA, let's see if you finish it," and strolled out. With that, I was even more determined to finish in four years, and I did.*

*Later that spring, plans for the Moorpark College Performing Arts Center were finally approved and funded. Construction began the next fall. Wow! Finally! After 16 years Les' dreams of having a real theater were actually going to come true.*

Monday, January 17, 1994. 4:31 a.m. A massive tremor strikes Los Angeles. We are jolted out of bed by a 6.7 magnitude earthquake.

The earth is rocking and rolling for a very long time. Everyone called it "The Big One."

I yell, "Earthquake!" and run towards the doorway in our bedroom for protection from any falling debris. I hear Shavonne screaming in fear inside her bedroom. I hear glass breaking, things falling off shelves and loud crashing sounds throughout our house.

Tyree and I rush to Shavonne's room. She tries to open the bedroom door but something inside of the room is blocking the way. Our dog, Nicky, inside the bedroom with Shavonne, is barking like crazy. Shavonne is crying and Tyree and I are pushing with all our strength to open her bedroom door so we can get her out.

The door opens a fraction of an inch. We push harder. Suddenly everything stops shaking. No more roaring, no more shaking. Dead silence. The only sound we hear is Shavonne crying from inside her bedroom. Super-mom Tyree pushes the door open far enough for Nicky to rush out followed by Shavonne. Tyree grabs her baby and hugs her.

I stumble in the dark down the hallway stepping on broken glass all the way into the kitchen where we keep our emergency flashlights. From that day forward we keep flashlights in every room of our home.

I grab a flashlight and rush back towards the rear of the house where our bedrooms are located. It's very quiet. No lights, in fact no electricity. I lead Tyree and Shavonne down the hallway to the front door. I shine my light around the living room and see broken glass everywhere. Pictures, wall hangings, and dishes all shattered. The floor is littered with debris. But thankfully none of the windows or glass patio doors have broken. Shavonne grabs the family earthquake kit from the hall closet as we head out the front door.

Shavonne's elementary school had done a wonderful job of discussing earthquake preparation. I admit if it hadn't been for her persistence we wouldn't have had our earthquake kit ready.

By now most of our neighbors are outside moving up and down the street asking if everyone is okay. An aftershock hits and suddenly we hear new screams until the aftershock is over. Again there's silence. Daylight is still a couple of hours away. Can't really see anything but we're aware that our neighborhood has suffered damage.

On our portable radio we hear the epicenter of the earthquake is located in Northridge, right in the middle of the Cal State Northridge campus, just a couple of miles from our home.

Sirens are heard. People mill around afraid to go back into their homes. I return from inside our house with bottles of water, some more blankets and several flashlights. For now, in the dark, all we can do is wait for daylight and wonder how much damage we've all suffered.

We have enough food to last a week, but with no electricity we don't know how long the refrigerator food will last. We have a few gallons of emergency drinking water and if needed we can take water from our swimming pool to use for the bathrooms. We have two propane tanks for our barbecue and feel confident that will last us a couple of weeks if used carefully. We also have lots of candles for nighttime use. We're okay for now.

But I'm really worried about mom. She's alone at her house in North Hollywood located across the Valley, and with no phone service we can't get in touch with her. So the three of us along with Nicky pile into our car and off we go to rescue Mom.

We find her frightened but otherwise unhurt. Her home is undamaged. I see only a few broken dishes and glassware. I also notice there isn't much damage in her neighborhood. We put Mom into the car and drive back to Chatsworth.

After one day electricity is restored, but it takes almost a week before we get back gas and water service. Aftershocks continue throughout the rest of the day. A question arises: after the Big One, when do you go back to work? I'm notified that Moorpark College classes will resume on Wednesday, January 19th. Aftershocks still occur throughout the 17th and 18th so I'm not sure I feel safe going back to work on the 19th but I go.

Moorpark College, Wednesday, January 19th, 8:30 a.m. I walk into the television studio and begin my first class of the day. Suddenly, the place is rocking and rolling. A large aftershock has hit. I look up and see all the studio lights swaying back and forth. In fact everything is swaying back and forth: lights, cameras, students. After 15 seconds the aftershock ceases and for a moment everything is silent. Absolutely no one speaks; everyone is standing or sitting with a dazed expression on their face. All eyes turn to me.

"Class dismissed," I say.

Everyone rushes out. As I'm leaving another strong aftershock hits. The college cancels classes for the rest of the week.

The 1994 earthquake was the most frightening natural disaster I'd ever been in. It also struck on January 17th... my 51st birthday. Happy Birthday to me!

*Because of the earthquake, Los Angeles Valley College suffered damage and the issues there caused other changes for me. A few weeks after the earthquake, the President at a sister college resigned due to the damage at his college and his home. My president was assigned to his campus.*

*A few days later I was sitting at my desk when I received a call from the Chancellor. He explained that some changes were being made and he wanted me to take over as acting president at Valley. I was stunned and immediately asked him how soon this would take place. I was hoping a few months. Instead, he said, "No, in a couple of weeks." Ouch! I was in the middle of preparing for qualifying exams at UCLA. In addition, our house had suffered damage from the earthquake that had occurred earlier that year. Cracks along the interior walls necessitated that the full interior had to be repaired and painted. Broken tiles in the kitchen and baths, and the concrete around the pool had to be repaired, along with other similar damage. I knew those repairs would be starting in a few weeks as well, which would mean preparing the entire interior of the house for painting, boxing our library, removing all the photos and picture we had hung on the walls and emptying kitchen and bath cupboards.*

*But what an opportunity. Some of my colleagues were sending out resumes left and right searching for presidencies, and here I had just been offered the opportunity to sit at that desk. Of course I would take it and this time the faculty overwhelmingly supported my appointment. I took office on April 14, 1994.*

*Serving as president was another new challenge for me, but I slid into the role very easily. I had difficult choices to make in the beginning, which included selecting staff to set up my administration.*

*The work included a lot of time in the community, as well as District and statewide meetings, but I enjoyed the position. My primary concern was always what we were doing to improve our services for students. I felt as long as that was my primary goal, I would be leading in the right direction.*

*A few weeks after I started as President, my brother, Robert, was found dead in his apartment. His death was sudden and it was determined later to be caused by severe liver disease. Clarence and I knew he drank more than he should and we supported his efforts to keep sober. Robert told me they had an AA Chapter at the aircraft plant where he worked, which was a little frightening to me because after all they built airplanes.*

*In retrospect I think he never got over his divorce from his first wife. The day he brought their newborn son home from the hospital, Robert said to me, "I will never do to my son what our father did to us, leave."*

*The way in which he said that stunned me and made me realize how much the death of our mother and the absence of our father had impacted his life. And yet, a few years later he was divorced. And while he did not desert his son, he became a part-time father, something that was still not enough and haunted him for the rest of his life. He was a fun-loving person and a wonderful big brother and I miss him daily.*

*It was because of Robert that we got our second pet. When the police discovered Robert's body, there was a six-week-old black kitten in the apartment. Robert had purchased him just a few days before, and the receipt was still posted on the refrigerator. What else could I do? The kitten came home with me. We named him Rocky, using the R for Robert. Since he was with Robert when he died, I liked to think a little piece of Robert was in Rocky's soul. He was with us for 19 years.*

*Toward the end of that summer, I realized that Shavonne's Bat Mitzvah was scheduled for December and that some planning had to occur. So in between dealing with our contractor, and my studies at UCLA, and my new position as acting President of the college, Les and I started planning for the December event.*

*While we were in the process of planning I had a very heart-wrenching dream. I was standing in my kitchen and my brother, Robert, was sitting at the table. We were having a nice conversation, laughing and having a good time.*

*Suddenly Robert looked at me and said, "You didn't invite me to Shavonne's Bat Mitzvah."*

*I said, "Of course I did, the whole family is invited."*

*"Yes, I saw everyone's invitations, but there wasn't one for me," he replied.*

*I stood, perplexed, wondering how I made that mistake. Then with a shudder I realized why and said, "But Robert, you died."*

*It was at that moment that I realized how deeply wounded I was by Robert's passing. He felt so present at that moment, yet I knew he was gone. I woke with a shiver, the scene still playing in my head and in my heart. He would not be there to share in this treasured family event. Rest easy, my brother.*

*When we were married, Rabbi Jacobs said we would blend our two cultures, and in planning Shavonne's Bat Mitzvah that is exactly what we did. The first thing we did was to settle on the invitation. We wanted something that spoke to her African American as well as her Jewish heritage.*

*We selected an invitation that was imprinted with a Tallit and added a strip of Kente cloth to the design. Truly a unique Bat Mitzvah invitation. Our friends from the Temple might not know what it was, but anyone who* knew what Kente cloth was would definitely understand.

We invited 200 family and friends to the service. Les' Uncle Sidney, Sidney's daughter Susan, and her two daughters flew in from New York to join the Wieders and the Countees at the celebration.

At the Shabbat services the Friday night before the Bat Mitzvah we all gathered at the synagogue. Uncle Sidney who was somewhat traditional in his ideas of Judaism was astonished to see our rabbi pick up his guitar and play during the service. This was not what he'd expected and he turned to Les and shook his head.

What we loved about Shavonne's Bat Mitzvah was the coming together of a truly multicultural group. It might have been the most diverse evening ever at the synagogue. One couple, friends who were from Senegal, came in full African regalia. They gave Shavonne an African drum as a Bat Mitzvah present because they told her one is needed in every home, most likely the only African drum received as a present that year among her B'nei Mitzvah friends. During the ceremony Les and I presented her with her tallit. I of course could not stop crying during my very short speech.

When it was time to pass the Torah scroll from generation to generation, it was passed from Uncle Sidney to Aunt Florence to Les' mom to Les and me and then to Shavonne, linking the generations.

When the time came for her to read from the Torah, she did a beautiful job, chanting her Torah portion. At the end of the services she read a poem she had adapted from a book called All the Colors of the Race by Arnold Adoff.

She spoke of the pogroms suffered by her ancestors in Hungary and the slavery that was suffered by her African American ancestors. After the reading, there was not a dry eye in the congregation.

The reception followed the service in the Temple social hall. The music was upbeat and the DJ kept everyone dancing until midnight. My favorite part of the reception was the candle lighting.

Shavonne lit 13 candles representing each year of her life, and upon lighting each one called up various family and friends to assist her in the lighting: her cousins, friends from schools, friends from Girl Scouts and Hebrew School, relatives from New York, carpool parents, aunts and uncles, and of course the final candle for mom and dad.

It was a very meaningful part of the reception and a way to say thank you to all of those who had been important in her life.

A dear friend of ours who attended the ceremony was a columnist for the LA Times. The following Monday morning he wrote a column describing the service and reception. It spoke of different peoples coming *together to celebrate a young girl's coming of age. We received numerous letters and calls from people in response to his column. It was a wonderful way to end a year filled with loss and accomplishments.*

# CHAPTER 13

## *Mathematical Retreats and a Presidency*

Over the years, I've always said the three most important things a father can teach his daughter are: one, how to make a martini; two, how to prepare a cigar; and three, how to bet the horses. Everything else her mother will teach her.

With that in mind while Shavonne was in middle school I decided to take her on a mathematical retreat. At least that's what I told Tyree. Actually, I had decided to take her with me to Del Mar Racetrack located just north of San Diego and teach her about odds and betting the horses. It was my way of having a special father-daughter weekend along with visiting a beautiful racetrack located next to the Pacific Ocean. When I told Tyree what I wanted to do she was, at first, confused but then caught on and laughed and said, "Have a good time."

Del Mar's season is held during the summer and the weather is always perfect. Shavonne and I drove down, checked into the hotel located directly across from the track and settled in for a weekend of betting the ponies.

When we arrived the races had already begun. I bought us tickets to the clubhouse and proceeded to teach her about odds and horse racing. It didn't take long for her to pick up the math involved and then start wagering. Of course she was too young to actually wager but she picked the horses.

For the next two days we went to the track, reviewed the odds, checked out the horses, then placed our bets. In the evenings we went to dinner at Bully's, a local bar and grill where the racing crowd gathered.

Did her math skills improve because of the experience? I don't think so, but it was a lot of fun, and she did learn how to play the horses.

*The mathematical retreats were a wonderful time for Les and Shavonne to spend time together, but it was also another example of Les' sensitivity. I was in the middle of some tough coursework in my doctoral program and this gave me some time to concentrate on my studies.*

*The year after we lost Robert, my brother-in-law, Tommy, succumbed to kidney failure. He had been on dialysis for quite some time, living with the difficulty of daily treatments.*

*I was in the process of applying for the permanent position of college president when he died. The interview process had begun and Beverly thoughtfully scheduled his funeral services the day after my interview with the selection committee. It was not the ideal time to interview for a presidency, but life does not always hand you ideal situations. Though carrying the sadness of Tommy's loss, I was able to get through the interview.*

*A year later we lost Uncle Herbert. He passed away quietly in his sleep at the age of 78. So many losses in such a short period of time—Aunt Rubey, Robert, Tommy, Uncle Herbert—had an effect on us all. After that there were several marriages in the family that countered the sadness of our losses.*

*In the summer of 1995 I was appointed as the permanent president of LA Valley College after having served as acting president for one year. I received the notice from the Board of Trustees just as we were beginning the 1995 Commencement Ceremony.*

*One of the first experiences I had as president was a visit from several of the Jewish faculty. I had no idea they would be so excited about my appointment. It was the first time Los Angeles Valley College would have a Jewish president. It was great that I was a woman, kind of nice that I was African American, but behind my office door there was a great celebration for the new Jewish president. I had to smile; it was a much bigger deal for them than apparently it was for the black faculty and staff, who did still give me individual nods, smiles and congrats.*

*Another fun part about being president was having a labor-management household. Les fell into the labor category and I, of course, was management. The faculty at Valley loved the idea that my husband was "one of them."*

*Every fall as president I gave an opening-day talk to the faculty. One year I told them that my husband had explained to me that the role of the administration was to provide the faculty with what they needed then get*

*out of their way and let them teach. I received a standing ovation. At the*
*next football game several faculty came up to him and patted him on the*
*back. They thought as long as I had the faculty influence at home I would*
*be okay.*

*Les performed another very valuable function for me. Over the years*
*he sat and listened to my practice sessions for every speech I had to give,*
*and there were a lot of them. When the presentations were for faculty, he*
*would review my remarks and let me know what to keep and what to toss.*
*It was so helpful having him as a sounding board.*

*He was also a wonderful escort for me for the numerous community*
*events I had to attend. The role of the president is pretty much a 24/7 re-*
*sponsibility, including weekends and evenings. Having to attend so many*
*community events took time and energy, but having someone to share the*
*travel with was very helpful. After a while I wasn't sure if the invites were*
*for me or him because if on the rare occasion I showed up without him, I*
*was always asked, "Well, where's Les?"*

*For me the presidency was a partnership, and having Les by my side*
*made the job much easier.*

*There were times I might have taken this partnership for granted be-*
*cause it was just the natural order of events for us. I never had to question*
*his support or commitment to my success at any level.*

At one time during the '90s every college in the San Fernando Valley
had a woman as president. Valley College, Pierce College, LA Mission
College and Cal-State Northridge were all led by women, and occasionally all four couples would end up at an event together. When that happened the four husbands would usually gather to have a drink and toast
our unique positions. Once we even talked about forming the First Gentlemen's Club and having a yearly golf tournament for charity. It would
have been great fun but alas it never happened.

Over the course of our life together, Tyree has been asked many,
many times how I feel about her being a college president. Well, the truth
is… I never once felt anything but pride. Tyree has always been a winner
and I've supported everything she's done. I always felt her success was
a shared experience for both of us… and it was fun being a First Gentleman.

As First Gentleman I attended formal events, cocktail parties, ban-
quets, award ceremonies, theater events, sporting events, concerts and of
course homecoming. I always enjoyed watching my wife work the room
at these events.

So what are the keys to being a successful First Gentleman? Well, you have to smile a lot, being a good listener helps, and you have to be able to carry on a conversation about lots of different topics; but mostly you just have to show up, be pleasant and show your support. After a few years some people would come up to me and ask me to relate something to Tyree. Occasionally some would ask me what Tyree thought about something and I'd always say, "I never speak for the president."

At many of the business black-tie events we attended I was usually the only person who had a career in the theater, which always made for interesting conversations. Most of the people were business leaders, politicians, or lawyers.

I was often asked how I direct a play or how I write one or where I get my ideas for a play. And of course there was always someone who would say to me, "You know, I've got an idea for a play."

Then they'd tell me their idea and afterwards ask if I might be interested in writing the script.

My answer was always, "Let me think about it first and get back to you." Everyone, it seemed, had a story.

Being First Gentleman was a role I played with great affection.

# CHAPTER 14

## *Life Goes On*

*A*s *an interracial couple we were continually asked, "What's it like?"
"What did his parents say?" "How did they treat you?" "What did your
family say?" By now we were well into our living routine and racial
issues that were interesting or maybe even challenging in the beginning
had subsided into normalcy.*

*We had been interviewed for a book titled* Mixed Matches. *It highlighted various interracial and interfaith relationships. For our story the
author concentrated on how we chose to raise a biracial child. We explained how important it was for her to be involved with each of our
extended families.*

*There are some African American kids who grow up in predominant-
ly white neighborhoods and who are totally out of touch with the black
community. Les and I definitely did not want that to happen. Our daughter could attend a birthday party in Malibu in the morning and be at her
cousin's apartment in South LA in the afternoon and not skip a beat. Both
were part of her world and she traveled between them with comfort.*

*Because of our interview in the book, later that same year we were
interviewed for* Good Morning America *regarding the O. J. Simpson trial.*

*We sat with two other interracial couples and were asked if the trial
was causing difficulties in our marriages. It was as if the interviewer was
hoping that like the rest of the city we were divided along racial lines.*

*Les explained to the interviewer that while we had an interest in the
trial, we were not fixated on O.J.'s innocence or guilt. We were busy go-*

*ing about our business being working parents. In no way was the trial*
*dividing our relationship. The other couples felt the same way. I'm sure*
*we were a disappointment to the interviewer.*

Not long after the book *Mixed Matches* was published, Joel Cohen,
the author, called to ask if Shavonne would speak at a conference being
held at Brandeis Institute in Simi Valley, California. Joel was to be the
keynote speaker on the subject of interracial marriage and Jewish-Afri-
can American relations in the US.

Previously after he interviewed us for his book, he told us that of all
the children of interracial couples he'd interviewed throughout the country, Shavonne was the most together kid he'd spoken with. He was very
taken by her eloquence when speaking about her family and mixed heritage. He had also read her Bat Mitzvah speech and was deeply impressed
by what she had written. So we spoke to Shavonne about his request and
she agreed to speak.

The day of the conference we drove to Simi Valley thinking she
would be speaking before a small group. When we arrived at the Institute
we saw the parking lot packed with cars. Once inside we saw over 250
guests waiting to hear Joel speak and of course Shavonne.

We were told that the host of the conference would introduce Joel,
who would speak first, and then Joel would introduce Shavonne.

When Joel was introduced I got nervous. I mean it's one thing for
your child to be asked to speak in front of family and friends, but to be
speaking in front of strangers is another matter. I wanted her to do well
and not stumble in her presentation.

Joel spoke for about 25 minutes, and when he was finished he abrupt-
ly sat down without introducing Shavonne. I looked over at Shavonne
wondering how this was going to work. Seeing that Joel had forgotten
to introduce Shavonne, the host went to the podium and called her up.
However, he neglected to give any background information about her, so
she was going up there cold.

Immediately I went into daddy-director mode and turned to Shavonne
and started to tell her what to do. As I began to speak she turned to me
and said, "Dad, I can do this." I stopped dead and looked at her as she got
up from her seat and walked to the podium. I looked over at Tyree, who
smiled at me, and I suddenly realized my daughter was ready to do this
without any help from her father.

Shavonne stood at the podium and told them why she had been asked
to speak and then talked about herself and her family and how she was
raised to appreciate both her parents' heritages. Then she gave her Bat

Mitzvah speech. Afterwards she took questions from the audience.

She was poised and confident. She answered questions thoughtfully and with humor. The audience was very impressed at what she had to say. She was wonderful.

When the speech ended many audience members came up to congratulate us on how well Shavonne had spoken.

Afterwards when someone asked Tyree if she was nervous when Shavonne got up to speak she told them, "No, not really. I knew she would do well. She's our baby. We raised her to be confident."

*In the fall, Les and Shavonne continued to be supportive of my numerous community activities and my doctoral studies. Shavonne was in high school and often after coming home would call me at work to ask what I wanted for dinner. By the time I came home, dinner was on the table; I could eat and immediately hit the books. Shavonne was now a big part of the cooking schedule in our home.*

*On Saturdays when she had soccer games, I would attend with Les, then afterwards head for the library or lock myself in my room at home to write.*

*Concentrating on doctoral studies was difficult during this time, but it was something I had to do. Many people begin doctoral programs and never finish, especially when they're working in full-time, demanding positions. Even with the wonderful support I had from Les and Shavonne, with all the demands of the presidency I found my progress was occasionally stalled.*

*What really spurred me on was my niece Danielle. She started a similar program at Pepperdine University a year after I started and I discovered she had caught up to me and might be finishing before I did. That woke me up. No way was my niece going to finish before me. So I put on my big-girl panties and got to it.*

*We both finished in May 1997, so of course we had a family party to celebrate. The theme, "Is there a Dr. in the house??? Yes, there are two."*

*I ordered my regalia special delivery so it would arrive in time for me to wear my doctoral robes to the June graduation at Valley College. As I marched in the procession, I thought of my grandparents and how proud they would be for their granddaughter.*

*The next spring Les decided it was time for our daughter to experience New York City and, of course, theater on Broadway. This would also be a time for us to connect with Les' past. We planned a trip to Ellis Island, the place where his father and Goldberger grandparents had entered into the United States. As we visited the Statue of Liberty and Ellis*

*Island, it was hard not to be caught up in the emotion they must have felt after their six-day journey across the Atlantic Ocean, coming to a new country hoping for a better future.*

*We spent quite a bit of time on Ellis Island. We were able to add Les' father's name to the list of immigrants that would appear on a new wall scheduled for construction in the Garden of Memory. (When we returned to New York in 2012 we were able to make a rubbing of his name on the wall.)*

*While in the city we took a walking tour of Harlem and stopped at the Schomburg Museum of African American History where Les did research for his play about Sojourner Truth. We also stopped at Temple Emanuel, the largest Reform congregation in the United States. We were also there on Easter Sunday and witnessed the Easter Parade on Fifth Avenue. What a show that was.*

*Finally, in addition to sharing this amazing city with our daughter and teaching her a part of her history, the highlight of the trip was five nights of theater. Through a friend we were able to get house seats for five shows, including* The Lion King *that had just opened. It was a wonderful New York experience.*

January 1, 1999, New Year's Day, 6:00 a.m. I get a call from the convalescent facility where Mom is recuperating from a fractured hip informing me she has died. Just like that. One moment she was alive and the next she was gone. For years her doctors had told us that she wasn't going to die from any of the ailments she had overcome: cancer, pneumonia, fractured hip. They said, "Whatever Hilda will die from will be something she never had any problems with in the past." They were right. It was her heart. That morning Mom had her one and only heart attack and she was gone.

After her funeral I thought about my parents, all the good times we had, all the trips, all the adventures. Only after they were both gone did I fully understand that all they ever really wanted for me was for me to be happy, which I have since learned is what all parents want for their children.

Mom's greatest desire was to be remembered. The day she died we had to smile at her timing. Now every New Year's Day we celebrate the New Year and remember Mom. She couldn't have picked a better date to be remembered. I love you Mom... and I'll always remember you.

*Being a college president afforded me the opportunity to have interesting experiences outside of running the college. Serving on various* boards was just one such example. I was appointed to the Board of Directors of one of the largest hospitals in the San Fernando Valley. As with many organizations where I served on the board, I found myself to be the only person of color, and in this case with the exception of the Director of Nursing the only woman. It was hard work with lots of materials to study, but I was fully engaged in the work and was soon elected as president of the board.

One of my favorites was the Foundation Board of Directors for Valley College. We raised funds to support academic programs and student scholarships. One of our alums, the actor Sean Astin, served on the Board. After Valley he matriculated to UCLA but remained loyal to Valley College. He was with us for a few years but then had to resign from the Foundation because he was going to be away for a while acting in this little movie called Lord of the Rings.

Sean had a connection with the Department of Defense and nominated me to attend a weekend at Fort Irwin in the California desert where the US Army tank corps trains. He assured me that it would be an amazing experience so I accepted the invitation. Unfortunately the trip was scheduled for December 1, 1999, Shavonne's 18$^{th}$ birthday. Fortunately she was in her freshman year at college and looking forward to celebrating her birthday away from home with her college friends. For the first time, we would not be celebrating her birthday with her. The trip to Fort Irwin would be a good distraction. Of course Les would be home alone with the dog and cat, but such is life. So off I went. I arrived at the Veterans Building on Wilshire Boulevard at 7:00 a.m. on Saturday morning and met the rest of a small select group going on tank maneuvers.

The group was transported by bus to Fort Irwin near the California/ Nevada border. The purpose of the trip was to have community leaders learn about the new army and an enriched training program that focused on improving performance by learning from mistakes rather than punishing soldiers if they made errors during training. We spent Saturday learning about the base and the basic training program.

At 4:00 a.m. Sunday morning we were taken out into the desert to observe tank maneuvers, and being the first weekend in December it was cold. The army had supplied a warm jump suit, gloves, helmet and jacket, but I remained partially frozen until about 11:00 that morning.

We rode a Hummer straight up the side of a mountain to reach our observation point. When a tank was "hit" it was out of the competition and the soldiers had to stay with their tank until the maneuvers ended. It was at that time that we had the opportunity to meet with the soldiers.

The men emphasized that their tank is their home and they had to stay *with it always. I had to struggle to climb on top, to get in, and to get out. The insides were very cramped. It amazed me how the soldiers jumped in and out like it was nothing.*

*We finished the exercise in the late afternoon and rode back across the desert to Fort Irwin. It was an amazing experience and I felt very lucky to have been given the opportunity to observe the training session.*

*A few years after my US Army adventure I was honored to be among seven college presidents who were selected to spend two days and one night on the aircraft carrier USS Abraham Lincoln. Hosted by a member of the California Community College Board of Governors, the presidents were given the opportunity to meet with the sailors and learn about naval operations on the ship.*

*I was somewhat reluctant to go. I would have to drive to San Diego by myself, then spend two days on an aircraft carrier; I just was not feeling it. Once again Les provided wise council. My sweet husband asked if I had lost my mind.*

*He said, "Do you have any idea how many people would kill for that opportunity?" So I packed up my car and drove to San Diego.*

*After a morning at the Naval Air Station North Island learning about our trip and an orientation on what we could expect, we flew about 100 miles off the Southern California coast in a C-2 aircraft to the carrier. When we landed we were immediately taken up on deck to watch planes land less than 50 feet in from of us. It was an amazing sight.*

*Afterwards, when we went below deck on our way to our briefing, I heard a voice call out, "Dr. Wieder." I turned and saw Alberto, a former Valley College student, who was stationed on the carrier. The other presidents were amazed and jealous. There were over 5,000 men and women on the ship and I ran into a former student. When his commanding officer discovered he knew me, his assignment was changed to be one of our escorts for our stay.*

*We had lunch together and had a great time reminiscing about his time at Valley College. We kept in touch and the following year when he was on leave I was able to take him to lunch along with my office staff. When the tsunami in Indonesia hit, the carrier was sent to the Indian Ocean to help with relief efforts. He sent me photos and emails describing what they found in that truly horrific event.*

*One evening I was able to actually sit in the Captain's chair and watch the planes land on night maneuvers. It was exciting. If a pilot was not successful and missed two landings, the plane was sent back to the mainland.*

*I was also among five visitors invited to have dinner with the Captain in his cabin. It was the same cabin where President George Bush had dinner after he landed on the carrier and said, "Mission accomplished."*

*The next morning we were jettisoned off the ship in a C-2 aircraft for the return flight. For my time on the ship I received a certificate that states, "Honorary Naval Aviator. In completing this remarkable feat, this Honorary Naval Aviator experienced deceleration from 105 to 0 mph in two seconds, and accelerated from 0 to 128 mph in three seconds, thereby gaining an understanding of the challenges and accomplishments of Naval Aviation." Impressive if I do say so myself.*

*My lasting memory of the trip was an unfortunate injury. When they buckled us in for the return flight, my left shoulder was not as tightly secured as my right, in that jettison take-off—something like going full speed then hitting a brick wall—my shoulder jerked forward. The result was a bruised rotator cuff that required a cortisone shot. Since I had signed a pound of paperwork absolving the US Government of any responsibility for injury or death on this trip, suing Uncle Sam was out of the question. So I took it in stride as part of the fun of the trip. Les was still adamant that the trip was worth the pain in my left shoulder. I must admit I had to agree with him.*

# CHAPTER 15

## Milestones and Heritage Travel
### 2003–2016

In June of 1999 Shavonne graduated from Chatsworth High School. Next step for her was college. Since both her parents worked at community colleges you'd think she'd first go to one of our schools then transfer to a university to complete her studies. Wrong. She selected the University of California, Santa Barbara (UCSB), one of the most beautiful campuses in the country. No complaints from me about her choice.

*Friends told me I would cry my eyes out when she went away. They were so wrong. Remember the TV commercial where the parents are measuring the room when the son goes off to college? That was us. Well, we didn't actually change the room, but we were very relaxed about her transition.*

*On the day we drove her up to UC Santa Barbara we saw this amazing view at the college entrance. The sun was shimmering on the water and the air was crisp and clear. What a beautiful place to live and study. We were both ecstatic that our daughter was having the college experience we both had always wanted.*

We were happy for her choice since she'd be just a 90-minute drive from our house. We figured we'd get to see her a lot. Wrong again. For most of her four years at UCSB we drove up occasionally. She was busy with classes, friends and work, but at least we talked regularly on the phone.

*During spring of her freshman year Shavonne managed to plan a surprise 20ᵗʰ anniversary party for us to be held at our house in early August. We're not sure how she pulled it off, but she did.*

*She designed and printed the invites in her dorm room. The invitations read, "You don't marry someone you can live with, you marry someone you can't live without." On the day of the party she got us out of the house for lunch and had family and friends come over to decorate and set up for the party. We were truly surprised; it was a great afternoon. We even jumped the broom after we renewed our vows.*

During the summers, Shavonne would come home for a week before going off to work as a counselor at Astro Camp in Idyllwild, California. At the end of summer when it was time for her to return to school she'd drive straight back to Santa Barbara with a laundry stop at home. Shavonne really enjoyed working at Astro Camp where she made life-long friends with several fellow counselors and campers.

Shavonne decided to major in Film Studies at UCSB. She loved movies and felt she could do well in that major. But, what to do with a BA in Film Studies when you graduate?

I asked her what she wanted to do in the film industry. She told me she wasn't sure. So I said, "Two people sit in a room across a table from one another at a studio. One person, a producer, says to the other, 'Give me 100 million dollars and I'll go off and make a movie that will win us an Oscar and make us billions.'

"The other person, a studio executive, sits there and thinks, 'Should I give this person the 100 million or the next person coming through the door?'"

"So who do you want to be?" I asked her.

After thinking about it for a few moments she answered, "I want to be the executive who decides who gets the 100 million." So I told her, "Then focus on the business side of the industry." She took my advice and went into marketing.

*When she graduated from UCSB she was offered a job to continue working at Astro Camp. Clearly she had fun working at the camp but we explained it was time to get a grown-up job and camp counselor was not on our list.*

*Then she told us she really wanted to work at DreamWorks. So did everyone else, we thought. Three nice Jewish boys started that company, and it would be a great place to work, but very hard to get into.*

*Well, what did we know, because by the end of the summer she was*

*there at DreamWorks working in the mailroom. How else does one get*
*started in Hollywood?*

*In 2001 the Board of Trustees of the Los Angeles Community College*
*District decided to raise funds for a building program to improve the nine*
*community colleges in our district. The three billion dollar bond measure*
*was successful and my life as a college president changed drastically.*
*After the election we immediately developed a campaign to revitalize Val-*
*ley. The college was sorely in need of repairs and new facilities.*

*Managing the bond program at Valley, a $350 million dollar oper-*
*ation, became almost a full time job. Les said, "Great, now you have*
*another full-time job to go along with your other two, running the college*
*and all of your community work."*

*I learned a great deal in a very short period of time about construc-*
*tion planning and architectural design. Most importantly the college fi-*
*nally began making much-needed repairs and renovations to the campus.*

*My top priority was renovation of the restrooms. Others were looking*
*for new buildings and so was I, but I also wanted refurbished restrooms.*
*So while we were designing new buildings, I was checking out every re-*
*stroom I went in, looking at faucets, towel holders, and the style of toilets.*
*Oops, this was not in my job description as president, but I spent a lot*
*of time on this issue. Then the district became very involved in ensuring*
*that all of our buildings met green building standards, so many additional*
*hours were spent discussing waterless urinals.*

*On a more serious side, I spent hours negotiating office sizes, where*
*windows should be located, which materials to use, always looking at*
*the financial bottom line while trying to maximize improvements to the*
*campus.*

From 1995 when the new Performing Arts complex opened on the
Moorpark College campus until I retired in 2005 I directed a series of
productions, mostly musicals that proved to be hugely successful both
artistically and financially. These shows were the foundation for the successful expansion of all the Performing Arts programs at the college.

Having the opportunity to work in a state-of-the-art theater complex
provided me with a new source of energy. The new complex had everything I'd hoped and wished for since I started teaching at the college in
1977.

Moving into the new facility and leaving our old small theater in the
Forum building was like moving directly from a bachelor apartment into
a mansion.

From the moment it opened and throughout the first year, the theater faculty walked around with wide smiles on their faces. The facility was a shot in the arm for all the performing arts but especially for us theater folk.

Beginning in 1999 with *Sweet Charity*, I directed in 2000 *Guys and Dolls*, 2001 *South Pacific*, 2002 *West Side Story* and 2003 *The Rocky Horror Show*. All played to sold-out houses.

In the spring of 2003, it came to me how to fix my Sojourner Truth script. I decided to have three actresses portray Sojourner at three different stages of her life.

It took me six months, from June to December, to write the new script. When I was finished I gave it to a producer friend to read. After reading it he told me it was the best script he'd read in a long time and I should produce it in Los Angeles. So the Sojourner Truth production was born.

Casting took place in Hollywood in the fall of 2004. In two weeks we went into rehearsals. By December the show was ready and in late January 2005 *Sojourner, The Story of Sojourner Truth* opened at the college for our "out-of-town tryout."

The production ran for three weeks selling out every performance. Reviews were wonderful. Once again, as with my play *Voices*, after every performance discussions were held about racism and slavery in our country.

In late February the production moved to the Hudson Theatre in Hollywood. The Hollywood trade papers, the *LA Times* and the *Daily News* carried rave reviews. The production became a hot ticket and the run was extended for two additional months.

As a result, the production received seven NAACP Image Award nominations: Best New Play, Best New Playwright, Best Ensemble Production, Best Director, Best Lighting, Best Musical Score and Best Set Design. It won for Best Ensemble Production. It also received three *LA Times* Drama Critics Award nominations for Best New Play, Best Director and Best Production.

I never would have thought I'd someday receive an award from the NAACP. Had I never met Tyree I would have never won this award. To me the award was for both of us.

The production was a very big boost for me personally and professionally. I had worked on this project for many years, going through numerous revisions, looking for the best way to present *Sojourner*'s story. To finally see it happen and then receive numerous award nominations was truly gratifying.

There's an old saying, "It may not happen when you want it, but when it does it's right on time." Well, I believe that's true. You never know when things are going to happen that will benefit you. But when they do you have to be ready to ride them for all they're worth. I did that with Sojourner and it was a great ride.

*After* Sojourner *closed Les and I took a long-overdue vacation, a cruise to Alaska. The scenery in Alaska was magnificent. It was a beautiful cruise and we loved all of the ports along the way. A well-deserved reward.*

*In July, I was asked to attend a conference in Beijing that focused on developing a community college-type system in China. Since Les was also a community college professor, he was able to attend with me. Meeting local educators and discussing how to develop a new system of higher education in China was a challenge, but the people we met with were so enthusiastic that the sessions were productive.*

*I sat in sessions during the day and Les, because he was not a participant in the conference but had accompanied me to the event, was out sightseeing with the spouses on the trip. We would meet up at dinnertime and he would tell me about all the fun he'd had during his outings while I'd been sitting in a conference room listening to endless speeches. Hmmmm... what's wrong with this picture? Fortunately I was able to get in some sightseeing as well.*

*I would say one of the most spectacular sights was the Great Wall of China. Climbing the Great Wall on July 4ᵗʰ was definitely a unique experience.*

*At first I told Les I didn't think I could make the climb so he went on without me, but as I sat there in the intense heat of midday, I realized what a mistake it would be for me not to do this. When would I be in China again? So I pulled myself up and climbed. It was well worth it, but the next day my knees were so sore I had to climb the stairs at the conference sideways. Still, I had traveled to China and I had climbed the Great Wall.*

In January 2005 I turned 62 and began thinking about retirement so I went to see the retirement counselor who told me I was eligible to retire at the end of the semester.

"You mean, I can retire right now?" I asked. The idea hit me like a lightning bolt. So right then and there, I decided to retire. I was ready.

I was ready because I was tired of the grind. After 28 years at Moorpark College, four years at Nordhoff and two years at LaSalle, I'd had enough. 34 years teaching is a pretty good run.

Everyone was surprised when I announced I was retiring. I mean everyone. Tyree and Shavonne were really shocked because all I'd ever said about retiring was I'd most likely retire in two or three years. Now I was leaving in three months.

My retirement party took the form of a "roast" and was held in the studio theater. The place was packed with current and former students as well as colleagues, friends and family. Three college presidents were also in attendance.

The roast was bawdy and pretty raucous but all in good fun. When it was over and I was alone cleaning out my office it hit me. I was finally leaving. Suddenly it seemed like my teaching career had gone by very fast.

In the fall of 2005, I was honored to receive the NAACP President's Award for my work at the college with African American students. I was deeply moved by the award and proud to receive it. Tyree, Shavonne and a large family contingent were there for the ceremony. It was one of the proudest days of my life.

*When Les made the decision to enjoy retirement, I knew I would most likely follow him in 2008. At the college, work was continuing on the bond program with the development of the college-building master plan and the design of several of our proposed new buildings. Along with my duties as president and overseeing the bond program, I was appointed by the Mayor of Los Angeles to the LA City Library Commission. The Commission was responsible for the operations and budget of the 72 branches of the city library. My experience on the Library Commission was remarkable. I worked with wonderful people and was very involved with City Hall, the Mayor's Office and the Library Foundation.*

*One of the things that Les and I both enjoyed about my time with the Library Commission was the opportunity to meet numerous authors as they came to book signings or were honored by the Library Foundation. We were honored to attend receptions or enjoy dinners with Tom Brokow, Walter Mosley, Quincy Jones, Toni Morrison, Salman Rushdie, Larry McMurtry and Kathleen Kennedy Townsend, to name a few. However, the highlight for me was meeting Justice Stephen Breyer. He was incredibly gracious and easy to talk with, sharing stories about his book,* Making Our Democracy Work: A Judge's View. *I had always been an admirer of Thurgood Marshall, one of the first African American heroes I had studied in school. Justice Breyer embodies the values associated with Justice Marshall.*

*I looked forward to my retirement in stages. I spent the first year figuring out what I wanted to accomplish over the next three years for the college. For me the most important concern was to leave the college with a revised, up-to-date college master plan that would be supported by the faculty and staff. I worked diligently with the faculty, staff and students to set the stage for that work to be done.*

*Looking back over my 14 years as college president, I had been presented with some incredible challenges, many of which were never written in the job description.*

*A few examples:*

*One Monday morning I walked into my office at 9:00 a.m. and there sat the Vice President of Operations and the captain of police. Already not a good sign. A small package in a brown paper bag was sitting on my office coffee table. I was told that one of our custodians had purchased an X-rated video over the weekend, and much to his surprise, when he viewed the movie, there in living color was our college used as the primary location for the shoot. The filmmakers, and I use the term loosely, had come on campus and shot all the exterior footage for the video. I called General Counsel. I asked about a cease-and-desist order regarding future sales. She said it wasn't worth it, so I then asked could we get some compensation for the use of the campus. That did not happen either.*

*On a sad note, one morning I was called to the football field because a former student had climbed the fence and hanged himself at the football stadium. I waited there until his mother arrived and witnessed her agony as the coroner came to remove her son. Several years after my retirement from LA Valley College I served as interim President at East Los Angeles College, and one day there a student locked himself in the stadium pool and committed suicide. How to handle events like these is never mentioned in any Presidential handbook.*

*But I've also experienced wonderful rewards. First and foremost was my satisfaction in ensuring that I always put the welfare of students above all else. This was extremely important to me because I knew it was what my grandparents would have expected of me, that I perform my responsibilities as president in the most meaningful way.*

*I often talked to Les, my ever-present sounding board, about my need to fulfill what I thought was my reason for being president. I was constantly looking for ways to improve what we did for students. Remember, I was once one of those students.*

*Years before at Compton Junior College I stepped into the admissions office and attempted to register for classes, not understanding a thing about what I was supposed to do. That difficult experience never left me so it became my mission to ensure that students at Valley College wouldn't suffer a similar fate.*

*The majority of my memories are of positive experiences, especially working with the students. I made it a point to maintain close contact with student leaders. I was especially concerned about student athletes. Many of them were students of color, and I was determined that they follow the mantra of being student athletes and not just athletes. I worked with the Athletics Director to establish a tutoring lab for the athletes and made sure the counseling department had a full-time counselor assigned to the athletics program.*

*Faculty referred students to me on a regular basis, especially female students and students of color who were intrigued that an African American woman was president of the campus. I always made time to sit and talk with students. My favorite question was, "You're president of the whole campus?" I even had business people ask me that question. I assured them that, yes, I was the president of the whole campus.*

*I announced my retirement for June 2008. The Vice President of Student Services, Yasmin, organized my retirement party. She felt I was due for a grand send-off. I thought we would have maybe 150 people. I miscalculated and 600 people attended my send-off.*

*Les gave me a bit of grief, saying, "You're always underestimating yourself. Of course everyone would want to be there."*

*It was truly a joyous celebration. I felt a genuine sense of affection from everyone in the room: my family, friends, co-workers, students, community leaders and Temple members. I was so happy that our daughter was there to witness the occasion and I was able to publicly thank Les, my partner and best friend, for his unwavering support of my work. The highlight of the evening was the announcement of an endowed scholarship in my honor.*

*The college magazine's feature article about my leaving was, "No Legend in the Fall." I was truly touched by the sentiment from the magazine staff. It spoke to me about how much the students appreciated my efforts on their behalf.*

*Right after my retirement from Valley College, Les and I took off for a driving trip to the Pacific Northwest, an attempt to make a clean separation from work. It was a wonderful relaxing drive and we visited friends along the way, former LA residents who now all seemed to have deer in their backyards.*

*In the fall we sailed through the Greek Islands on a Clipper Ship with a group of eight to help Cousin Sheila celebrate her birthday. We started with a few days in Athens where we visited the Theatre of Dionysus, the birthplace of Greek Theater. Les was very happy. We then sailed to six island ports. Cruising along under full sail was really exhilarating. We ended the trip with a stay in Venice.*

One afternoon we visited the Jewish Ghetto and discovered a little shop where we found an illustration of Shavonne's Bat Mitzvah Torah portion. How amazing was that? It was totally unexpected but the perfect gift to bring home.

When we returned from our sailing trip we took off for a drive on the East Coast to experience the wonder of the fall leaves, something we were not able to do before because of our work schedules.

The leaves were magnificent. Along the drive, I kept checking out the homes that carried Obama for President signs and was very happy to see many of them as we drove through New York, Connecticut and Massachusetts. We returned home just before the presidential election, and in November the nation elected our first African American President, a day I will never forget.

In January on inauguration day we hosted an "Obama Brunch." The party started at 7:00 a.m. and lasted until the President and First Lady danced at the Inaugural Ball. Almost everyone who came brought a bottle of champagne to the celebration, and before the very long day ended we had emptied all of them.

As the President was being sworn in, Les put his arm around me and we shared that historic moment as we sipped champagne. I thought of my grandparents and realized they needed to be a part of this moment. I went in the hallway, took their pictures off the wall and placed them on the table in front of the television so they could witness history. Somehow it made me feel better that they could experience this event with me.

I was truly enjoying retirement, however, 14 months later, I found myself back at work. No, not because I was bored. The District Chancellor left and the Board was in need of an interim Chancellor while they conducted a search. They asked and I said yes to a one-year appointment. I was the first African American woman to hold that position.

A few months after that assignment finished I worked as a consultant at LA City College for about six months. And just when I thought I was really finished, I stepped in as the interim President of East LA College for one year. After that, I stopped. Time to move on to all of the personal projects I had put on hold, genealogy, piano, writing, and more travel.

In 2010 we celebrated our 30th wedding anniversary and Shavonne received her MBA degree from Redlands University. To celebrate both events we booked a trip to South Africa for October. But first Les and I went with a group from our temple, led by our rabbi, to Israel. Visits to Israel and South Africa began what we called our heritage travels, the opportunity to see firsthand where our ancestors had lived.

One of my cousins had moved to Israel in the mid-1980s and lived

*in a city just outside Tel Aviv. She too had married a Jewish man and he
had decided to "make alilyah." That is, return to Israel. The move was
truly an adventure for her and their five children, with a sixth being born
in Israel after their move.*

*She wrote to me about her concerns with issues like suicide bombers
but also how her neighborhood was constantly on the lookout for strangers and worked together to protect one another. She felt her children were
growing up in a loving community and a country steeped in history. After
five years in Israel they decided to return to the US. While living there had
been a good experience for the family, they both missed their families.*

*When I stepped off the plane in Israel I felt an energy I had not felt
before. I had read so much about this country that had known conflict
throughout its history. As we traveled the country and I learned so much
more about the history I was amazed that so much had been developed
from the sprawling desert.*

*Masada held a particular fascination for me. I was astonished to
learn how it was built and how life was sustained on this mountaintop
above the Sinai Desert*

*Our trip to the Western Wall was indeed a highlight. Touching the
actual wall of the second temple built in Jerusalem in 70 CE and leaving
my handwritten prayer in the cracks was a sobering experience. After my
visit to Israel I felt a connection to the history, the land and the people.*

We loved Tel Aviv, a beautiful modern city located right on the Med-
iterranean Sea. Haifa is a striking seaport city. The Golan Heights are
impressive and Eliat located on the beaches of the Red Sea is a stunning
beach city. But the most impressive city was Jerusalem.

In Jerusalem everywhere you step you place your foot on Biblical
history. For me the most impressive place was the Western Wall. Standing on ground that was so important to Jews gave me a deep feeling of
belonging to the Jewish people.

*In October we took our celebration trip to South Africa with Shavonne
and our niece, Danielle. After traveling 27 hours we arrived in Cape
Town and spent four days touring the city and surrounding countryside.*

*Next we visited the township of Soweto and all the popular attrac-
tions in the area. From there we flew to Kings Camp for our safari.*

*The camp was located just outside Kruger National Park. We spent
five days on safari, which was one of the highlights of our entire trip.*

*Seeing "the big five" animals out in the bush was an amazing adven-
ture. Each day we saw herds of elephants, water buffalo, antelope and*

*zebra. We saw lions and leopards and even came upon a pack of wild African dogs as they tracked a leopard. The animals, camouflaged in the late-summer vegetation, made me understand what it meant to be in "the bush."*

*From Kings Camp we flew to Victoria Falls in Zimbabwe where Shavonne bungee-jumped off the 400-foot Victoria Falls Bridge. For some reason I was not nervous but I should have been. Les took photos of the entire jump. Afterwards when she got back to us the first thing she said to Les was, "Okay, now it's your turn, Dad."*

*"Yeah, right," was his response.*

*From there we traveled to Botswana where we went on a water safari on the Chobe River. We encountered a herd of hippos, some very fierce-looking crocodiles and hundreds of elephants.*

I remember saying to Tyree and Shavonne on our first morning driving through the bush while following a female leopard and her cub, "We're in Africa chasing leopards! Awesome!"

One of the coolest parts of our safari was our daily five o'clock celebration. Every day at five in the evening our guide would stop our Range Rover, pull out a picnic basket and make us cocktails at sunset. "Cocktails at sunset in the bush" was one of my favorite safari memories.

*In 2013 we decided it was time to travel to Hungary, specifically Budapest, the last known address of Les' family in Europe. Shavonne traveled with us to visit the homeland of her grandparents. Our tour included stops in Prague and Vienna.*

*Each city was magnificent but honestly Vienna was my favorite. The broad tree-lined avenues were beautiful. An evening Mozart concert at the Schonbrunn Palace was a once-in-a-lifetime experience.*

*The highlight for Les was walking along the boulevards in Budapest where his grandparents had traveled. We had a private tour of Jewish Budapest and visited the Dohoney Synagogue where Les' grandparents had worshiped.*

*We were very fortunate that our guide was able to introduce us to the research office at the Holocaust Memorial where we were able to learn that several Wieders were listed in the historical records as residents of Budapest. Some buildings in the Jewish neighborhood still have bullet holes from World War II, not repaired and left as a memorial of the city's struggle against the Nazis toward the end of the war.*

*One of the most enjoyable things we did while there was take a Culinary Walking Tour of Budapest. It was a tour of various eateries around*

*the city where we sampled a variety of Hungarian cuisines and wines.*
*You can learn a lot about a country and its history by way of food.*

One of Tyree's retirement plans was to get involved with genealogy, so she signed up for Ancestry.com. From that website she has been able to get an enormous amount of information about both our families. I have always known that my family, both sides, came from the same region in Hungary and were of course Jewish. Tyree was not sure which part of Africa her ancestors had come from though there was that family legend that a fiddle player from Madagascar was put on a slave ship to exercise the slaves and was trapped on the ship and later sold in America. She took a DNA test to confirm that legend. I followed suit regarding my ancestors from Hungary.

My DNA showed that I was 97% Eastern European Jewish and 3% from the Caucasus Mountain Range. No surprises there.

Tyree's test came back 63% African, mostly from the Congo with a small trace from Asia which related to Madagascar. But then a real surprise turned up when her DNA also showed she was 22% Irish. Not European but specifically Irish—through her great-grandfather William Henry Warren, née Wilson, we learned. Wow!

Once we found out that Tyree and Shavonne had Irish blood I said, "Heritage trip! We have to go to Ireland!"

In the spring of 2016, Tyree, Shavonne and I went to Ireland on our final family heritage trip. What did we discover in Ireland about Tyree's side of the family? Not much, but we did have a chance to see the country and get to know its history and people. We learned a great deal about Guinness beer and good Irish whiskey. I felt the family heritage trip to Ireland was a great success.

# CHAPTER 16

## *Reflections*

From 1977 until I retired in 2005 my life was everything I'd dreamed about. As a theater artist I finally felt I'd proven my worth. As a teacher I'd received awards and recognition. As a father I'd seen my daughter grow into a beautiful successful woman. And as a husband I'd watched as my wife's professional career soared. Also during that time my love for my wife grew deeper.

My life's journey has been an interesting twisting road. It has brought me love and adventure, failure and success. It has been full. Retirement hasn't stopped me from seeking new adventures.

Looking back I see clearly that the most important moment in my life was when I met Tyree. She is my love and my life. She is my best friend. She has given my life purpose. She makes me laugh. I make her laugh. I have her back, she has mine. I love her. She loves me.

One of the cornerstones of our relationship was when I learned to say, "You're right and I'm sorry." That phrase means so much to us because I've recognized she usually is right and I am usually sorry. Not as easy to say as one might think but it's very important to our relationship or any relationship for that matter.

Growing up, our early lives showed no inkling that the two of us would ever meet. Maybe it was in the stars. Maybe it was fate. Maybe it was destiny. Maybe it was the hand of God. Who else could have arranged it?

So what's the secret for our long and loving relationship? How did we manage to merge our lives, our heritage and religion into what has become Les and Tyree? Laughter, trust, respect, support and romance all contribute to the success of our relationship, and of course luck had a lot to do with it as well. You never know when that special person will walk into your life.

*Our story* Matzo Balls and Cornbread *covers our family histories and our life together. It has been a wonderful journey. We have been so blessed to come from strong families who supported us in our personal and professional lives.*

*As Shavonne stated at her Bat Mitzvah, her circle includes Golde Meir and Moses, Sojourner Truth and Martin Luther King Jr. Bringing our histories together has informed both our lives and opened us up to understanding the world in a way we would not have had we not been together. We know that our family and friends have also benefited from our coming together.*

*Discovering our connection on that sunny day in Ojai was the beginning of this story; a story that validates the fact that it is possible to find a soul mate in life, a best friend and a confidante; a story that confirms that finding a person who shares your values and principles allows for happiness in a world that also offers challenges. Not only do we finish each other's sentences, we begin each other's thoughts. And we laugh, more than anything we laugh. It's what makes our hearts happy, laughter and unconditional love.*

*Our greatest joy has been our loving daughter. She has grown up to become an amazing person: smart, funny, loyal and a compassionate individual. We could not be prouder of the woman she has become.*

*Matzo Balls and Cornbread is truly a love story. It's about how two people who came from very different worlds were lucky enough to meet for lunch one day in Ojai and never looked back.*

# PHOTO ALBUM

# THE WIEDERS AND GOLDBERGERS

**ABOVE:**
Grandparents
**Leopold** *(1867–1920)*
**and Regina Wieder**
*(1869–1950)*

Grandparents
**Lipot** *(1885–1924)* **and**
**Eleanor Goldberger**
*(1888–1964)*

**LEFT:**
The Wieder Family
*Miami, Florida, 1953*

The Goldberger family
with Les sitting
on the floor
*New York, 1946*

**ABOVE:**
**James Wieder, 2<sup>nd</sup> from left top row**
*Soccer Team, 1933*

**MIDDLE:**
**Hilda Goldberger, front row center**
*New York Hungarian Festival, 1926*

**RIGHT:**
**James and Hilda Wieder**, *1979*

# THE COUNTEES

**Grandfather Arthur Lorenzo Countee**
*(1897–1967)*

**Grandmother Ethel Rubey Countee,
"The Nightingale of Kansas City"**
*(1896–1979)*

**Beverly, Pat, Charles Henry, Ethel, Arthur, Rubey Eulalia, Noyal,** *1954*

**Great-Grandfather**
**Charles Henry Countee** *(1874–1956)*

**Great-Grandmother**
**Rebecca Eulalia Countee** *(1874–1910)*

**Great-Grandmother**
**Rose Ellis Rubey** *(1877–1958)*

**Great-Great-Grandfather**
**Rev. Robert Nelson Countee** *(1845–1909)*

# THE WARRENS

**Great-Grandparents**
**Ella Bandy Warren** *(1868–1967)* **and William Henry Warren** *(1865–1942)*

**Father**
**Clarence Nokomis Warren Sr.**
*(1924–1990)*

**Grandfather John Herman Warren** *(1905–1986)*

**Clarence Nokomis Jr., Tyree Oneida, Robert Nelson**, *1949*

**Mother
Oneida Countee Warren**
*(1925–1949)*

**Beverly Countee, Robert,
Tyree, Clarence Jr.**
*1951*

# TYREE, LES, AND SHAVONNE

**Les Wieder**
*1958*

**Tyree Warren**
*1965*

**Les and Tyree**
*Jamaica, 1982*

**Tyree, Shavonne, Les**
*1983*

**TOP:**
**Shavonne's MBA**
*University of*
*Redlands, 2010*

**LEFT:**
**Heroes' Square**
*Budapest, Hungary,*
*2013*

# ACKNOWLEDGMENTS

Wʀɪᴛɪɴɢ our memoir was a task that allowed us to re-visit our lives together over the past 39 years. Since memories aren't always as accurate as we would like, a great resource were the journals and calendars we kept over the years. They provided us with an excellent road map of our lives together. But there were also several individuals who gave us support and helped us with our book.

We'd like to thank the following individuals: Billie Greer, who read our first draft and gave excellent suggestions on what we needed to do to make our book better; Abbey Klein, Shelia Troupe, Fran Krimston and Cathy Meyers for their review and comments; Marv Zuckerman, who introduced us to Daniel Weizmann, who recommended our editor; and finally Pablo Capra our editor, who gave us invaluable assistance in formatting and editing our manuscript into book form.

Then there was our family. For Les, his mom and dad provided detailed stories about their life together over the years that added a wonderful texture to the Wieder/Goldberger history.

For Tyree, conversations with her brother Clarence, sister Beverly, cousins and other family members who shared their memories of the Warren/Countee history and contributed their comments to her narrative.

There was also encouragement from our family and friends that helped complete this journey. We are grateful for all of their love and support.

And finally we thank our daughter Shavonne, who inspires us to cherish our past and look forward to our future.

# ABOUT THE AUTHORS

LES WIEDER is a retired theater arts college professor and an award-winning theater director and playwright. He is a past recipient of the President's Award from the NAACP for "his mission to advance the opportunities available to citizens of all races, genders, ethnic and social backgrounds."

TYREE WIEDER, Ed.D. is President Emeritus of Los Angeles Valley College where she served for 14 years. She also served as Chancellor of the Los Angeles Community College District, and President of East Los Angeles College. She is the first African American woman to serve as the head of these three institutions. She has received numerous awards for her work in the community and was President of the Board of Library Commissioners for the City of Los Angeles.

THE WIEDERS have been married for 37 years and have one daughter.

Made in the USA
Las Vegas, NV
03 November 2023

80182966R00132